**Pro Tips for Taking Great Pictures
with Your Digital Camera**

SHOOTING | DIGITAL

Pro Tips for Taking Great Pictures
with Your Digital Camera

SHOOTING DIGITAL

Mikkel Aaland

SYBEX®   San Francisco • London

Associate Publisher: DAN BRODNITZ

Acquisitions Editor: BONNIE BILLS

Developmental Editor: JIM COMPTON

Production Editor: DENNIS FITZGERALD

Technical Editor: FRED SHIPPEY

Copyeditor: LINDA ORLANDO

Book and Cover Designer: LORI BARRA, TonBo DESIGNS

Electronic Publishing Specialist: JAN MARTI, COMMAND Z

Research Assistant: ED SCHWARTZ

Managing Photo Editor: LIZ GRADY

Graphic Illustrator: ERIC HOUTS, EPIC

Proofreaders: EMILY HSUAN, ERIC LACH, LAURIE O'CONNELL, NANCY RIDDIOUGH,
MONIQUE VAN DEN BERG

Indexer: TED LAUX

Front Cover Photographers: TERRY SCHMITT (TOP AND BOTTOM LEFT PHOTOS);
LEE-CARRAHER PHOTOGRAPHY (BOTTOM MIDDLE PHOTO),
"SAPPHIRES ETERNAL" ETERNITY BANDS BY ANNE MARIE FINE JEWELRY DESIGN;
JOHN ISAAC (BOTTOM RIGHT)

Back Cover Photographers: SCOTT HAEFNER, BRUCE AVERA HUNTER,
WENDI MARAFINO, TOM MOGENSEN

Library of Congress Card Number: 2003103565

ISBN: 0-7821-4104-8

Manufactured in the United States of America

10 9 8 7 6 5 4 3 2

To Rebecca, Miranda, and Ana

Acknowledgments

A lot of people made this book possible: I'd like to first thank Bonnie Bills and Dan Brodnitz of Sybex. Rarely does an author get as much support and encouragement as these two have given me. I'd also like to especially thank the following Sybex people for their commitment to making this a great book: Jim Compton, Dennis Fitzgerald, Amy Changar, Margaret Rowlands, and Yaniv Soha.

Thanks, of course, to Studio B's Neil Salkind and David Rogelberg, who counsel me well.

Fred Shippey, the technical editor for this book, did much more than just provide technical advice, and for that I am most grateful. Special thanks to Ed Schwartz, my trusty assistant, who took so much of the load off my shoulders. Liz Grady found and contacted many of the contributing photographers and was a joy to work with. Linda Orlando is credited as the copyeditor, but she did much more and the book is better for it.

The book would be very slim if it weren't for the advice and contributions of its contributors: Richard Anderson, Morton Beebe, Robert Birnbach, Rudy Burger, Craig Carraher, Tinnee Lee, Doug Clark, Jorge Colombo, Bruce Dale, Dave Drum, Peter Figen, Bitsy Fitzsimmons, Helmi Flick, Kate Grady, Scott Haefner, Dave Harp, Scott Highton, Jack Holm, Bruce Avera Hunter, John Isaac, Leonard Koren, Wendi Marafino, Tom Mogensen, Richard Morgenstein, Michael Reichman, Mark Richards, Steve Rosenbaum, Doug Salin, Terry Schmitt, Chester Simpson, Carol Steele, Andrew Tarnowka, and Chris Wahlberg. Their names and contact information are found at the end of the book. I encourage you to go online and explore more of their wonderful work.

I'd also like to thank: Monica Suder, Michelle Vignes, Alexis Gerard, Karen Thomas, John Knaur (Olympus), John McDermott, Paul Persons, Michael Langberg, Luis Delgado, Mark Brokering, Richard Koman, Bernard Ohanian, Hunter Freeman, Paul Agus, Michael Borek, Tony Barnard, Jim Kane (Nikon), Jacques Gauchey, Cotton Coulson, Joy Tessman, Matt Dibble, Daniel Watz, Sean Parker, Laura Levy, Sebastian DeWitt, Maggie Hallahan, Eric Hyman (Bibble Labs), Eric Zarakov (Foveon), Beth Avant (Sony), Pam Barnett, Peter Skinner, Kris Aaland, Michael Taggart, Sr., Steve Schneider, Michael McNamara, Kakul Srivastava (Adobe), Saurabh Wahi (Nikon), Amy K. Podurgiel (Nikon), Jane Kimberly Foley (Nikon), and John Edling (Dycam), who all provided valuable advice and information.

Thanks also to Leo Laporte, a true lover of photography, for his wonderful foreword and Michael Rogers, who has shared the digital path with me for so long. Super special thanks to Lori Barra of TonBo designs and Jan Martí of Command Z who have made yet another beautifully designed book.

Last but by no means least, thanks to my wife Rebecca Taggart and my daughters, Miranda Kristina and Ana Mikaela, who make it all worthwhile.

—MIKKEL AALAND, SAN FRANCISCO, 2003

Foreword

The power of the computer revolution is simple: once you convert real-world objects into bits and bytes, anything is possible. Nowhere is this more apparent than in photography.

Digital photography represents the latest step in a technological revolution that began almost two centuries ago with Louis Daguerre's silver chloride prints. Daguerre amazed the world by fixing the light from a pinhole camera onto a piece of glass, thereby preserving a moment in time for an eternity.

Today an inexpensive digital camera can transform that light into electrical impulses with accuracy and brilliance that even film can't match. It can store hundreds of images on a sliver of silicon no bigger than your thumbnail. Those images can easily be sent across the country in seconds, be shared with hundreds of people at once, and even be modified to create an utterly new reality. The tools and skills necessary to do all this are within the reach of nearly anyone. You hold in your hands the book that will unlock those skills for you.

It's fitting that the author himself has traveled a similar path. Mikkel Aaland has worked as an itinerant photographer, making pictures much as his 19th century counterparts must have, in a makeshift studio-on-wheels, capturing images of anyone with a few dollars to spare. After nine years on the road, the result was his 1981 book, *County Fair Portraits*.

Shortly thereafter, another legend, Ansel Adams, told Mikkel that if he were beginning all over again he'd be shooting digital. Mikkel took the great man at his word and became one of the first to use, and write about, digital photography.

When Photoshop was first released in 1990, Mikkel reviewed it. In 1992, he wrote *Digital Photography*, one of the earliest books published on the subject, and he has written half a dozen more since. He has worked as a professional photographer, using top-of-the-line digital equipment, and as a proud husband and father he has captured his own life with the same consumer-grade cameras the rest of us use. He's also been teaching digital techniques on TV for the past several years on my show, TechTV's *The Screen Savers*. There is no better guide to the magical transformation of light and dark into bits and bytes.

Photography, from the Greek for "writing in light," has rewritten our notion of time and history. Digital photography is reworking our notion of reality itself. One of the great technological innovations of the 19th century is once again leading the way in the 21st. Here is your chance to be a part of the revolution—to start *Shooting Digital*.

Leo Laporte

LEO LAPORTE

Contents

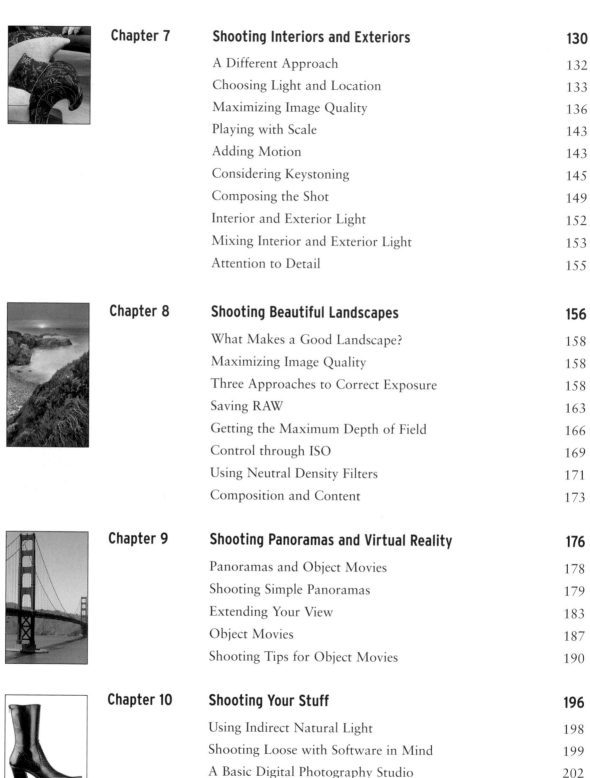

"Shooting Digital is for people who love photography and who have had their passion for shooting pictures rekindled by the simple act of buying and using a digital camera."

Introduction

Recently I ran into an old friend who proudly showed me his new digital camera. He'd been serious about his picture-taking, but several years ago his interest waned and he packed away his darkroom equipment and his fancy 35mm SLR. The thrill was simply gone.

Now he has rediscovered his love for shooting pictures and he carries his digital camera everywhere. He loves the immediate gratification of seeing his shots displayed on the LCD. He loves not paying for film or processing. Every day he is delighted to discover something new he can do with his camera. He's purchased a photo-quality printer and learned some basic software image-processing skills. He's even sold a few prints and had an exhibit at a local coffee shop.

As he talked and his enthusiasm grew, I could see that he had done more than rediscover a love for taking pictures. Through the digital camera, he is able to see the world anew.

I also feel this way about shooting digital, and that's why I wrote this book.

Shooting Digital is for people like my friend who love photography—and who have had their passion for shooting pictures rekindled by the simple act of buying and using a digital camera. It is also for people who aren't satisfied with only point-and-shoot photography. It's for people who want to get the most out of their digital camera, regardless of model.

This is not a book for everyone. I've done my best to explain features and concepts specific to most digital cameras. However I've taken the liberty to assume that readers already have a grasp of basic photographic nomenclature and know something about topics such as f-stops, shutter speeds, and focal length.

I've been working on this book for a long time. In fact, you might say it started on August 24, 1981, when Sony issued a press release announcing the "Revolutionary Video Still Camera Called Mavica." I had already been introduced to the concept of digital photography by the photographer Ansel Adams, so I was primed for the announcement of a filmless camera that required no developing. My first thought was, "No more darkroom chemicals!" My fingers were already brown, and my lungs ached from too much exposure to the caustic chemicals. This thought was followed by a vague sense that this was much more than an environmental issue: it was something quite extraordinary. It was many years before a true "digital" camera was introduced to the consumer market. (The Sony camera was actually a still video camera, which produced analog images, not digital images.) In 1991, the Dycam digital camera was marketed. It captured only a mere 376 × 240 pixel resolution in grayscale and was limited in many other ways, but it was quickly followed by improved cameras from other manufacturers.

I wrote a detailed outline for this book in 1997. It stated very clearly that this would be a book that focused primarily on the shooting aspects of digital photography. Through real-life case studies of photographers, I envisioned an extremely practical book that would help serious amateurs and professionals alike transition from the world of shooting film to the world of shooting digital.

Back then I had a problem—my talent pool was shallow. Aside from a few high-end studio photographers and some newspaper photographers, professional photographers were not willing to pay roughly $20,000 to equip themselves digitally. The simple point-and-shoot digital cameras hitting the market were promising, but they lacked the user controls and resolution that serious photographers needed.

Well, times have changed. The same cameras that cost $20,000 back in 1997 have fewer features than models now costing $1,500. Consumer digital cameras are greatly improved and their popularity has surpassed sales of film cameras. An entirely new category of digital cameras has emerged, the so-called prosumer digital cameras. These digital cameras are loaded with features, and the images they produce equal or rival the quality of film. The cost of professional digital cameras has come down to the range where an independent freelancer can buy one. My talent pool has broadened correspondingly.

 Note: Be sure to visit **www.shooting-digital.com**, the companion website for this book, which will provide you with the latest up-to-date information on digital cameras, accessories, software, and much more.

This book contains the collective wisdom of over 30 contributors, many of whom are professional photographers shooting exclusively digitally. I spent countless hours with these contributors harvesting a wealth of tips and advice that they were so generous to share, and I greatly appreciate their contributions. (Biographies and contact information for the contributors is included at the end of the book.)

It is my profound hope that their experiences and mine will help you ramp up your own shooting skills and show you how to get the most out of your digital camera. It is also my hope that the stunning images they contributed will inspire you to go out and make your own.

Good luck and happy shooting!

—MIKKEL AALAND, SAN FRANCISCO, 2003

John Isaac

Before You Shoot

You'll increase the odds of making great digital photos if you take a few moments to ground yourself in some basics. It's useful, for example, to understand why shooting digital is inherently different from shooting film. And even if you already own a digital camera, you should know whether the camera you are using—or the one you are thinking about upgrading to—is really the right digital camera for your needs. This chapter will get you started on the road to making great photos with your digital camera.

1

Chapter Contents

Mikkel Aaland

Bridging the Film/Digital Gap

Since most of us come to the digital world from the world of film, it's comforting that much of the nomenclature of digital photography is familiar. Digital cameras have lenses, f-stops, and shutters just like traditional cameras. Light is captured and recorded. Images are stored and shared. Many film photographers entering the digital camera world will quickly get up to speed because of the many similarities between digital and film photography. However, it is important to know that the differences are also great, and if you apply your old knowledge indiscriminately to the digital world, you are likely to get unsatisfactory results or not fully utilize the capabilities of the new medium. Let's look at some of the similarities and differences.

Capturing Light: Electronic vs. Chemical

Both digital cameras and film cameras capture and record light. However, film cameras rely on a chemical process. Silver halide crystals change when struck by light, forming a latent image that is revealed upon development with a chemical agent. Figure 1.1 summarizes this familiar process.

Figure 1.1: Film is both a capture and a storage device. The image is revealed upon chemical development.

Digital cameras rely on a much more complex system that includes several interconnected electronic components and sophisticated image processing. Let's look at this system in more detail.

The Digital Capture and Storage Process

Digital capture starts with the sensor chip. This chip contains an array of photoreceptors, each capturing one pixel of the ultimate image. The number of receptors in the chip is what determines the camera's maximum resolution. In most systems, a layer of filters is applied over these receptors (see Figure 1.2), so that each one can capture only one of the primary colors—red, green, or blue. These colors are the basis of the RGB color model used in all computer imaging. Electronic processing, either in the camera or in a computer, then combines these separate R, G, and B values into RGB pixels in the image.

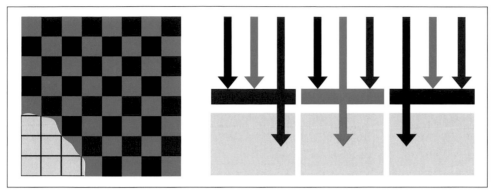

Figure 1.2: In a typical sensor, red, green, or blue filters cover individual pixels (photoreceptors) in a tiled mosaic pattern (left). The filters allow one wavelength of light to pass, and a given pixel therefore records only one color (right).

The processing of the digital data from the sensor is the most complex part of the process, and also the most variable. Unless you've chosen to save the image in the RAW file format, the camera's onboard processor will organize the separate R, G, and B pixel values into RGB data and a perform variety of other steps before assembling the final image. This processing may include compression (in the JPG file format) or no compression (in the TIF file format). You'll learn more about these formats in Chapter 8's "Know Your Camera: File Formats" sidebar, and in the Zooming In appendix under "RAW Data Revealed."

After light is captured by the sensors and the processing is complete, the information (data) is passed on in digital form to some sort of built-in memory system or, more commonly, to an external storage medium such as the commonly used SmartMedia or CompactFlash card.

The sensor and electronic system that carry out the task of digital processing and storage are built entirely into the camera and cannot be easily swapped and upgraded. By comparison, film has individual characteristics dependent on brand and manufacturer, and those characteristics are independent of the camera itself. You can easily switch from a fine-grained film to a fast, grainy one by simply replacing one roll with another in the camera.

Comparing Resolution

Film resolution, expressed as resolving power, is a function of the size and structure of the silver halide particles (Fine, Medium, or Coarse), the emulsion thickness, and the actual size of the film (35mm, 120mm, etc.). Digital camera resolution is based on the number of pixels contained in a particular sensor. The number of pixels is expressed either as an "A × B" form with "A" representing the number of pixels in the width and "B" the number of pixels in the height of a sensor (for example, 2560 × 1920 pixels) or as a total number of pixels (for example, 4,915,200 pixels, or more simply, 4.9 megapixels).

In general, the more pixels a sensor is capable of capturing, the finer will be the detail that is recorded. I must qualify this statement though, because there are some sensors on the market—notably ones created by Foveon and Fuji—that squeeze more color data from each pixel, thereby making a side-by-side, pixel-to-pixel comparison between sensors less meaningful. (Read more about this in Zooming In under "Sensors Expanded.") Sometimes the documented number of pixels may include pixels that aren't even actively used, introducing yet another variable.

Some of the earliest digital cameras captured only 640 × 480 pixels (.3 megapixels)—just enough pixels to fill a small computer monitor, and barely enough to produce a decent 3" × 4" print. Nowadays a typical 3-megapixel consumer digital camera captures around 2048 × 1536 pixels, which is plenty enough resolution to produce a decent 8" × 10" print. Table 1.1 shows what size prints you can reasonably expect to produce from various resolutions. Note that these are general guidelines and actual results will vary depending on the type of digital camera and output device used and other qualities of an image such as sharpness, color, and content.

Print Size (inches)	Need at least
3" x 5"	.6 megapixels (900 x 675 pixels)
5" x 7"	1.3 megapixels (1280 x 960 pixels)
8" x 10"	3.2 megapixels (2048 x 1536 pixels)
11" x 14"	6.1 megapixels (3008 x 2000 pixels)
16" x 20"	11 megapixels (4064 x 2704 pixels)

Table 1.1: Optimal pixel resolutions needed for desired output specifications (assuming 200dpi print resolution)

Note: Roughly speaking, it requires a digital camera capable of capturing approximately 6 megapixels to match the resolving power of a medium-grain 35mm film. Other digital camera variables such as lens quality, sensor characteristics, and image-processing capabilities make a difference as well.

Considering Exposure Latitude

Many sensors don't have the exposure latitude between light and dark that film provides, and sensors aren't capable of producing good results in low-light situations as successfully as some films can. Professionals, of course, have found ways around these limitations and I'll pass on their knowledge in the appropriate sections. Of course it is also important to keep in mind that this is a temporary situation. While we've approached the limits of what film can do, the capabilities of electronic capture will likely surpass those of film.

Bottom line: Unlike film cameras, digital cameras depend on a complex array of electronic components, all of which contribute to image quality—or lack thereof.

Lenses: Getting the Numbers Right

Digital cameras, just like a film cameras, rely on lenses to collect and focus light onto the sensors. If you've used a 35mm film camera, you are probably familiar with how lenses are numerically differentiated in terms of focal length. (*Focal length* is the distance between the optical center of a lens and the medium that captures the image—either the film or sensor surface.). For example, a lens with a focal length between 40mm and 55mm is considered "normal" and covers a field of view similar to human vision, about 50 degrees. Focal lengths less than 40mm are considered wide angle and focal lengths over 55mm are considered telephoto, with a narrower field of view. A lens designated as wide angle will expand the field of view, and long telephoto lenses narrow the field of view and appear to bring far objects close. Zoom lenses provide a range of fields of view, often going from wide angle to telephoto. A versatile zoom lens might provide a range of focal lengths, say from 28mm to 200mm. And so on.

> **Note:** Because the sensor of a digital camera is physically different and responds to light differently than film, digital camera lenses are often designed from the ground-up to take into account these differences. Some camera manufacturers are more successful than others in producing lens/sensor combinations that contribute to overall image quality. If you use a digital camera that accepts interchangeable lenses, it is important that you choose lenses carefully. Not all lenses will give you optimal quality. A lens that works fine with a film camera can produce color aberrations, flare, and lack of sharpness when used with a digital camera.

When shopping for a digital camera it's natural to want to compare focal lengths of digital camera lenses with those of familiar 35mm film cameras. But although a digital camera's "normal" lens will capture approximately the same field of view as a film camera's "normal" lens, the physical focal length considered normal is usually much shorter. (Because of this difference, it's typical to refer to "35mm equivalent" focal length when discussing lenses for digital cameras, and I'll use that term throughout this book.) A 50mm lens that is considered "normal" for a 35mm film camera would be considered a telephoto lens for many digital cameras.

Why? Because most digital cameras use sensors that are smaller than 35mm film—sometimes only a quarter of the size—and the smaller the sensor, the shorter the normal focal length. Figure 1.3 illustrates this point. With the same physical focal length, a 35mm film camera (which has a 24mm × 36mm frame size) would show a somewhat larger field of view, with less magnification, than a digital camera with a relatively large sensor (such as the Nikon D100, with a 23.7 × 15.6mm sensor). With the 5.27 × 4mm sensor on the Minolta DiMAGE X, we have a much smaller field of view and more magnification.

Figure 1.3: The same focal length will produce different fields of view depending on the size of the sensor/film.

Different digital cameras use different size sensors, so focal-length equivalents will vary. For example, 30 mm is considered a normal focal length for the Nikon D100 while 7 mm is considered normal for the DiMAGE X. For now, most camera manufacturers provide 35mm focal-length equivalents when necessary, either on the lens housing or in the manual. If you can't find the 35mm focal-length equivalent for your particular camera, you can refer to the owner's manual or to the manufacturer's website. With some digital camera specifications you will see a number referred to as a 35mm "multiplier factor." Multiply this number by the focal length of your lens to get a 35mm film equivalent. For example, if the multiplier is 1.5 and you are using a 100mm focal length, $1.5 \times 100mm = 150mm$, which is the 35mm equivalency.

Note: Because digital camera manufacturers calculate 35mm equivalents using different criteria, allow for up to a 15% variation when comparing one digital camera's equivalent focal length with another's.

If all else fails, there is a relatively straightforward relationship between the diagonal dimension of a sensor (or film) and what is considered a normal focal length. If, for example, the diagonal measurement of a sensor is 12mm (as it is for the sensor used in the Nikon Coolpix 990), then the normal focal length is 12mm. (The Nikon actually comes with an 8mm–24mm zoom lens, which translates to 38mm–115mm in 35mm film equivalence). The diagonal measurement for the sensor in the 14-megapixel Kodak Professional DCS Pro 14n digital camera—and the Canon EOS-1D—is the same as 35mm film—about 43mm—which explains why a 50mm "normal" lens on the Kodak and Canon cameras will provide the same field of view on a 35mm film camera. (Many people have been taught that a 50mm lens is a normal lens for a 35mm camera, but as you can see by the math, 50mm doesn't fully represent the normal human field of view. Many pros consider a 35mm lens "normal" for a 35mm film camera.) Some manufacturers list the diagonal measure of a sensor with the camera's specifications.

Note: Lens zoom capabilities are sometimes expressed in multiplication style, such as 3x or 6x. This refers to zoom range, starting at the widest angle. A 40mm, 4x lens, therefore, has a range of 40mm-160mm. A 35mm, 10x lens has a very large range, from 35mm-350mm. Digital zoom is something altogether different. It has nothing to do with the lens itself, but refers to software interpolation that occurs after an image has been captured.

Knowing what you do now, you'll better understand why it's rare to find a digital camera equipped with a lens that has less than a 30mm focal length equivalent. Only the more expensive digital cameras with larger sensors give you the option of wider lenses. Even then, if you place a 12mm fisheye lens on, say, a Nikon D 100, it will still be equivalent to only about 20mm on a 35mm camera—which is wide, but not super wide. (Accessory, add-on lenses can extend the wide-angle capabilities of many digital cameras to a degree; however, there is some tradeoff in quality.)

Bottom line: Focal length equivalents will vary between different digital cameras with differently sized sensors. Don't expect a 1:1 relationship between the angle of view of a lens used on a digital camera and the lens used on a 35mm film camera. Finally, the smaller the sensor, the less chance your camera will provide an effective wide-angle view.

Aperture and Depth of Field

It's not only focal length numbers that are different in the digital and film worlds. Aperture comparisons between a digital camera and a 35mm film camera—at least when it comes to the depth of field—won't always give you the same results either.

Apertures, which are found in most lenses, work in tandem with shutters to control the amount of light that passes through to the sensor or film. Aperture size is expressed as f-stops, with "f" representing the focal length of a lens. f/2, therefore represents an aperture diameter that is 1/2 the focal length of the lens, and f/16 is an aperture diameter that is 1/16 of the focal length of the lens. f/2 is wider than f/16 and allows more light to pass through the lens. Theoretically, an f/5.6 setting on any lens, on any camera—digital or film—will always let in the same amount of light.

Depth of field is the range of acceptable sharpness in front of and behind the plane of focus. As you'll see throughout the book, the ability to control depth of field—either to isolate a subject from its background, or to put more objects in focus—is an important creative technique.

As most of you probably already know, wider f-stops yield a limited depth of field, while narrower f-stops increase the depth of field.

But depth of field is not determined only by f-stop. It's also determined by the focal length of a lens (longer lenses produce less depth of field); the distance from the lens to the object (the closer the lens is to the subject the less depth of field); and, just as importantly for the purpose of this discussion, by the size of the sensor—or for that matter, the film. (For a very technical discussion of this topic I invite you to visit my website: **www.shooting-digital.com**.)

From a purely practical point of view, the smaller the sensor your digital camera uses, the more depth of field is produced for any given lens, f-stop, or distance. Depth of field, therefore, varies from one digital camera model to another—and rarely will you get what you might expect without some experimentation.

Later in the book, I'll give you a way to test your digital camera and lens for depth of field, and I'll show you ways to deal with more depth of field than you want (☞ "Know Your Camera: Controlling Depth of Field" in Chapter 2). For now, just know that this is a potential issue with huge implications, especially, for example, if you are shooting a portrait and you want the background to go more out of focus and it doesn't.

Bottom line: The amount of depth of field produced by your digital camera might not be what you expect. You'll need to experiment.

Shutters: Another Way to Control Light

Digital cameras need shutters to control light just like film cameras. Some digital cameras use a shutter that is mechanical, not unlike the shutters used in a film camera. The shutter—be it a leaf shutter or a focal plane shutter—controls the amount of light that strikes the sensor. The faster the shutter, the less light is allowed past; the slower the shutter, the more light. Remember from basic photography that varying the shutter speed and changing the f-stop is how you get more control over the amount of light hitting the film or sensor, and also how you can stop or blur action or control depth of field.

Some digital cameras use the sensor itself as a shutter. This requires a special sensor but essentially the pixels themselves are told electronically when to turn on and when to turn off. As you can imagine, using this electronic method can produce much faster speeds than anything mechanical. Engineers for Olympus, for example, have produced speeds of 1/18,000th of a second. Speeds like this are inherently impractical because they require so much light (and such a wide aperture). Using sensors as high-speed shutters in this way has its tradeoff: it lowers the effective resolution of the sensor.

From a practical point of view, the key things to keep in mind when looking at the capabilities of a digital camera shutter are:

- Just like with a film camera, an important creative option can be using a digital camera that provides some control over a range of shutter speeds—especially if you are shooting action. Most prosumer and professional digital cameras come with a shutter priority or manual mode. Rarely do consumer-level digital cameras offer such options.

Note: Throughout the book you'll see reference to digital cameras as *consumer, professional,* or *prosumer.* These distinctions are rough, and some digital camera models overlap categories. Generally speaking, however, consumer digital cameras are tailored to users who prefer mostly point-and-shoot capabilities. Prices range from $100 to $400. Prosumer digital cameras offer more user control, a wider variety of features, and to a certain degree, higher pixel counts. (At some point, when all digital cameras contain film-equivalent or higher pixel counts, this will be less of an issue.) Prosumer digital cameras generally start at around $500 and go to about $1,500. Professional digital cameras combine user control and higher pixel count with speed of use and responsiveness and durability. These cameras typically have interchangeable lenses, although this feature is also starting to appear in some prosumer models. Prices for these kinds of digital cameras start at about $1,500 and the sky is the limit.

- At this time, most prosumer and professional digital cameras feature shutter speeds in excess 1/1000th of a second, which is plenty fast for most shooting situations.
- Although extremely slow shutter speeds are an option on most digital cameras, keep in mind that shutter speeds slower than 1/15th of a second often introduce electronic "noise," which shows up as blotchy patterns in continuous-tone areas. Some digital cameras offer noise reduction modes, with some tradeoff in quality.
- Some mechanical shutters provide faster synch speeds when used with electronic flash. This can be important if you are trying to balance flash with bright daylight.

Bottom line: Just about everything you know about film cameras and shutter speeds will apply to shooting digital.

Metadata

One of the biggest differences between film cameras and digital cameras is the amount of metadata generated. Metadata is information encoded onto the film or into the digital file. Some film cameras embed the date and time a picture was taken, and with a special data back you might be able to encode some other type-based information. This is nothing compared to the data that is typically encoded by a digital camera.

Digital camera manufacturers have standardized the way this metadata is saved into a format called Exchangeable Image File or "EXIF" for short. To read this EXIF data, you'll need imaging software such as Photoshop or Photoshop Elements, or the imaging software that often comes with a digital camera.

Not only can you use EXIF data to see what type of digital camera was used, but you can see the date, f-stop, shutter speed, ISO, and the fact that a flash was on or off. Some of the higher-end professional cameras such as the Nikon D1X even allow you to hook up a global positioning system (GPS) to your camera so you can encode in the EXIF metadata the exact spot in the world where you shot a particular image.

Metadata is used by printing software to determine print resolution. It can help you organize your digital images and even make you a better photographer by giving you a handy reference to your camera settings.

Beyond Film

There is a point where the electronic and chemical worlds completely diverge. For example, most digital cameras are equipped with an LCD screen that provides near-instant image playback. This may sound like a small thing, but in reality preview ability has important significance. As you'll see throughout the book, LCD previews can be used in a variety of ways, from displaying technical data on the quality of an image to precise framing, to ice breakers that help your subjects relax as you photograph them.

Another area that has no counterpart in the film world is file formats. Most digital cameras give you a choice of how you want the digital data saved. You can opt for a small file size via various JPEG file format compressions, or for high quality—albeit large files—saved in the TIFF file format. Some cameras even allow you to save the pure, unprocessed data that comes directly from the sensor. This RAW data, as it is called, can then be processed on a desktop computer with imaging software more sophisticated than the processing in the digital camera itself.

Control over white balance is another point of divergence between digital and film. Shoot daylight film under tungsten or fluorescent lights and you'll get a greenish cast. With a digital camera you simply adjust the white balance—or let the camera do it for you—to compensate for the different light values.

Digital also goes beyond film with the capability of many digital cameras to capture full-motion video and sound. As you'll see in Chapter 4, many photographers are using their digital cameras to create short 15- to 30-second clips that have both practical and entertaining value.

The Right Digital Camera

Digital cameras come in all sizes, shapes, and prices, with various types of features. There is no such thing as a single *perfect* digital camera, regardless of cost. However, there is such a thing as the *right* digital camera for you, and it all depends on your needs.

An expensive, professional digital camera with interchangeable lenses may not be the right camera if you are running out the door to shoot your child's first day at school and you really need only a lightweight consumer digital camera that fits in your pocket. On the other hand, if you are shooting fast moving action, you may be satisfied only with the responsive controls typical of a professional or prosumer-level digital camera.

Before I get really specific about matching your needs with the technical aspects of digital cameras, I want to remind you (and myself) that there is much more to making good photographs than the technical details. In the process of focusing on a camera's capabilities and features, it's easy to "lose the forest for the trees." The fact is, some of the most memorable images in history were taken with cameras that we might consider crude: think Matthew Brady and his Civil War photographs, or Edward S. Curtis and his American West images.

Sure, the right tool for the right job is preferable, but as you'll see throughout this book, a creative person can overcome many of the limitations of a less-than-perfect digital camera. I learned this lesson many years ago, when one of my mentors, Gordon Clark, encouraged me to spend a few days shooting everything with a 200mm telephoto lens, even close up portraits. It wasn't easy, but I soon learned to compensate and actually came up with some decent images. When I went back to using other lenses, I saw the world in a whole new way and my photographic abilities were vastly improved.

Matching Your Needs to a Camera

The following section matches the desirable features and specifications of a digital camera with several general photographic shooting categories. (These categories are the subject matter of Chapters 2 through 10 of this book.)

Hopefully—in lieu of recommending actual camera models and manufacturers—this summary will give you a start toward learning what to look for in a digital camera and ultimately you won't buy more or less camera than you need. For readers with needs not met by a single digital camera, I suggest considering acquiring multiple cameras. As digital cameras continue to drop in price this becomes a more and more realistic option.

With the exception of the landscape/architecture category, I don't get into pixel resolution. Sure, pixel resolution is an important criteria in choosing a digital camera—and for that reason I address it elsewhere in the book—but the amount of pixels you need really depends on what you are doing with the final image, and not so much on the subject of what you are shooting.

Important Features for Shooting Portraits–Chapter 2

Portraits generally benefit from using longer-than-normal focal lengths. The focal length need not be to be too long: a typical portrait lens is anywhere from 85-135mm (35mm equivalent), well within the capability of most zoom lenses included with most digital cameras. Accessory add-on lenses can extend less-than-optimal lens capability but with a tradeoff in quality. Another important feature to look for in a digital camera is aperture priority metering. With the choice of f-stops comes the ability to control depth of focus, which, as you will see in Chapter 2, is useful. (Some consumer digital cameras lack this option but include a so-called portrait-shooting mode, which essentially selects the widest possible aperture to diminish the sharpness of the background.) LCD preview capability is absolutely a must when shooting portraits. Most digital cameras come with this feature, but some LCDs are bigger and more easily viewed than others. If you choose to use external electronic strobes for your portraits, and you need to trigger the strobe from the camera, a digital camera with a PC synch outlet is convenient. (There are ways around this, which you'll see in the appropriate chapters.)

Important Features for Photographing Children and Events–Chapter 3

Children move constantly, and so do guests at weddings, birthday parties, and other events. Many times they move very quickly. Some digital cameras are more responsive and better equipped than others to shoot subjects that move. Anyone who has digital folders full of out-of-focus shots or just-missed moments knows very well what I am talking about. (I go into a lot of detail about digital camera shutter-release-lag in Chapter 3.) Camera response is therefore a very important thing to consider when looking at the specs of a digital camera. Another thing to consider is an effective built-in flash. Some built-in strobes are more powerful than others. Some are more accurate than others. If the built-in strobe isn't enough, does the camera have the capability to accept an external dedicated strobe? Not all do.

You'll definitely want a wide-angle lens capability if you are shooting groups. Most digital cameras feature wider-than-normal focal lengths, but is it wide enough? (This is where going to a camera store and picking up the camera to test it is invaluable.) As you will see in Chapter 3, some photographers find it handy to frame difficult-to-get shots with LCDs that swivel and move independently of the camera lens.

Important Features for Shooting Fast-Moving Action—Chapter 4

Shooting things that move *really* fast—i.e., cars, horses, athletes, etc.—is very challenging, and nearly impossible if your digital camera is not up to it. An ideal action digital camera will first of all be extremely responsive. There are lots of tests for this but the bottom line is this: when you turn on the camera, does it respond immediately? When you press the shutter release does the camera respond quickly, and continue to respond? The camera should have shutter speeds in excess of $1/1000^{th}$ of a second and a shutter priority mode. It should have a burst mode capable of capturing three or more frames per second. (More is better, of course.) It should have a fast zoom lens capable of 200mm (35mm equivalent) or longer focal length and a fast autofocus with assist. Ideally, it will have some type of image stabilization option to minimize camera or movement shake. (Usually this is built into the lens). It should have higher ISO option settings (up to 1600 ISO) to enable fast shutter speeds. And last of all, an ideal action digital camera should be lightweight and have a sturdy and durable body construction. Yeah, I know, you are going to pay for these features. But they really make a difference.

Important Features for Shooting Minimovies—Chapter 5

Not all digital cameras offer a minimovie option. Ironically, the more expensive the digital camera or the more professional it is, the less likely it is that the camera will have the capabilities of capturing these short but extremely useful full-motion sequences. After you read Chapter 5, I think you will agree that having this capability is extremely attractive.

Important Features for Travel Photography—Chapter 6

Travel photography includes just about every photographic category you can imagine, including portraits, landscapes, and action. This makes selecting an appropriate digital camera all the more difficult. You will need an extremely versatile camera—for example, one that includes a zoom lens with a wide range of focal lengths. (Add-on lenses are just one more thing you have to carry and they can be easily lost.) You'll also want a digital camera with reasonable power consumption. It's nice if it uses commonly available batteries.

An on-the-road digital camera is also ideally durable and lightweight. If you are traveling to certain parts of the globe, you don't want a flashy camera that says, "hey look at me!" Making backups of your digital images is always important but when you are on the road it is particularly challenging. Some digital cameras store data on durable mini CDs; others have dual memory slots so you can make backup copies from within your camera. (Digital wallet-like devices are always an option, but again, they mean one more thing to lug around and possibly lose.)

Important Features for Architecture and Landscape Photography–Chapters 7 and 8

Up to this point I have not brought up image quality as an issue. However, when you turn your lens to landscapes and architecture photography, image quality becomes a critical part of the success of your work. Not only does the camera you use need to have the capability to produce high-quality images, you also need to know how to get the most quality out of it. This subject is dealt with in great detail in Chapters 7 and 8. Higher pixel counts in excess of 4 megapixels are definitely a plus. World-class optics are also important. You'll want more camera controls—including, ideally, both exposure and white-balance bracketing. You'll also want the ability to save your image files in a variety of file formats, including the extremely versatile RAW data format, which you'll hear a lot about throughout the book.

Important Features for Panoramas–Chapter 9

Another way to extend the ability of your digital camera is through special software that stitches multiple images together and creates either a panorama or an object movie. (All of this is detailed in Chapter 9.) Just about any digital camera can be used to create simple panoramas. However, if you want to create professional quality panoramas or object movies, you'll need a digital camera that has exposure and focus control overrides. You'll also need to use a tripod, and it really helps if your digital camera comes with the appropriate screw mount.

Important Features for Tabletop and Close-up Photography–Chapter 10

You'll see in Chapter 10, Shooting Your Stuff, that shots of inanimate objects under natural light can be made successfully with just about any digital camera. However, for more flexibility and ease of use with studio lights, certain features in a digital camera are desirable. For example, a digital camera with a PC synch outlet for a strobe trip cord is very handy. Nearly all professional digital cameras and many (but not all) prosumer-level digital cameras have one. Not so with consumer-level digital cameras. They almost never have one. There are workarounds if your digital camera lacks this outlet, as we see in Chapter 10. An accurate viewfinder is always helpful when shooting objects. Only SLR digital cameras or cameras with electronic viewfinders have accurate viewfinders. The workaround to this is to use the LCD display for framing, but this uses a lot of battery power. Macro lens capabilities can be very critical, especially if you are shooting small objects such as coins and stamps. Close-up attachments are an option, but sometimes they are cumbersome and not nearly as effortless to use as a digital camera with a good macro lens. Wide-ranging zoom capabilities are also useful. Longer-than-normal focal lengths flatten perspective, which is often desirable. Wide-angle capabilities are also useful.

Knowing Your Digital Camera

You may be surprised to hear that many of the professional photographers featured in this book used cameras not labeled "professional." But even a point-and-shoot camera in the hands of a professional can be effective. It's not just a matter of having a "good eye." A pro also knows one thing that many others don't: understanding both the strengths and weaknesses or your equipment is critical. A weakness can be overcome only if you know it exists.

In short, it's not the digital camera that makes a great photo; it's the relationship between the photographer and the camera—one based on knowledge and experience—that produces the best results.

Take shutter lag. Many digital cameras suffer from it. You press the release button expecting to get the shot, only to see later that the camera actually released the shutter a good second or so later. What can you do if you own such a camera? Well, first of all you need to find out how bad the lag is. I learned a very simple test from my *Los Angeles Times*' friend, photographer Tony Barnard. Sitting at a coffee shop in San Francisco, he showed me the test found in Chapter 3, "Testing for Shutter Release Lag." Once you figure out the lag, if any, you can learn to anticipate a shot.

Knowing your camera is such a huge and important subject that I've devoted a whole series of sidebars to it throughout the book. (In fact, it's one of three topic areas that I'll cover in sidebars throughout the chapters; you'll meet the other two shortly.) In each chapter you'll see a sidebar titled, "Know Your Camera," and you'll find technical explanations that you can apply to just about any digital camera.

Know Your Camera sidebars include:

- General Quality Test (Chapter 1)
- Controlling Depth of Field (Chapter 2)
- Testing for Shutter Release Lag (Chapter 3)
- Frame and Focus (Chapter 4)
- LCDs (Chapter 5)
- What Goes Wrong with Digital Cameras (Chapter 6)
- The Sensor Inside (Chapter 7)
- File Formats (Chapter 8)
- Lenses (Chapter 9)
- Built-in Flash (Chapter 10)
- Adjusting White Balance (Chapter 11)

Know Your Camera: General Quality Test

There are many things to consider when determining the overall performance of your digital camera. How does it perform in low light? How well does it handle a wide dynamic range of light? Are the colors accurate? How well does the autofocus work? How well does the exposure system work? Is the camera responsive? Increasingly, camera reviewers are establishing standardized tests that answer these and other questions and publishing their findings on the Web and in print.

You can easily test for yourself at least two important quality issues: image sharpness and color fringing. (You'll need an image processing program such as Photoshop, Photoshop Elements, Paintshop Pro, Picture It, or proprietary software that comes bundled with many digital cameras.)

To start:

1. Pick a scene that includes a lot of color and detail, such as the one shown here.

2. Use your camera's controls to select the highest resolution setting. If you can, set your camera to save your file in the TIFF format. If you must save your image as a JPEG, use the best quality setting, meaning less compression. (Since this is a test of the imaging capabilities of your digital camera, saving your data in RAW data format isn't as useful. RAW data, an option in mostly higher-end digital cameras, generally isn't touched by a digital camera signal processor, and therefore doesn't suffer or benefit from onboard, on-the-fly image processing.)

3. Place your camera on a tripod and make an exposure. Since this is a general test, it's okay to use your camera's autoexposure settings.

4. Now open your image with an image processing program.

5. Using magnification and navigation tools, zoom into the areas with most detail. Look for **Sharpness or lack thereof**. For example, look at the image on the left. When magnified it appears sharp, a result of both good optics and appropriate camera image sharpening. The image on the right, may at first glance look "sharper" than the one on the left. But it's actually been over sharpened by camera processing, and upon magnification appears quite pixelated.

An image that appears soft or out of focus might be a result of poor optics, or it may not. Many digital cameras apply a slight blur to the image during onboard image processing to prevent color fringing. Also keep in mind that sometimes what you see as sharpness is really just increased contrast, again produced by image processing. Don't panic if your test image looks too sharp (contrasty) or too soft. Many digital cameras allow you to select from a variety of sharpness settings. Refer to your camera manual.

6. Now find an area with an abrupt color transition. Look for **color fringing**, which is often found at the color transition areas where interpolation can lead to color artifacts and loss of image detail. The image on the left below, for example, suffers from a lot of color fringing while the image on the right displays a more acceptable level of color fringing. There isn't much you can do about color fringing except, if possible, save your images in the RAW data format and process the images outside the camera. (☞ "RAW Data Revealed," Zooming In.)

Software Solutions

The potential of imaging software is something to always keep in mind while shooting. Knowing what can and can't be fixed will streamline the way you shoot, and ultimately make you a better photographer.

There are many commercial imaging software applications. Some of the more popular ones include Photoshop, Photoshop Elements, Paint Shop Pro, and Microsoft Picture It. Many digital cameras come bundled with one of these software packages, or a manufacturer's own basic imaging software. I've written books on using Photoshop and Photoshop Elements, so I am partial to those programs.

Throughout the book, I've devoted a second series of sidebars to many of the most common photographic issues that imaging software can address. These sidebars are titled "Software Solutions" and marked with an icon like the one in the following sidebar, and they cover a wide range of software-related issues, including:

- Changing Pixel Count (Chapter 1)
- Blurring a Background (Chapter 2)
- Digital Fill Flash, Fixing Red Eye, and Sharpening an Out-of-Focus Image (Chapter 3)
- Changing a Background and Adding Motion Blur (Chapter 4)
- Grabbing Stills from a Minimovie (Chapter 5)
- Changing the Quality of Light (Chapter 6)
- Fixing Keystoning (Chapter 7)
- Fixing Exposure (Chapter 8)
- Changing an Object's Color or Texture (Chapter 10)
- Removing Noise and Other Artifacts (Chapter 11)

Having noted what can be fixed with software, it's equally important to know that sometimes it is difficult or impossible to fix an image with software, such as times when you have:

- Radically distorted images caused by a wide-angle lens or faulty optics
- Radically overexposed or underexposed images
- Bad facial expressions or other subject-induced problems
- A blank image, as in leaving a lens cap on (you'd be surprised...)
- A totally out-of-focus image (software sharpening works only to a degree)
- Not enough resolution (software interpolation adds only pixels, not details)

Software Solutions: Changing Pixel Count

You can use software such as Photoshop, Photoshop Elements, and Genuine Fractals to increase or decrease the number of pixels generated by your digital camera. This is useful when you want to make an image smaller for the Web or for e-mail, or if you want to increase the perceived resolution. Remember, when you increase resolution this way, you are adding only pixels, not detail. Also keep in mind that when you interpolate data up or down, your image invariably "softens." I always suggest when using Photoshop for example, to apply a slight Unsharp Mask filter when you finish resizing.

Accessories That Make a Difference

Accessories extend the capabilities of digital cameras, sometimes quite profoundly. Custom-fitted underwater casings, for example, open a new world of visual exploration. Wide-angle lens attachments help overcome many of the optical limitations of digital cameras. Special LCD shades make it possible to review images even in the bright sun.

Important accessories are mentioned throughout the main text of the book, but whenever you see a sidebar with this icon ( ) you'll find additional information on accessories that I feel make a difference. These include:

- Add-On Lenses (Chapter 2)
- Removable Memory Storage (Chapter 3)
- From the Kitchen Drawer (Chapter 4)
- Batteries (Chapter 5)
- Backup Devices (Chapter 6)
- Tripods (Chapter 7)
- External Light Meters (Chapter 8)
- Commercial Rigs for VR Photography (Chapter 9)
- External Artificial Lights (Chapter 10)
- Underwater Casings (Chapter 11)

Finding Up-To-Date Information and Support

Hardly a day goes by without a new digital camera or accessory hitting the market. We are in an explosive and exciting time and it's hard to keep up. The information presented in this book is meant to be timeless (within reason), giving you solid tips and advice on the process of shooting digital. For up-to-date information on specific cameras, printers, and other products related to digital photography, I suggest you visit the companion website for this book, **www.shooting-digital.com**. There you'll find links to websites that offer timely information. You'll also find links to user forums where you can read what other impartial users have to say, and links to workshops and classes that I've found particularly useful. I'll update the links as need be. You'll also find links to many of the sources mentioned throughout the book.

Although websites are very useful for comparing prices and specifications, ultimately you'll want to see or touch a piece of digital photography equipment. It's especially important to hold a digital camera and gauge how it fits and feels and to see whether or not the controls are intuitive, or if the LCD is bright or big enough. National store chains such as Ritz Camera and CompUSA are good places to start for so-called consumer and prosumer digital cameras. Stores that offer professional digital cameras are rarer, but can be found by checking local Yellow Pages listings under "Photography." I've provided links to stores around the country at **www.shooting-digital.com**. Trade shows are another excellent venue for viewing and touching equipment, so I've also included links to trade shows such as the Photo Marketing Association (PMA) and Photo Plus East.

Shooting Great Portraits

A digital camera's instant feedback and interactivity makes it easier than ever for you to create memorable portraits. This chapter shows how to set up and how to shoot—and just as important, how to work with your subject during those stages. You'll see examples of different types of portraits and learn how each one was created.

Chapter Contents

John Isaac

The Digital Photographer and the Subject

Digital cameras can fundamentally change the way portraits are made. That's because a good portrait is more than a simple document of a person's face. Implicit in every portrait is a relationship between photographer and subject. When you shoot digital, your ability to interact with your subjects is expanded. By showing them the results on a screen and eliciting a response, you get the subjects more involved in the process. With an improved relationship between you and your subjects, both you and they are more relaxed and your actions more fluid. As well, with the ability to preview an image, you can be confident that you've got the right smile and the right look and not spend any more time than is necessary.

In the next sections, you'll get specific tips on working with your subject before and during the shoot.

Preparing for Your Shoot

Often portrait shooting sessions are set up in advance, which means you have time to prepare. Even if your portraits are taken on impulse, such as the one shown in Figure 2.1, there are things you can do to make sure you won't miss that once-in-a-lifetime shot.

Figure 2.1: John Isaac's moving portrait of a Kenyan man and his village was taken with an Olympus E-20, using a wide-angle add-on lens.

Your Camera and Equipment

To start, get to know your digital camera's features and limitations. This means:

- Know your camera's lag time. Many digital cameras have an annoying pause between the moment the shutter release is tripped and the moment the shutter actually releases. This is frustrating, but if you are aware of the lag you can anticipate the right moment to trip the shutter and improve the odds of getting the shot you wanted (☞ "Overcoming Camera Lag" in Chapter 3).

- Know how much battery life you have. Carry backups. Earlier digital cameras were energy hogs and you got only a limited number of shots before running out of juice. Newer camera models are more efficient, and batteries have also improved. Still, starting with fresh batteries and bringing backups can make a photo shoot go much smoother. Keep in mind that the more you share your LCD images with your subject, the faster the batteries will drain (☞ "Accessories That Make a Difference: Batteries" in Chapter 4).

- Know how many images your camera is capable of recording. This calculation is based on the capacity of your memory card, the actual sizes of your image files, and your choice of file formats. Although the precise number of images you need will vary depending on your subject, it's best if you don't have to stop in the middle of a shoot to erase unwanted shots or switch memory cards (☞ "Accessories That Make a Difference: Removable Memory Storage" in Chapter 3).

- Know your lens (or lenses). Many portraits are taken with a longer-than-normal focal length, which flattens and compliments facial features. Shooting with a less-than-normal focal length (wide angle) may cause unwanted facial distortion if you aren't particularly careful. Most consumer and prosumer digital cameras are equipped with zoom lenses that provide desirable longer-than-normal focal lengths. If you are shooting a professional digital camera with interchangeable lenses, then you have plenty of choices.

- Know whether your digital camera is capable of creating a shallow depth of field. The less depth of field you can create, the more you can isolate and draw attention to your subject (☞ "Knowing Your Camera: Controlling Depth of Field" later in this chapter).

- Make sure that external strobes (if you use them) connect and work properly with your digital camera. Not all digital cameras come with synch connections but there are ways around this (☞ "Accessories That Make a Difference: External Strobes" in Chapter 10).

- Know that your digital camera is capable of producing enough resolution for your output (☞ Chapter 12). Keep in mind that resolution can be enhanced up to a point with good results, depending on the portrait.

The Location

If possible and appropriate, take the time to scout out a location before you shoot. There are several thoughts to keep in mind while searching for the perfect location:

- If you prefer to shoot the portrait using natural light, scout out suitable spots. Be sure to take into account the time of day and the relative position of the sun.
- If you are shooting with external electronic strobes or incandescent lights that don't operate on batteries, look for places that are large enough for all of your equipment and offer electrical outlets. (Portable power sources are an expensive alternative.)
- Pay particular attention to potential backgrounds. You'll likely want something that doesn't overwhelm your subject.
- In all cases, look for places that offer privacy so you can concentrate on your equipment and your subject without interference from curious onlookers.

Preparing Your Subject

Whether you meet your subject in person or talk with them on the phone before hand, be sure to find out what they are planning to wear. Rules of good taste aside (hey, who am I to judge?) there are some technical things to keep in mind: plaids are almost always a potential problem. Electronic sensors consist of fixed, parallel strips of light-sensitive pixels, and busy patterns, such those found in plaids, can cause distracting moiré patterns. Also, because digital cameras often blow out highlights, I discourage subjects from wearing a lot of white, especially white hats.

It's helpful to know your subject's physical characteristics before the day of the shoot. Although there is a lot you can do with strategically placed or diffused lighting and camera angles to diminish double chins or soften the glare from overly active sweat glands, you might consider bringing a professional stylist along to the shoot. Stylists are listed in the Yellow Pages or in web search engines as "Stylists." When the budget is tight—which is most of the time nowadays—I carry a small makeup kit consisting of powder, a soft application brush, a mirror, and an assortment of lipsticks. I've also suggested to clients that they stop at the Macy's or Neiman Marcus cosmetic department for a tune-up before meeting me for a shoot.

 Note: *The Art of Makeup* (Harper Collins, 1996) and *Making Faces* (Little, Brown, 1999) by Kevyn Aucoin are both beautiful and practical books that'll give you many useful tips on basic makeup techniques.

Working with Your Subject During the Shoot

When I am shooting a portrait I try to engage my subject in conversation. What I discuss with my subject varies, but I poke around until I find something that takes their mind off the moment. I also involve them in the shooting process, sometimes even handing the camera to them and encouraging them to take a shot of me. Other ways to involve the subject include:

- Showing them the LCD display. Most digital cameras come with LCD displays that range in size from 1.5 x 1.8 inch to 3.5 x 4 inch. (The larger the LCD, the easier it is to view, but the more power is consumed.) To improve the LCD viewing in strong outdoor light, I suggest you use some sort of light shield. I use the commercially available Hoodman (see Figure 2.2), but you can also make your own with scissors, tape, and cardboard. You can also make it easy for people (and yourself) to see the image by using a reading magnifying glass, which is commonly available at pharmacies.

Figure 2.2: The commercially available Hoodman, shown here attached to a Nikon camera, makes viewing and sharing the LCD in bright light much easier.

- Hooking the digital camera to a TV monitor. Many digital cameras have a composite video out port, which makes it possible to view the images on just about any TV monitor. Keep in mind that often the ideal portrait orientation is vertical, so if you view a vertical shot on a TV monitor you'll either have to turn the TV on its side or turn your head sideways.

While shooting, display confidence. Even if you are nervous or normally shy, if you've followed my suggestions and feel prepared for the shoot, confidence should come naturally. If you exude confidence, you'll be amazed at what people will do when you tell them to do something. This is especially important when you are shooting a group shot and you need to stage manage a room full of unruly people (☞ "Group Portraits," later in this chapter). Believe me, if you have a camera in hand and you show confidence, people will respond. I had the privilege of shooting a group portrait that included the former President of the United States, Jimmy Carter. Yes, even the former President of the United States responded when I told him to move into another position. He also yelled to me to step back, which I did, right into a tree...I love that guy!

What You Can and Cannot Fix

Finally, keep the potential of imaging software in mind when shooting. Specifically you should know that even after you take the photograph, you still can:

- Easily remove redeye caused by a direct flash
- Remove or diminish the effect of distracting backgrounds
- Soften skin and remove blemishes
- Fix contrast, exposure, and color problems (to a degree)
- Sharpen out-of-focus images (to a degree)
- Correct distortion caused by a wide-angle lens or faulty optics (to a degree)
- Blur or remove a distracting background
- Diffuse the harsh effects of direct strobes

On the other hand, keep in mind that it's difficult or impossible to fix:

- Radically distorted images caused by a wide-angle lens or faulty optics
- Radically overexposed or underexposed images
- Facial expressions that express displeasure or tension between you and your subject

If possible, it's always best if you get the shot right in the first place.

Software Solutions: Blurring a Background

One of the easiest ways to diminish the effect of an overwhelming background is to blur it. Using Photoshop Elements (or Photoshop), here's what I did to improve the image shown on the left here.

1. I selected the subject using the Lasso selection tool.
2. I then chose Select ➤ Inverse to make the background the active selection. I then slightly feathered this selection by 2 pixels (Select ➤ Feather) to soften the transition between the foreground and background.
3. To give the picture more depth, I applied a Gaussian Blur to the background (Filter ➤ Blur ➤ Gaussian Blur). I set the Radius at 13.5 pixels. The final image is shown on the right.

Making Head and Shoulder Shots

One of the most commonly used portraits is the so-called "head and shoulders" shot such as the one shown in Figure 2.3. You see these portraits everywhere: with job promotion notices, in passports, and accompanying resumes. Digital cameras combined with some basic photography techniques can make it easier than ever to create these shots. Here are four variations, using different digital cameras and different lighting sources.

Using Window Light with Reflector

This is one of my favorite methods of making a head and shoulder shot. It is also one of the easiest. All it requires is a digital camera, a window transmitting natural light, and some sort of reflector or bounce light. For the shot shown in Figure 2.3 I used my prosumer Olympus E-10, a 4-megapixel digital camera with a mounted 35-140mm equivalent zoom lens. However, this technique will produce great pictures even with a consumer-level digital camera.

Figure 2.3: Indirect window light mixed with reflected light from a gold reflector produces a flattering effect.

I started by choosing my background carefully. I made sure I had a large, plain area to frame my subject. As I describe later in the chapter, the lens on the E-10, even when set to the widest aperture, doesn't blur the background as much as expected and an in-focus, cluttered background would have been distracting. Although I could have fixed a distracting background later using imaging software, it would have been time-consuming to do so. It was much easier to find an appropriate background before taking the picture.

I always vary the position of the camera in relation to my subject's head until I find the most flattering angle. If you look at the image shown on the left in Figure 2.4 you'll see why. In this case, shooting down on my subject emphasized the high fore-head, and shooting up, as shown on the right, didn't help either. For this situation straight on was best. You'll have to experiment to find the most photogenic angle for your subject. This is something you can do without firing a shot. You should be able to see what works and what doesn't through the viewfinder.

Figure 2.4: Vary the angle of the camera, looking for the most flattering perspective. The shot on the left wasn't bad, but it wasn't as flattering as shooting straight on. Shooting upward produced the unflattering shot on the right.

To distribute light evenly over the entire face, which is very important, considering the capabilities of most digital cameras, I use a 32-inch hand-held gold or soft white reflector—available at professional camera stores or on the Web. The reflector I use folds up nicely and can be easy carried anywhere, as shown in Figure 2.5. (Refer to **www.shooting-digital.com** for commercial sources.) You can also use a standard white piece of paper or stiffer, white foam board if you want, although you won't benefit from the warm light produced by the gold metallic surface of the commercial reflector. I find fold up reflectors so convenient I always carry a smaller, 22-inch version in my camera bag. It's convenient when you have someone to hold the reflector for you but I've learned to both hold and aim the reflector with one hand while holding and shooting my camera in the other. Some photographers tape reflectors to walls, railings, or trees, or lean reflectors on chairs or poles when available.

Figure 2.5: Commercial reflectors fold up for easy storage and carrying.

The E-10 provides different exposure mode controls and I chose Aperture mode. In this mode I select the aperture and the camera selects a corresponding shutter speed to produce the correct exposure. I almost always select the widest open aperture setting or a nearby setting (in this case I set the aperture to f/2.4) and check that the shutter speed is fast enough to avoid camera-induced blur (☞ "Reducing Camera-Induced Motion Blur," later in this chapter). Even if your digital camera doesn't give you different exposure modes to choose from, and you use a reflector and a long or telephoto lens setting, and follow the rest of my suggestions, you'll probably get good results with the standard automatic exposure setting.

In this example my subject is standing, but they could just as well have been sitting as long as the light from the window strikes their face and they are comfortable.

The following is the EXIF metadata for my shot:

Focal length=24mm (90mm equivalent)
F stop=f2.4
Shutter speed=1/100th
Flash: Off
JPEG Quality: High
Resolution= 1600 x 1200
ISO=80

I've explained why I chose f/2.4 and as you can see, the corresponding shutter speed was 1/100th of second. You can also see by the EXIF data that my focal length was 90mm equivalent, meaning I could safely hand hold the shot. 90mm equivalent is considered a medium-long focal length, which is possible on most digital cameras. Wide angle lenses tend to distort the face unless the picture is shot straight on. (See Figure 2.6.) Longer focal lengths flatten and flatter facial features. Just remember that the longer the focal length, the more chance of camera shake.

Figure 2.6: Wide-angle lenses can cause distortion, especially when shot from above or below the face.

You'll also notice that I set my camera to produce a JPEG file. Most of the time, with shots like this portrait, I don't have a problem using the JPEG file format, even though some information may be lost during compression. I take a lot of shots when I am shooting a portrait, and by using JPEG I can fit a lot more images on a memory card. Also, many times, the head and shoulder shot is used small, whether it is on the web or in print, and resolution/quality isn't as critical. Of course, if you are planning on greatly enlarging your image, or if you want every pore, wart, or freckle to be perfectly sharp, then save the file as a TIFF or even in the RAW format, if your camera allows it (☞ "Know Your Camera: File Formats" in Chapter 8).

How many shots does it take to get it right? That depends on the subject, of course. You can always shoot until you run out of memory or your batteries go dead. But I often stop well before that. The beauty of the digital camera is that I can see my results immediately and stop when I've got a good shot, and therefore save time for both my subject and me.

One last thing: I always try to fill the frame with my subject's head and shoulders. I mean, why waste pixels on space that I'll likely throw away later? I know that some point-and-shoot digital cameras won't let you get closer than four or five feet, so filling a frame with a sharp image isn't always possible, but do the best you can.

Bottom line: Use a wide f-stop, telephoto lens setting, and a reflector to evenly distribute light on your subject's face.

Reducing Camera-Induced Motion Blur

Motion blur caused by camera shake is common when you shoot a long focal length lens combined with a slow shutter speed. What constitutes a slow shutter speed? It depends on the focal length of your lens and your ability to hold the camera steady. Generally speaking, the shorter the focal length, the slower the shutter speed you can use before you get camera blur. That means when you've set your zoom to the widest angle, you can actually get away with shutter speeds as slow as 1/20th of a second. Conversely, if you've zoomed into telephoto setting, your shutter speed should be faster than 1/100th of a second. Because there are so many variables to take into account, it's best to experiment with different focal lengths and—assuming you have control over the shutter speed—with different shutter speeds, using the LCD readout for immediate feedback.

Of course, you may still get motion blur if your subject moves, but that is another story. Some digital cameras offer an image-stabilization feature. When activated, image stabilization makes it possible to handhold at much slower shutter speeds.

You'll minimize the chance of camera shake by holding the camera with both hands, with your left hand supporting the lens. Obviously, this technique is valid only if your digital camera has a protruding lens. Most digital cameras are built with right-handed people in mind, and the shutter release is situated accordingly. Two steps are commonly required to release the shutter and take a picture: a slight pressure on the trigger sets the auto focus and exposure measuring in motion, and then slightly more pressure actually releases the shutter. Don't jam your finger down on the shutter release; you'll end up with camera shake and possibly an out-of focus-image, improperly exposed as well. Instead, press the shutter release slowly and firmly. If you are especially worried about camera shake, hold your breath before pressing the release. You might also find it useful to brace yourself against a wall, pillar, or other fixed object.

Using On-Camera Strobes

Camera-mounted strobes often produce light that is harsh and unflattering, as shown on the left in Figure 2.7. The larger, more diffused a light source is, the softer the quality of the light it produces. There are several ways to soften strobe light and reduce its harshness, such as "mixing" strobe light with ambient light, as shown on the right in Figure 2.7. You can also diffuse the strobe light with translucent material, or, if need be, place your finger partially over the flash to cut down on the intensity. If possible, you can sometimes aim the strobe at a ceiling and bounce the light down onto the subject. However, keep in mind that if a ceiling is anything other than white, a colorcast will be created, which can be corrected by adjusting your white balance setting but with some effort. Whenever possible, I've found it useful to use camera controls to dial back the intensity of a strobe by about 1/4 of a stop. Not all digital cameras give you this kind of control, though, and you'll have to consult the manual to see if this is possible with your digital camera.

Bottom line: On-camera strobes can be used for making portraits if diffused or mixed with ambient light.

Figure 2.7: The shot on the left was taken with an onboard flash. Nothing was done to diffuse the flash or diminish the harshness. The shot on the right was taken with the same flash aimed directly at the subject, but this time the light was diffused with tissue paper and mixed with ambient light.

Accessories That Make a Difference: Add-On Lenses

You can extend the lens capabilities of some digital cameras that don't accept interchange-able lenses by using add-on lenses such as the one shown here.

Add-on lenses are available with wide angle, telephoto, or close-up capabilities. Some of these add-on lenses are built specifically for one camera model or one brand; others are made to fit a variety of digital camera lenses but require additional adapters. In all cases, you should research a particular add-on lens before purchasing. Consider the following:

- Quality varies widely from model to model, and from manufacturer to manufacturer. Often you get what you pay for.
- Unless your digital camera is an SLR type, expect to use the LCD monitor for viewing.
- Watch for vignetting—as typified by darkening the edges of an image, most noticeable at wider apertures—and overall loss of lens speed.
- Consider that add-on lenses add weight to your system, and are one more thing that can be lost. Use a soft pouch or other suitable means of protecting the add-on lens during storage or travel.
- Consider that the cost of a required adapter sometimes exceeds the cost of a particular add-on lens and adds yet more weight and one more thing to lose.
- Close-up attachments can be bulky and reduce the amount of light received by the camera. They are usually made for only one camera model. Many digital cameras must be in the fully zoomed position to prevent vignetting.

Using Continuous Light Sources

As an alternative to an electronic flash, you can use light sources that are on continuously.

Bruce Avera Hunter, former National Geographic photo lab technician turned professional photographer, shot the portrait shown in Figure 2.8 with a prosumer Nikon Coolpix 990 digital camera and four halogen lights with directional barn doors that came from a discarded copy-stand system. He shot the portrait for the Discovery Channel's Discovery Health Online Body Challenge in his basement studio in Maryland. The portrait is one of many "before and after" shots from a series on weight management. Once again, the techniques illustrated in this example can be applied to consumer, prosumer, and professional level digital cameras alike.

Figure 2.8: This portrait, shot for the Discovery Channel, was shot by Bruce Avera Hunter in a makeshift basement studio using a Nikon Coolpix 990 and four continuous light sources.

Continuous light sources, like the ones Bruce used for this shot, are an inexpensive and good alternative to studio strobes. Not only do they produce a pleasing, consistent light, but also they are more manageable than studio strobe systems, which typically cost several thousand dollars as opposed to several hundred. If you are lucky like Bruce, you might find an old set of lights in the trash or at a flea market or on eBay for a song. You won't need an additional flash meter to measure the light when you use continuous light sources, and it really doesn't matter what color temperature the lights have as long as you adjust your camera's white balance settings accordingly. Halogen works well, but tungsten and even fluorescent can work just as well. Although the lights themselves are relatively inexpensive, you'll also have to spend money on accessories such as light stands, extension cords, barn doors, and diffusion material. Lights with cooling fans generally cost more. (See **www.shooting-digital.com** for commercial sources.) One disadvantage to continuous lighting sources is that the heat they produce can be distracting to a subject and produce noticeable perspiration. To avoid this, use the lowest possible wattage or block the heat with diffusion material.

Bruce set up one 500-watt light to the left of this camera, which was mounted on a tripod, and one to the right. He diffused the light by dangling a beige sheet from his ceiling a safe distance in front of each light, creating a very desirable effect, similiar to one created using a soft box. To diffuse the shadow from the background—another beige sheet—Bruce situated a 300-watt light next to the light on the camera's right side, and aimed it at the stucco ceiling. The bounced light diffused the shadows cast by the subject on the background and lightened the top of her head slightly. The fourth light, 500 watts, was situated directly behind the camera and bounced from a silver car sun shield toward the subject's face. This is the light that gave her eyes a nice sparkle and filled the dark areas under her eyes. (Bruce's setup is shown in Figure 2.9).

Figure 2.9: The setup for Bruce's shot.

Bruce had his subject hold up a white card, which he then used to make a custom white balance setting (↩ "Know Your Camera: Adjusting White Balance" in Chapter 11).

At first he used his camera's spot metering option to make an exposure, but when he noticed in the LCD preview that it was producing an image that was too dark, he switched to the camera's Matrix setting, which worked great. His shutter, as revealed by the camera's EXIF data, was 1/68th of a second; the f-stop was 3.4 and the focal length was 14.1mm (or 70mm equivalent). Bruce used an AC adapter so he didn't have to worry about his batteries going out in the middle of the shoot.

Bottom line: Continuous light sources are an inexpensive alternative to external strobes and can be used with nearly all digital cameras without additional cords, flash meters, or other strobe lighting accessories.

Working with a Soft Box and Reflector

Photographer Richard Morgenstein shot the moody head shot of an artist shown in Figure 2.10 with a Canon G1 prosumer digital camera. He used just one main light provided by a powerful professional electronic strobe encased in a soft box, and a reflector to bounce some light into the shadow areas. Soft boxes, which are commercially available, produce a soft, less defined shadow-edge light much like the light seen on a cloudy day. Richard's setup is shown to the left in Figure 2.11, and to the right is a generic image of a soft box. The subject straddled a chair about 12 feet from a store-bought background made of gray cloth. By keeping his subject this far from the background, Richard avoided having light spill onto the background.

Figure 2.10: This moody portrait was made by Richard Morgenstein using an electronic strobe and a soft box to diffuse the light. A reflector to the right provided a slight fill.

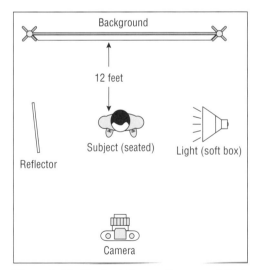

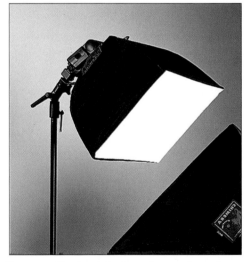

Figure 2.11: To the left is a diagram of Richard's setup. To the right is a photo of an electronic strobe and soft box.

Generally, when shooting portraits with a digital camera, it is desirable to keep your lighting ratio to a minimum, creating *flat lighting* (in the vernacular of professional photography). In other words, adjust your lighting sources—be they strobes or continuous lights—so that they produce light in equal values evenly across the face. This is important because digital cameras don't have the dynamic range of some films, and you'll lose detail either in the shadow areas or in the highlights, if the intensity of light varies too much. However, there are times when this rule should be broken, and that is what Richard has done. If Richard had added another strobe light to fill the right side of the subject's face he would have created a good but not great portrait. The drama in this case comes precisely from the strong contrast between light and dark, which is emphasized by the digital camera's limitations.

Chances are, you don't own a soft box, and have never even used one except perhaps in a photography class. It may seem that a case study involving a discussion of soft boxes and professional strobes may belong solely in the realm of the professional photographer. But the fact is, soft boxes provide a beautiful, diffused light that is ideally suited for shooting digital. They can be used with more inexpensive continuous light sources as well and there are even soft boxes made specially to fit over small, external strobes like the ones that mount to the top of your camera. If you are serious about shooting portraits, and serious about shooting digital in general, I suggest you explore the option of investing in a soft box, along with appropriate light stands to hold the boxes in place. I've noticed that more and more lighting equipment manufacturers—who used to cater only to professional photographers—are tailoring soft box prices to the budget of the serious amateur. Again, go to **www.shooting-digital.com** for referrals to manufacturers.

There is another important issue raised by this case study. How do you fire an external strobe from a digital camera that isn't equipped with a flash synchro socket? All professional digital cameras and many prosumer digital cameras come equipped with a socket that connects an external strobe via a cable to the camera shutter release. If your digital camera isn't thus equipped, you have a couple of options. First, if your digital camera has a hot shoe for mounting an external strobe, you can purchase an adaptor that turns the hot shoe into a flash synchro socket. (This is what Richard did with his Canon G1 to make the portrait shown in this case study.) You can also use the camera's built-in strobe to fire the external flash unit; most external flashes have a "slave" mode that commands the strobe to fire when another flash is flashed (☞ "Accessories That Make a Difference: External Artificial Lights" in Chapter 10).

Bottom line: Soft boxes provide even, diffused light, perfect for shooting digital. But remember, although an even lighting ratio is usually desirable, the best image may very well be one that doesn't follow the rules.

Note: Backdrops for portraits can be bought or self-made. They can be paper, cloth, or any other material, and there are no hard rules. I often use commercially available seamless paper that comes in varying widths from 4 feet to 10 feet, and in rolls, like paper towels. (See **www.shooting-digital.com** for sources.) I've also painted my own backdrops using canvas (which can be expensive) or bed sheets (less expensive but not as durable or as easy to work with because they crease and fold easily). I suggest avoiding busy patterns that distract from the subject. When you shoot, place your subject several feet away from the background to avoid shadows, unless that is what you want.

Environmental Portraits

It's one thing to take a simple head and shoulders shot where you are focusing on the face and trying to remove anything extraneous. It is quite another thing to attempt to create a portrait that gives a glimpse into a person's personality and shows an environment at the same time. These portraits become a narrative and often tell an entire story in a single glance. Like the head-and-shoulder shots described earlier, there are many ways to take an environmental portrait, with natural light or with strobes.

Figure 2.12: Chester Simpson made this environmental portrait at a Civil War reenactment by combining natural light with a portable strobe light.

Daylight with Camera Strobe

Chester Simpson made the portrait shown in Figure 2.12 with a Canon D-30 digital camera, a relatively modestly priced professional camera that accepts interchangeable lenses. It was shot in 2001 at a reenactment of the Battle of Bull Run in Leesburg, Virginia. Chester used a Canon 540 portable strobe mounted directly on his camera and balanced the light from the strobe with the soft ambient light of the tent. As discussed earlier, combining strobe light and ambient light is very effective. If Chester hadn't used the strobe, the subject's face would have been too dark or the environment around him too light. Since Chester often shoots "off the cuff," he relies mostly on the camera's automatic settings and a quick glance at the LCD preview screen to make sure the exposure is in the ballpark. Chester also used the automatic white balance settings and used Photoshop later to fine-tune the color cast. Chester almost always saves his data in the RAW format and converts it later using the Canon software that came with his camera. The RAW format is like shooting negative film, he says. It gives him more room for exposure error (☞ "Know Your Camera: File Formats" in Chapter 8). This format produces a 3.4M file for each image and Chester uses a 1G microdrive to save his images.

Bottom line: Using a fill flash in bright outdoor light will likely improve a portrait. Check with your digital camera's manual to learn how to set the flash to fill flash mode.

Beauty from Window Light and Reflector

John Isaac made the stunning portrait shown in Figure 2.13 of his friend Carmen who dances for the American Ballet Theatre. By positioning her on the floor, John both put emphasis on his subject and also gave a hint of the dancer's world.

He used an Olympus E-20 digital camera. His background is actually the floor, and he positioned his friend near a window that provided the light you see on her face. He taped a gold reflector to a pole located to his right. The 33-inch reflector filled Carmen's shoulder with a gold light. He then perched on a stool and shot from above. Again, this technique will produce great pictures, even with relatively simple digital cameras with no adjustments.

Bottom line: Backgrounds can be anything, as long as they don't take attention away from the person you are photographing.

Shooting in the Bright Light of Day

Figure 2.1 at the beginning of this chapter shows an environmental portrait taken by John Isaac while shooting for a book titled *A Day in the Life of Africa* (the portrait wasn't used in that book). Once again he used the Olympus E-20, but this time he used a 24mm equivalent add-on lens. He was literally only a few inches from the subject's face, but because he shot straight on there was little of the distortion typical of a wide-angle lens shot angled up or down. It was taken in bright sunlight and John actually exposed for the highlights, knowing that the dark areas of the image would be too dark but he could lighten them later in Photoshop. He shot at f /11 which, combined with the wide angle lens, put both his foreground and background sharply in focus. In this case, because of the composition and the strength of the man's face, the background doesn't overwhelm or intrude. In fact, the background tells us much about the man, including where and how he lives.

Bottom line: It doesn't matter which digital camera you shoot with; use wide-angle lenses carefully. Aim straight on and you'll lessen the chance of facial distortion.

Figure 2.13: This simple but beautiful portrait was made using only window light and a reflector. (Photo by John Isaac)

Group Portraits

Shooting groups of people can be especially difficult, especially if you are working with a group of people who are busy, or who don't want to be together.

Professional photographer Mark Richards took the group shot shown in Figure 2.14 for *Time* magazine at San Francisco General Hospital, using a Canon D-30 digital camera. Mark used two strobes, one aimed toward the subjects and one behind, which provided the strong foreground shadows. The front strobe was encased in a soft box that provided soft, flattering light on the faces. Fill light came from the white walls hence no second front light needed. A diagram of Mark's setup is shown in Figure 2.14.

Mark set his camera to manual exposure mode and used a strobe meter to calculate the exposure values for the shot. He used f/11 at 1/180th of a second. When Mark is really busy and doesn't have time to mess with a strobe meter, he simply sets his f-stop and shutter speed based on personal experience and uses the camera's LCD histogram read-out to fine tune the exposure (↶ "Software Solutions: Fixing Exposure" in Chapter 8 and ↶ "Reading Histograms" in Zooming In.) Like other professionals mentioned in this chapter, Mark consistently underexposes his shots to ensure that detail is not lost in the highlights. This was especially important in this situation, with the white hospital jackets.

Mark actually dropped to the floor to get the interesting angle and used his 17-35mm zoom lens set to 17mm for the shot. (The Canon D-30 has a 1.6 lens multiplier, so the 35mm equivalent for this shot was about 27mm).

Mark saved the shot as a high-quality JPEG although nowadays he mostly saves his work in the RAW data file format, opting for even higher quality possibilities. (It helps that he also has traded in his Canon D-30 for the Canon D1, which allows him to save both RAW and JPEG versions of the same image.)

Shooting portraits is Mark's specialty and when it comes to shooting groups he acknowledges that the technical aspects are only part of the challenge. When it comes to arranging and working with his subjects he says, "You've got to set the tone immediately. Think of yourself as a director on a set. Make the people in the shot pay attention to you by saying just that. Tell them, 'Hey, we are doing a picture. You are the stars. Work with me. Let's do this right.' Get your subjects onboard, and you'll make a great photo."

Bottom line: When shooting groups, get everyone to listen to you and the rest is relatively easy.

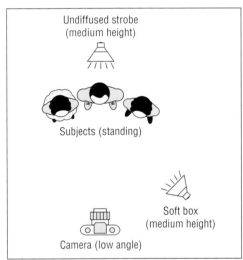

Figure 2.14: The group shot above was taken by Mark Richards for Time magazine, shot with a Canon D-30 digital camera. The diagram shows Mark's lighting setup.

Know Your Camera: Controlling Depth of Field

When you focus your camera and lens on a particular point, you expect that point to be sharp. However, depending on several variables, objects in front or behind that point may also be sharp. In a portrait, you often want only the subject to be in focus. How much of an image is in focus and how much isn't is referred to as *depth of field*.

The exact amount of depth of field is a function of several factors: lens f-stop, lens focal length, the camera's distance from the subject, and the size of the camera's sensor that determines the specifications of a particular lens. However, in general, wider apertures such as f/2.8 and f/3.5 produce less depth of field, while narrower apertures such as f/8 and f/16 increase the depth of field and place more things in focus including distracting backgrounds. Longer-than-normal focal lengths combined with wide apertures decrease the depth of field. Remember from Chapter 1 that "normal" focal lengths are determined by the physical size of the sensor in your camera.

Aperture control is available with most prosumer and professional digital cameras via an aperture priority or manual mode. You are more limited if you are using a consumer level camera without these capabilities, although you still have options. (More on that shortly.)

It's very important that you get to know how much control you really have over the depth of field. Digital cameras don't always produce what you expect, especially if you are coming with expectations from the world of 35mm film cameras. (We got into this subject briefly in Chapter 1.)

This image was shot with an Olympus E-10 at f/2.2 with a focal length of 25mm (approximately 100mm equivalent). Notice the background.

Now look at this image.

It was shot with a Nikon D100 digital camera at f/3.5. The background is even blurrier. What is going on here? Both shots were made with a large aperture, which, in combination with a longer focal length should reduce the depth of focus (in theory). It turns out that the Olympus camera uses a smaller sensor than the Nikon. Two different formats and two different results.

How do you know what result your camera and lens will give you in a similar situation? Assuming you have control over the aperture (via aperture select or manual modes), simply select the widest aperture. Set your focal length to the longer end of its zooming range. Look at the results in your LCD. Remember, the LCD doesn't show all the pixels the camera captures so sometimes you may need to open your image file in a computer with image software to get a better sense of what is going on.

What if you don't get the results you want? Or what do you do if you are using a camera that doesn't give you control over the aperture setting? How can you get less depth of field? The easiest way, if your camera is capable of it, is to increase your focal length. (This also increases the chances of motion blur, so be sure to hold your camera extra steady). Get as close to your subject as you can. The closer the camera is to an object, the less depth of field you will have. You can also just try to make sure the background doesn't have any busy, distracting patterns. This won't affect the depth of field, but it's an effective workaround. Finally, a lot can be done later using selective blurring techniques with imaging software.

Later I'll get into the issue of increased depth of field, which is useful when you are shooting buildings or landscapes, or certain product shots.

Photographing Children, Pets, and Social Events

What does shooting digital photographs of children, pets, and social events have in common? Making a good photo often means capturing a fleeting, sometimes spontaneous moment. Not only does this challenge the skills of the best photographer, but it also challenges the technical abilities of many digital cameras. In this chapter we will look at ways to meet— and overcome—these challenges as well as learn some neat tricks that'll give your photographs more zing.

3

Chapter Contents

Beating the Odds
Overcoming Camera Lag
Photographing Children
Photographing Pets
Photographing Social Events

Mikkel Aaland

Beating the Odds

It's one thing to be lucky and get the perfect shot of your son or daughter hitting a home run for the first time at a Little League baseball game, or capture your cat when it is holding still and looking at you at the same time, or catch the exact moment when a bride throws the bouquet in the air. It's another to consistently use a digital camera to make photos that overcome the odds.

When shooting subjects that don't hold still, pros know it's absolutely critical to:

- Position yourself and your camera in relation to the subject carefully, and with forethought.
- Learn to anticipate the right moment to shoot through careful observation and knowledge of the subject.

Figure 3.1: This shot required careful positioning, anticipation, and a wild pitch. (Photo by Doug Salin, shot with an Olympus Camedia C-3000Z)

Look at Figure 3.1. This was a fortunate shot but no accident. Professional photographer Doug Salin carefully aimed his consumer-level Olympus Camedia C-3000Z digital camera through the chain-link backstop fence at his 14-year-old son Zachary. He zoomed the lens close to its maximum 96mm (35mm equivalent) focal length. Once he had framed the shot so that his son, the catcher, and home plate were all visible, he pressed the shutter release halfway to pre-focus the lens on his son. Doug then took his eye from the optical viewfinder and turned his attention instead to the pitcher and the ball. He kept his arm and hand holding the camera propped firmly against the chain link fence and his finger pressed halfway on the shutter release. Even though the camera was "focused and primed" to shoot, Doug knew there would be a lag between the time when he pressed the shutter release all the way and the time when the shutter actually released. Like any good baseball batter, Doug knew he would have to anticipate the second when the ball would pass over the plate, and actually trip the shutter well in advance of that moment. He tried a few pitches, missing the perfect moment. But when the pitcher unexpectedly threw a wild pitch, Doug was ready, and caught his son leaping in the air just before the catcher caught the ball.

Some other technical details: Doug used the C-3000Z's aperture priority mode and set the aperture to f/6.3. This resulted in a shutter speed of 1/200th of a second, plenty fast enough to catch his son jumping but not quite fast enough to completely freeze the action of the ball. Doug also used the C-3000Z's exposure compensation to underexpose the image by 2/3 of a stop. Through trial and error, he learned to bias the C-3000Z's exposure, otherwise the camera consistently overexposed most shots.

By the way, Doug actually specializes in architectural photography, not shooting Little League baseball. We will see more of his professional work in Chapter 7.

Overcoming Camera Lag

There is nothing more frustrating than aiming your digital camera at a decisive moment, pressing the shutter release and having nothing happen—no shutter release, no flash, nothing—until the moment has passed.

This is the dreaded shutter release lag that is common to so many digital cameras, including the camera Doug used in the opening example. Although shutter release lag can be severely limiting, there are ways of dealing with it, as we just saw with Doug's shot of his son at the plate.

First, not all digital cameras suffer from this technical annoyance. For example, most professional digital cameras are extremely responsive and the Fuji FinePix S602 is particularly responsive for a consumer-level digital camera. Newer models such as the prosumer Canon G3 suffer less than their predecessors, but, for now, the chances are pretty good that the digital camera you are using lags between the instant you press the shutter release button and the actual moment the shutter is released and an image captured. In all fairness to digital cameras, many film cameras, especially the ones with complex electronic autofocus circuitry, also suffer from shutter release lag to some degree.

In the next sidebar, "Know Your Camera: Testing For Shutter Release Lag," you'll learn an easy way to quantify shutter release lag on your camera. You may already know that your camera lags, but the test should help you determine how much lag really exists.

So what do you do if you have this problem? Short of going out and buying a better digital camera, you can:

- Get really good at anticipating shots.
- Exert control over the situation. For example, command people to hold still, or re-create the shot you missed.

- Lower your expectations of getting exactly the shot you want every time. Or, a more positive way of looking at this is to learn to appreciate an element of unpredictability—after all, sometimes the shot you actually get is more interesting than the one you intended.
- Press your shutter release button part way to pre-focus and "prime" the electronics for a quick release. For many digital cameras there will still be a lag when you press the release fully, but not as extreme.
- Check for updates of your digital camera firmware.

  I'll elaborate on these suggestions later in the chapter.

Note: Digital cameras contain programmable memory chips not unlike a computer's ROM or PROM chips. From time to time digital camera companies—like computer companies—provide firmware updates, which update the camera's memory chips' coded instructions and improve or correct how certain functions are performed. These updates—available via the manufacturers website—don't change fundamental specifications of a digital camera (resolution, lens speed, etc.), but they can, for example, improve camera response time, extend memory card support, support different color modes, and update EXIF data support.

Other Performance Issues

There are a couple of other digital camera performance-related issues you may have encountered that can affect your ability to capture a decisive moment. Slow camera start-up is one. Suddenly a good shot presents itself and you turn on the power to your camera. Several seconds later, the camera is still not fully powered up and the shot is gone. Keeping your camera in so-called "sleep mode" can minimize this irritating characteristic of many digital cameras. However, with many digital cameras there still is a lag while the camera wakes up. And even in sleep mode you are using precious battery power. Assuming you've determined this to be a problem—easily tested, by turning on a digital camera's power and waiting—the best solution is to learn to anticipate your shots and have the camera fully powered on in advance and ready to go when the shot presents itself.

If your digital camera uses an electronic viewfinder rather than an optical one, or if you are framing the scene through the LCD preview monitor, there is yet another annoying lag that occurs when you try to zoom quickly from either wide angle to telephoto or from telephoto to wide angle. This lag—which can be characterized by a jerky, uneven sequence of images—is especially disconcerting if you are used to the smooth action and immediate feedback you often get with an optical viewfinder. There is not much you can do about this, except get used to it or switch to a camera with an optical viewfinder. However, electronic viewfinders do have their advantages. For example, more often than not you get exactly what the sensor sees with little image cropping; also, you can view in real time the effects of various exposure settings.

Enough about the limitations, er…*quirks* of digital cameras. Let's move on to the fun stuff.

Know Your Camera: Testing for Shutter Release Lag

When you press the shutter release button on a digital camera, you set in motion a sequence of complex electronic events. Depending on your digital camera and your settings, light is metered and a shutter speed determined and set; focus is determined and the sensor circuitry enabled. This sequence can take time, and if your subject has moved or changed expression, you won't get the shot you want or expect.

How do you determine how much lag your camera has? These specifications aren't usually readily available from the manufacturer, unless they are especially good. Camera reviewers sometimes give this information, but usually only if the digital camera is notably good or notably bad.

Here is a simple shutter release lag test that requires the help of an assistant. Depending on the features of your digital camera you may want to perform the test more than once. For example, try it once with your camera set to auto focus, once in manual focus, and once with your camera set to auto focus but with the focus pre-focused and locked. (Check your camera manual to see if your camera offers these options.) It is best to perform the test using sufficient natural light, with the flash turned off. Keep in mind that this is only a shutter release lag test; it doesn't tell you anything about how quickly—or in many cases, how slowly—your digital camera processes and stores the image file after you've taken the picture.

1. Have your assistant put his finger to his cheek, as shown on the far left.

2. Tell your assistant that on the count of three, you want him to to take his finger away from his face in one smooth motion. Begin counting, and at the exact count of three you press the shutter release button just as your assistant moves his finger.

3. Take a look at the results in the LCD preview window and note where the assistant's finger is. If it is as shown in the middle, your camera lag time is minimal. The image on the right shows what happens with a digital camera that has a really long lag time.

For a more accurate test, go **www.shooting-digital.com** and download the "Shutter Lag Release" tool. You'll have a choice between using an animated GIF or a QuickTime movie to test your camera. Follow the accompanying instructions.

Photographing Children

It's relatively easy to make an ordinary photograph of a child. Scrapbooks are full of them. The child, with a forced smile, stands stiffly and stares into the lens of the camera. It's quite another thing to make a photograph that evokes much more than just time and place—one that captures the natural emotion of childhood.

A digital camera—slow response time notwithstanding—can help you go from taking mundane, ordinary shots of children to extraordinary ones. With none of the economic consequences associated with film, and with the benefits of immediate feedback, shooting digital offers you a creative license that you may not have had since…well, since you were a child yourself and dabbled in ink and paint.

Combine a newfound creative freedom with the following shooting advice and you've got a winning combination:

- Always carry a camera with you. The best shots come at unexpected times and places. (You can buy digital cameras that fit in your pocket and still produce decent quality.)

- Shoot on the children's level. Digital cameras with tilting viewfinders make it easy to do this.

- Play around with your digital camera settings. With digital cameras, there are few costs for making mistakes. Be open to lucky accidents.

- Stop shooting when a child starts complaining. My dad never listened to me, and see what happened? One of the reasons I took up photography was just to get on the other side of the camera.

- If you can't capture the "decisive moment," consider using a digital camera's movie mode (☞ "Minimovie Case Studies" in Chapter 5 for an example of a child bobbing for apples at a birthday party).

- Hand the digital camera to the child and let them shoot. Hey, you'll be surprised by what they come up with!

Now let's apply this advice to some real-world situations. Keep in mind that many of the following techniques used to photograph children can be applied to other kinds of photographic situations as well.

Zooming for Emotion

It was the first day of the New Year, and raining lightly. We were determined to spend the day outside, so we bundled the girls in rain gear and headed for the Presidio, San Francisco's former military base near the Golden Gate Bridge.

I've always believed that what you do on the first day of the New Year sets the tone for the rest of the year, and being outdoors was a good start. I turned my digital camera toward my six-year-old daughter and got the shot shown in Figure 3.2. It's all there—the umbrella, the puddle, the hint of rain—but there is nothing special about the shot.

Figure 3.2: This ordinary shot needed improvement.

Then, as I looked at the preview in the camera's LCD, I asked myself: what can I do to make this more interesting? I had a kind of epiphany when it occurred to me I could do whatever I wanted, with little or no consequences. I wasn't going to run out of film; I had a 64MB SmartMedia memory card in one slot, and a 340MB microdrive card in another. (The Olympus E-10 I was using accepts both CompactFlash and SmartMedia cards.) I remembered an old trick I'd read in a photo magazine—select a slow shutter speed and zoom the lens while the shutter is being released. I had avoided trying this technique with my film camera because it required a lot of shots and even then you were never sure you got the shot until the film was developed. But, hey, I was shooting digital! No problem. I explained to my daughter what I wanted to do and then I had her run toward me with her umbrella open. I set my camera to shutter priority, and set the shutter to 1/4 second (f/11 was set automatically by the camera to make the correct exposure). Then, with the lens set to wide angle, I tripped the shutter and zoomed in as my daughter ran toward me. I did this several times until the LCD preview confirmed that I had gotten the shot I wanted; you can see it in Figure 3.3.

Bottom line: Experiment! Experiment! Experiment! Use the LCD to get immediate feedback and don't worry about film and developing costs.

Figure 3.3: By zooming the lens while I released the slow shutter, I got this image.

Focusing in Low Light

The end-of-summer camp party was held outdoors, at night. It was dark except for a few Christmas tree lights, and as you can see on the left in Figure 3.4, my Olympus E-10 had trouble focusing in autofocus mode, even with help from an infrared focus assist. I set the camera to manual focus and found a spectacular highlight about five feet away to focus on. Instead of re-focusing every time a happy camper went by, I simply gauged the distance between me and my subject, and then made sure that distance was about 5 feet before pressing the shutter release button. To make the shots even more interesting, I used my camera controls to set the flash to a "Slow Synchronization" setting. With this setting, the shutter remains open a couple seconds after the flash fires, thereby creating the trails of ambient light you see on the right.

Not all digital cameras have this feature and some manufacturers call it by other names such as "Night portrait" (Minolta) and "Twilight portrait" (Sony). If your camera has a manual mode, you can recreate the look by setting your shutter speed to 1 or 2 seconds. Your f-stop setting will depend on the characteristics of your flash and the camera itself but it's easy to try different settings, view the results, and try again if needed. Try moving the camera slightly while you shoot, for even more outrageous lighting effects.

Bottom line: Low-light situations are difficult for even the best autofocus systems. If possible, set your digital camera to manual focus and determine the focus by distance or by aiming and focusing on a spectacular highlight.

Figure 3.4: Autofocus didn't work in the low light (left). I set the camera to manual focus, prefocused, and then used the Slow Synchronization setting to get this more interesting shot (right).

Shooting from a Different Perspective

A common rule of thumb is to not shoot down on kids. Instead, try to shoot at their level. That's not always easy, especially if you are like me and your knee joints aren't as young as they used to be. Digital cameras often feature LCD monitor screens that flip into different positions, allowing you, for example, to hold the camera at your waist and look down at the monitor to get the shot, or hold the camera out at odd angles and still easily view what the lens sees.

Doug Clark, a professional photographer living in Seattle, used a prosumer Canon G2 digital camera with its "vari-angle" LCD to get the shot of his sister's two-year-old son, Clark, shown in Figure 3.5. He placed the camera on the ground facing the child, then swiveled the LCD up so he could see the image clearly. He set the camera to Program mode and let the camera figure out the correct f-stop and shutter speed (1/60th of a second and f/2). When he saw the pensive expression he was looking for, he released the shutter. As you'll see later in this chapter, Doug also uses this method to get great shots of pets, and in Chapter 4 you'll see how he uses it to get a great bowling shot. Doug has shot 4,500 images in the last nine months with his G2, including digital photos of his honeymoon that were posted on the Web for all of the family to see. Doug says he is now spoiled and can no longer afford to shoot film, except when he is being paid by a client to do so. Doug likes to refer to his G2 as a "stealth camera" because when he turns off the audible sound it's as silent as the famous Leica 35mm rangefinder camera, which has been used for decades to get some of the world's finest photojournalistic shots.

Bottom line: Vary the camera's position in relation to your subject—especially when photographing children.

Figure 3.5: It's easy to get a different perspective if your monitor tilts. (Photo by Doug Clark)

Overriding the Flash

Electronic flash alone will often produce a sharply contrasted image, as the one shown in Figure 3.6. In this case, I actually like the effect, but many times the effect is not desirable. With most digital cameras, you have control over whether or not a flash fires. If you leave the flash set to automatic, the flash will fire when the onboard electronics determine that the light is too low to produce a sharp, properly exposed image. Don't be intimidated by low light situations and use a flash just because your camera says you should. I turned off the flash on my Olympus E-10 for the shot in Figure 3.7 of my daughter as she heads into the bathroom bathed in a soft light. My f-stop was 2.2 and my shutter speed $1/8^{th}$ of a second and I had to hold the camera very steady, but I like this photograph much more than the shot taken with the flash.

Figure 3.6: With the camera's flash settings set to automatic, the flash automatically fired in this low-light situation.

Figure 3.7: By turning off the flash and relying instead on the natural light, I still got this shot.

Of course, turning off the flash and depending totally on existing light brings up two important issues: white balance and sensor sensitivity settings. Even though I left my white balance setting at "automatic" in the second, non-flash shot, the image has a color cast and no pure whites. Fortunately it is a warm color cast that actually enhances the effect of the image. However, if a pure white had been important I would have taken the time to use a predefined white balance setting or make a custom one (☞ "Know Your Camera: Adjusting White Balance" in Chapter 11). Most, if not all, prosumer and professional cameras provide custom as well as predefined white balance settings. These options are rarer in consumer-level digital cameras, which usually rely on an automatic, albeit less precise, white balance adjustment.

Sensor sensitivity is expressed as an ISO (International Standardization Organization) number and can also be controlled on most prosumer and professional digital cameras. The higher the ISO number, the more the information coming off the sensor is amplified. When listening to a weak signal on your radio, if you increase the volume level, you not only increase the volume of the program but also increase the volume of the static or noise. The same thing happens with your digital camera: the higher the ISO setting, the more likelihood there is of including distracting and unwanted electronic "noise" in your picture. The optimal ISO for most digital cameras ranges from 80-200. I could have set my ISO as high as 800 on the Olympus (the high end varies from model to model) but I chose instead to leave the ISO at its default setting of 80. If I had set the camera to ISO 800 I could have used a faster shutter speed or a narrower aperture and still gotten a proper exposure. However, if I had done so, not only would the shot have been less interesting, but also my image quality would have suffered. You will see in subsequent chapters how increasing ISO can be used very effectively.

Bottom line: Just because your camera indicates you should use a flash doesn't mean you should. Live dangerously! See what happens if you leave it off.

Kids Photographing Kids

I love what happens when a young child is handed a digital camera and encouraged to take pictures of their friends and siblings. They come up with some interesting shots on their own, and I am always inspired by just watching them shoot fearlessly with no preconceptions or prejudices of what an image should look like.

Figure 3.8 shows a photo taken by my six-year-old daughter with a Kodak DX 3500, a 2.2 megapixel digital camera I bought for her for $50. It's not a photograph an adult would make purposefully. But my daughter, viewing an earlier shot in the LCD monitor that included an accidental intrusion of her finger, liked what she saw, and created a whole series of "finger-in-lens" shots. I especially like the way her finger balances the composition and puts focus on her friend, who is obviously hamming it up for the camera.

Bottom line: Don't hog the digital camera! Give the kids a chance. You may start the next Ansel Adams or Dorothea Lange on his or her path.

Figure 3.8: My daughter shot this carefully composed photo of her friend Bella with a Kodak DX 3500 I bought used for $50.

Keeping the Cost Down

A year ago I bought my daughter a point-and-shoot film camera and both she and I got tired of it quickly. I was tired of the film and developing costs, and she was frustrated that she couldn't see immediate results. She'd seen me shooting digital most of her life, so looking at an LCD screen was natural to her. I didn't want to spend a lot of money on a digital camera and the "Barbie" type of digital camera with its 640×480 pixel screen resolution wasn't going to satisfy her need for higher quality prints. (Ah, the burden of having a professional photographer for a father!) Then I discovered a shopping secret: buy last year's floor models at large electronic and office supply stores like Fry's, Office Max, Staples, Circuit City, or Best Buy. Besides the $50 Kodak I bought for my daughter, I've gotten great deals on an a couple of Olympus digital cameras, and my goal now is to collect enough of these low-cost digital cameras to outfit my daughter's first grade class.

This is what I do: I head straight for the digital camera section and ask for the manager. Then I ask him or her politely if he or she has any display models for sale. I explain that I want them for my kids. Usually the cameras are hidden under a counter, out of sight and wrapped in bubble wrap. I always carry my own batteries and both a CompactFlash and a SmartMedia memory card to test drive the camera. Most of these used digital cameras, but not all, are sold "as is" without cables, instructions, warranty, or memory. (This doesn't present a problem, though; you can find the instructions on the manufacturer's website and buy discounted memory later.) If the camera works, I figure there isn't much that will go wrong later. I try not to pay over $75, regardless of the camera. Obviously, it helps if you know something about last year's models before you start bartering and I suggest you do your homework on the Web before venturing out to the store. While you are negotiating with the manager (or sales person), it doesn't hurt if you make them think you'll be buying accessories from them as well. Even if you have no intention of doing so, this might inspire them to give you a better deal on the camera.

Photographing Pets

When it comes to making good digital photos of domestic animals, there isn't that much difference between photographing them and photographing children. Both rarely hold still, so getting a good shot is a combination of luck as well as skill.

Of course, having said this, not all pets (nor all children for that matter) are the same. Photographing haughty cats can be much more challenging than shooting, say cuddly dogs...as you will see.

Digital Cats

"Cats: my camera loves 'em, but they don't always love it back," says Helmi Flick about her favorite portrait subjects, which can be as challenging to capture as they are photogenic.

Helmi shot the cats shown in Figures 3.9, 3.10, and 3.11 with an Olympus C-5050 digital camera using the lighting setup shown on the right in Figure 3.9.

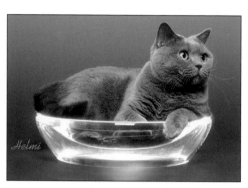

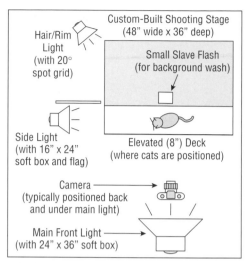

Hair/Rim Light (with 20° spot grid)

Custom-Built Shooting Stage (48" wide x 36" deep)

Small Slave Flash (for background wash)

Side Light (with 16" x 24" soft box and flag)

Elevated (8") Deck (where cats are positioned)

Camera (typically positioned back and under main light)

Main Front Light (with 24" x 36" soft box)

Figure 3.9: This British short hair was photographed by Helmi Flick using the simple portable studio setup shown on the right.

Figure 3.10: This brown-spotted Bengal cat was also photographed by Helmi Flick.

Figure 3.11: Helmi's comical shot (left) resulted from a fortuitous mistake: a long exposure setting. The "whirling" cat was later stilled with a faster shutter speed (right).

Cats are just about all Helmi has shot since May 1999, when her husband bought Helmi her first digital camera to reduce her film and processing expenses. "I enjoyed shooting my own kitties before that, in spite of all the film I blew on bad shots to get that rare keeper. But the move to digital really opened the door for me. Being able to shoot hundreds of frames a day at zero cost, and being able to instantly see why most of them were flawed in time to reshoot them accelerated my learning curve tremendously. Working digitally gave me the confidence to turn my passion into a profession."

One year later Helmi began working the cat show circuit in Texas and neighboring states as the "official show photographer." Her husband, Ken, who shares her passion for cats and photography, travels with her, setting up their lighting and staging gear and working with Helmi as her "roadie, gaffer, grip, technical advisor, and cat wrangler."

At a cat show, Helmi and Ken set up their lights, typically three studio flashes and a small battery powered slave, and their custom built shooting stage (see Figure 3.9 for a diagram of this setup) in a room off the main show hall that provides some insulation from the distracting sights and sounds of the show activities. Covering the 48"-wide stage is a fabric backdrop. Helmi's material of choice is a stretchy fabric with a suede texture, pulled tightly to eliminate wrinkles and shadows. She uses backdrops of various colors depending on the color of the cat.

Helmi begins with these camera settings:

- Focus Mode: Auto
- White Balance: Daylight/electronic flash setting or custom set to an actual white card reading with studio flash illumination
- Exposure Mode: Manual, with shutter speed set to 1/200th sec for reliable flash sync

She then takes a few test shots of a stuffed toy cat stand-in to determine an ideal exposure balance between the relative light levels of her studio flashes and her camera's f-stop. Whenever the background color or cat color changes, Helmi will recheck and readjust her light levels and camera aperture.

When Helmi is satisfied with her lighting and exposure settings, Ken has the cat owner bring the cat in and place it on the stage. Both he and Helmi spend a few moments making friends with the cat and allowing it to get comfortable with them and the setting. The interval required to put a cat at ease varies by breed, individual personality, and age (kittens are easy). It can range from 30 seconds to "never."

Helmi then positions herself 4 to 8 feet from the cat and prefocuses her camera so that when the ideal shot presents itself, she can seize the moment without that lengthy shutter lag time that plagues digital cameras. "In cat photography," Helmi says, "that elusive 'moment' is frustratingly brief, and without Ken's support as my cat wrangler, I could wait for its arrival for days!" Ken coaxes the cat into the desired pose or position and then uses a "cat tease," which might be a feather or some sparkly Mylar streamers on the end of a stick, to attract the cat's attention toward the camera or wherever they want it to look. "When Ken 'makes' the shot," Helmi says, "I just need to be ready to take it." Working as a team like this, they put the cat through a variety of traditional poses as well as attempt to capture some playful action shots that express their subject's "catness."

Helmi encourages the cat's owner to be present during the photo session to ensure that she is getting the kind of poses they want. And when she has taken around 20 shots or so, she will invite the owner to immediately review those images and choose the ones they wish to have printed. For this review, Helmi connects her camera to a TV monitor and shows her customer VGA versions of what she has taken. "I lock in the images the customer selects," Helmi says, "In order to distinguish them from the outtakes. Then I download the image files from my camera to my notebook computer."

When the show is over, Helmi says her work has just begun. "Those cat photographers who shoot film are mostly done after shooting at a show. They drop their negatives off at the lab for processing and then pick up the prints and mail them out to their customers as proofs. I submit my image files to the lab for printing just as they do, since I always deliver conventional 4 × 6 photographic prints, not ink jet images. But I never submit raw unretouched image files for printing and I never deliver 'proofs.'" Because working with digital files enables Helmi to retouch and refine her raw images, she always takes advantage of that capability in order to deliver portraits that are the best images they can be without altering the physical appearance of the cat or doing "cosmetic enhancements" that would compromise the authenticity of her work. "Delivering every print as a finished portrait requires countless hours at my PC and adds tremendously to the time I have invested in each shot," Helmi admits, "and it certainly hasn't made me rich yet. But if I'm putting my name on a print, I wouldn't want it to be any less than I can make it."

Bottom line: Follow your passion and see where it leads!

Of course, you don't have to set up a studio like Helmi and her husband to get great digital photos of cats. Figure 3.12 shows a more candid shot of an ordinary but very special cat, Carlton, taken by Doug Clark using a tilted LCD screen and his Canon G2 placed on the floor.

Bottom line: Again, perspective makes all the difference.

Figure 3.12: This image was produced by placing the digital camera on the floor in front of the cat, using the tilted LCD monitor to frame the image. (Photo by Doug Clark)

Digital Dogs

Compared to photographing cats, dogs are a piece of cake. Tell them what to do, and most of the time they will do it. You could probably even hand a dog a camera and they'd take the photo for you! Well...not really, but you get the idea.

Peter Figen, a professional photographer best known for his high-end advertising work, shot the two images shown in Figure 3.13 of his studio-mate's dog, Mocha, using an older high-end professional digital camera, the Fuji FinePix S1 and a Nikkor 80mm-200mm zoom lens. (Just to demonstrate how quickly the market changes, this 6.1 megapixel digital camera, based on the Nikon N60 body, which takes Nikon lenses, initially sold for around $4,000. You can buy the body now for around $1,300 new, and I'm sure it'll be even cheaper by the time you read this. Of course, you'd need to add the price of a lens to the cost.)

Figure 3.13: Peter Figen captured two views of his studio-mate's dog Mocha with a Fuji FinePix S1.

Peter often turns his camera on Mocha, a likeable Shepherd mix that spends all day at the studio. Photographing Mocha is a welcome contrast to many of his stressful professional studio shots. Peter gets his best shots when he "sees the world as the dog does," which means he is often on his knees following Mocha around. For the shot of Mocha running, Peter set his camera to aperture priority mode and set an f-stop of 4.0. In aperture priority mode, the Fuji—like all digital cameras with this option—sets a corresponding shutter speed for the correct exposure. If the light values change, the camera automatically updates the shutter speed for the correct exposure while leaving the f-stop setting constant.

This is a good opportunity to emphasis an important point. Professional photographers like Peter know the importance of choosing an appropriate exposure mode. Exposure mode options are offered in all professional digital cameras and most of the advanced consumer digital cameras as well. The most common exposure mode options include:

- Shutter priority, where a shutter speed is selected and the camera selects a corresponding aperture. As light values change, the shutter speed remains constant while the aperture settings change automatically as needed.
- Aperture priority, such as the mode Peter selected for this example.
- Manual, where the photographer chooses both the shutter and aperture settings based on either suggested exposure readings from the camera or an external light meter.
- Programmable mode, which "intelligently" chooses a combination of shutter and aperture settings based on certain criteria, including the focal length of a lens.

Peter chose an aperture of f/4 because he wanted just a shallow depth of field to minimize the effect of the background. In the shot of Mocha running, there was plenty of light, so the resulting camera-selected shutter speed of 1/512th of a second was fast enough to stop Mocha in action. Shutter release lag isn't a noticeable problem for the Fuji, according to Peter. For the shot of Mocha sitting, the f-stop was the same, but the camera—because of slightly less ambient light—automatically compensated by selecting a slightly slower shutter speed of 1/395th of a second. By the way, for the first shot the focal length was 168mm, which (because the Fuji camera has a 1.5 multiplier) translates into a 35mm equivalent of 252mm. The second shot was taken at 125mm focal length, for a 35mm equivalent of 187mm. (↶ Chapter 1 if you need a refresher on focal-length equivalence and multipliers.)

Peter says that even with the higher pixel count of the Fuji camera, he always shoots his images as closely cropped as he can. Shooting "loose" is easier, but if you have to crop your image later you might not have enough resolution for a good print. Although for most of his professional assignments Peter saves his digital images in the RAW file format, when he shoots Mocha or other similar personal shots, he sets the camera to save in the high-quality JPEG mode because it cuts down on the file size and speeds up the processing time of the camera so he can shoot more images faster.

Bottom line: For more creative control, you'll need a digital camera offering different programmable modes so that you can choose the shutter speed or f-stop.

Software Solutions: Digital Fill Flash and Fixing Red Eye

It's not always possible to take a perfectly exposed image, or avoid red eye from an on-camera strobe, or have every shot be perfectly in focus. No worry. Don't erase those less-than-perfect shots. Imaging software can help.

Digital Fill Flash

If you must shoot outdoors in the direct sun, use a fill flash to soften hard shadows, or use some kind of reflector that bounces the sun into the shadows. If you can, move the subject into the shade. If all else fails and you get a shot like the one shown on the left, you can always use a digital fill flash. Digital fill flash is a simple feature commonly found in programs such as Photoshop Elements, Picture It!, and Paint Shop Pro. If you are using Photoshop you'll have to use a combination of Levels adjustments to balance the foreground light with the background. On the right, you can see the same photo after using the Photoshop Elements Fill Flash command.

Red Eye Removal

Red eye occurs when light from an on-camera flash reflects off the back of the eyeball, giving a person or animal a demonic look. Many digital cameras have a red-eye reduction mode option to combat this problem. In this mode, the strobe goes through a pre-flash routine: the strobe rapidly fires a burst of short pulses of light that close the pupil and then, after a second or so, the main flash fires and the shutter releases. The disadvantage is obvious: shooting is slowed considerably. Instead of using red-eye reduction, consider fixing it later with imaging software. The image on the left below, with red eye, was fixed using Photoshop Elements' Red Eye Brush tool, to get the image shown on the right (Picture It! And Paint Shop Pro also have tools for removing red eye. Photoshop doesn't, although you can use other methods such as Desaturate to remove red eye.)

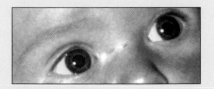 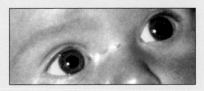

Software Solutions: Sharpening an Out-of-Focus Image

Out-of-focus photos are common, almost as common as photos with fingers placed accidentally in the frame. Imaging software can fix an out-of-focus image, but only to a degree. On the left is a shot that I sharpened using Photoshop Elements' Unsharp Mask filter. I know the name of this filter sounds counterintuitive, but it is based on a traditional film compositing technique that creates a blurred negative version of the image. It then averages this copy with the original and through three controls—Amount (percentage), Threshold, and Radius—gives you precise control over the amount of sharpening and the way the sharpening is applied. The resulting image is shown on the right. Keep in mind that sharpening through image processing is ultimately achieved by increasing contrast between adjacent pixels, and if you try to "sharpen" too much, you just end up with a very contrasty image.

Photographing Social Events

A social event—be it a wedding, or a press conference, or a retirement party—can present a variety of shooting situations. The event you're trying to immortalize with photos might be boring and mundane (think people sitting around a table eating, or "grip-and-grins" as people shake each other's hands and smile at the camera). On the other hand, you might end up doing quite a bit of nail biting to get the pictures you're aiming for. (Think cake cutting or award giving, and someone yelling, "YOU HAVE TO GET THE SHOT!")

Shooting social events can be very stressful, especially if you are the photographer expected to get the perfect shot. By shooting digital, and knowing from the LCD whether you have the shot or not, much of the anxiety is removed. However, as I've said throughout this chapter, the task of shooting moving subjects poses its own set of problems for users of digital cameras, which I'll focus on later in this section.

Generally, when it comes to shooting social events—and I've shot my share of them—consider these suggestions:

- Take charge and act as though you belong there. (And if you are not the primary photographer, get out of the way of the person who is!)
- Pay attention to the dress code and blend in with the crowd.
- Alternatively, if the situation warrants it, wear something or carry something that sets you apart as THE photographer. Sling around a big, fancy, expensive camera, or have an assistant dote over your every move. The point is to have people take you seriously.
- In some situations, it helps to think of yourself as entertainment. At the very least, the fact that you are there taking photos can make an otherwise boring event seem more important.
- Follow my advice in Chapter 2. Know your camera, carry spare batteries, and use the LCD preview as a device to loosen people up.

Above all else, respect the wishes of those you are photographing and only photograph as long as they want you to. Just because you are shooting digital and don't have to worry about the cost of film doesn't give you a blank check for taking as many pictures as you want. People tire of having a camera in front of their face all the time, and if you are shooting with a flash, you can become especially annoying to the people around you. Once you've lost the respect of the people you are photographing, you likely won't get a good shot anyway.

Anticipating Gestures and Mannerisms

I was hired by a national union to shoot pictures of a reception for California's Governor, Gray Davis. It was a typical social event, lots of grips and grins between the governor and his well-wishers. Up to that point I was shooting film—which is what the client wanted—but when the governor stepped to the podium to give a short speech, I shot digital as well. The client wanted digital so they could post the governor's speech immediately on their website. On the left in Figure 3.14 is a really good example of what I have been talking about all through this chapter. I pressed the shutter release button of my Olympus E-10 at a moment when the governor made an interesting gesture. By the time the shutter released, you see what I got. It took several minutes of carefully watching the mannerisms of the governor before I figured out that whenever he gestured with his arms, his facial expressions changed so quickly that I could never predict what I'd actually get by the time the shutter released. I watched and waited, getting to know his pacing and mannerisms. As you can see on the right, I finally got a decent shot of him just after he had made a particularly popular statement and had paused for a moment to enjoy the audience reaction. It's not the best shot in the world, but it wasn't my job to make the governor look goofy. Most people, especially professional politicians and speakers, have predictable gestures and mannerisms that become apparent upon observation. Even if your digital camera doesn't lag, you can use this knowledge to make more interesting photos.

Bottom line: The road to great photography begins with observation. Spend time watching and getting to know your subject before pressing the shutter release button.

Figure 3.14: I pressed the shutter release button, but by the time my camera shutter actually opened the governor had moved on to the awkward pose on the left. After carefully watching his gestures and mannerisms, I anticipated this moment and—even with shutter release lag—managed to get the good shot shown on the right.

Shooting Grips (or Hugs) and Grins

Look at the image on the left in Figure 3.15. I shot this at my high school reunion with an Olympus C-2500 L digital camera. I set the camera to automatic and got a halfway decent shot, even though my high school mates' dark hair blends into the dark background. What could I have done to get a better shot? If you look at the image on the right, you'll see a very similar type of shot taken at an awards ceremony with another Olympus camera, the E-10. I did two things differently that resulted in a better shot. Instead of relying on the camera's normal flash mode, I left my E-10 set to Program mode but set the flash to "slow"—just as I did in the previous example on focusing in low light—so the ambient light would "mix" with the strobe. I held the camera very steady, and since I shot at a wide angle and far enough back, I minimized movement-induced blur. Using the on-board camera strobe, which fires at several thousandths of a second, also helped prevent the blur usually associated with slow shutter speeds. By shooting this way, the camera actually revealed the ambient light in the back as well. Not all digital cameras offer "slow" flash settings, but you can get a similar result if you have a Shutter- priority option and select a shutter speed of, say, $1/15^{th}$ of a second. If you have a manual exposure option, simply set your f-stop and shutter speeds to expose for the ambient light and use your flash in automatic mode. The other thing I did was to ask the subjects to move into a position that placed the strong ambient light behind them. (They were originally standing in front of a dark wall.) It pays not to be shy in situations like this, especially if moving people around just a little makes for a better photo. Now, with the camera exposing for the ambient light, and with a strong ambient light behind them, there is a nice sense of depth that I didn't get in the first example. By blending flash with ambient light, I also avoided the harsh look associated with direct flash.

Bottom line: Don't be shy. Move people into a position that makes for a better shot.

Figure 3.15: With the flash set to normal and no ambient light behind, there is little distinction between foreground and background (left). By setting the flash to Fill mode, and positioning the subjects in front of a strong ambient light source, the photo has more depth (right).

Digital Weddings

There are many ways to approach shooting a wedding, ranging from formal poses of groups and individuals to a looser, more photojournalistic approach, where events dictate the shot rather than rigid social rules of who should be photographed with whom. Most wedding photography nowadays consists of both approaches. Often a professional photographer is hired to shoot the formal shots, while a friend or relative is designated to shoot the candid shots.

A Professional Approach

British photographer Carol Steele shot the beautiful wedding photo shown in Figure 3.16. Carol is a professional photographer who, after over 10 years shooting film, has turned completely to digital. Her Bronica medium-format film camera now gathers dust on the shelf. This shot, for example, was taken with a Nikon D1X, a professional digital camera with a 42-105mm equivalent zoom lens, set to its 45mm equivalent. She used Aperture priority setting and the exposure was 1/160th of a second at f/5.6. (Most of her wedding shots are done using this lens or a 24mm equivalent lens.)

Granted, Carol is using top-of-the-line digital equipment but her shooting tips for aspiring digital photographers are useful regardless of which digital camera is used.

Her most valuable suggestion for readers of this book, in my opinion, has to do with flash settings. She most often uses a Nikon SB 80 DX detachable strobe, which, like so many strobes—even built-in ones—generally is set by default to shoot "too hot." As a general rule of thumb, Carol always uses flash controls to dial back the intensity of her strobe. In the previous example, which was shot outdoors on a sunny day, she adjusted the strobe setting by minus 1.3 stop. This is just enough flash to fill some of the shadows, but not enough to overexpose other light details, such as a white wedding dress. (She also reduced the camera's exposure by dialing in a -0.3 EV exposure compensation which further reduced the possibility of a blow out of the very light areas of the wedding dress.) When the day is overcast, Carol needs only to dial back her strobe about minus .3 stop, just enough to provide a highlight kick to the eyes. (Most prosumer and some consumer digital cameras provide control over the strobe intensity. Consult your manual for instructions.)

Figure 3.16: A professional approach to wedding photography. (Photograph by Carol Steele)

Carol also suggests:

- If you aren't the hired professional, don't get in the way. Instead, focus your camera on the unusual stuff that happens away from the bride and groom.
- Know the limitations of your digital camera. (You've also heard this from me plenty of times!)
- Back up your shots. Carol carries two 1GB microdrive cards and two 512 MB CompactFlash cards, and at least three times during the wedding she takes a break and downloads the data into a laptop where she makes back-up CDs.

Carol saves her data in the RAW file format and uses an Auto White Balance setting with a -3 override. This gets her in the ballpark for most images so that only minor tweaks are needed later with imaging software.

Note: For a more detailed discussion of the RAW format, ☞ "Know Your Camera: File Formats" in Chapter 8. For a more detailed discussion on white balance, ☞ "Know Your Camera: Adjusting White Balance" in Chapter 11.

Bottom line: You'll get better results from your camera strobe if you slightly dial back the intensity slightly. Most prosumer and professional digital cameras offer this capability. See your camera's manual for details.

A Candid Approach

In Figures 3.17 and 3.18 you see the results of a completely different approach to shooting a wedding, The images were made by a non-professional (although a self-described "photo-enthusiast"), Bitsy Fitzsimmons, with her Canon G2, a prosumer-level digital camera. On the left in Figure 3.17 Bitsy captured a "let your hair down" side of an otherwise formal wedding. The revealing moment could only have been captured by an intimate friend or relative, and the photograph makes a nice compli ment to the staged shots taken by the professional on hand.

Figure 3.17: On the left, a candid moment shot by Bitsy Fitzsimmons with a Canon G2. Bitsy got the shot on the right by holding the camera over her head and framing with the swivel LCD.

Bitsy (who, for the sake of full disclosure, is my wife's aunt) has been an avid film photographer for years. Recently, for Christmas, she received a digital camera as a present and within in a week, she was up to speed and is now a die-hard convert to digital. I've witnessed her photography improve dramatically since she started using the digital camera. She claims the improvement comes from the immediate feedback provided by the LCD screen, but I thinks it's also because she just plain enjoys shooting more images and has a great time e-mailing her beautiful work to all of us relatives. And as we all know, practice helps make perfect...

Getting the shot shown on the right in Figure 3.17 was more of a technical challenge. Bitsy found herself in the back of a crowd of well-wishers blocking her view. Bitsy isn't really a shy person, but instead of pushing her way to the front of the crowd, she found it a lot easier to simply raise the camera over the crowd and use the swivel screen in the back of the camera to frame and focus the shot. Many—but not all—digital cameras have similar LCD swivel capabilities, which is an invaluable feature if you are often in situations were eye-level viewing is not possible. Bitsy has gotten so used to framing her images using the LCD that she rarely uses the Canon's optical finder. She also likes the fact that the LCD displays the image exactly as it is captured, as compared to the finder, which doesn't accurately reflect the actual image area. Bitsy prefers to frame tight so she doesn't have to crop the picture later and lose valuable pixels, so it is especially important that she knows exactly what she is getting.

Figure 3.18: This image was shot by holding the camera into the aisle (Photo by Bitsy Fitzsimmons).

The shot of the two children coming down the aisle shown in Figure 3.18 also benefited from the LCD swivel screen. Bitsy poked the camera into the aisle as the children walked by, and by viewing the LCD, she knew when to press the shutter release button.

What's the first tip Bitsy offers when asked about shooting weddings? "During the wedding ceremony, for God's sake, turn off the camera's built-in sound! The beeps and chimes and snaps can be more annoying than a ringing cell phone." Thankfully, it's not hard to follow Bitsy's advice: most digital cameras have a sound on/off option. Check the owners' manual, or be prepared for the consequences.

Bottom line: Just about any digital camera in the hands of a wedding guest will often produce the most memorable wedding shots of all.

Accessories That Make a Difference: Removable Memory Storage

Sometimes referred to as digital film, memory cards or memory sticks are storage devices that hold the digital data produced by a digital camera. A few types of memory devices are shown here.

Removable memory storage devices come in a variety of formats and the most commonly used are the SmartMedia and CompactFlash cards, MultiMedia/SD cards, and the Sony Memory Stick. The xD-Picture card, used by companies such as Olympus and Fuji, is one of the newest formats and is about the size of a postage stamp with an image storage capacity of up to 8GB. The Sony MVC-CD series digital cameras use a 156 MB (8cm) CD-R or or 156MB (8cm) CD-RW disc, both of which are extremely durable but do not have the higher read/write speeds of the other solid-state devices. Some digital cameras are capable of using more than one format, usually SmartMedia and CompactFlash, but for the most part, one format is used.

Memory devices come in a variety of storage sizes ranging from 8MB to 1G. Devices that hold more than 1G are expected on the market soon. They are also rated by read and write speed, just like the hard drive in your computer. Prices (and quality) depend on the type of card, the storage capacity, and the read/write speed. Just like computer memory, digital camera memory is constantly getting bigger, faster, and cheaper.

Not only can these cards fit right into the digital camera, but also readers are available to connect the cards to a computer just like any external memory device. There are even readers available that allow you to hook your memory device directly to a TV monitor.

What can go wrong with digital camera storage media? With normal use, not much. Most of the devices are solid state, and quite durable. However, the IBM Microdrive, which fits in the CompactFlash slot of many, but not all, digital cameras, is really a mini hard drive and is therefore vulnerable to impact. (The Microdrive also eats up more power than a typical CompactFlash card.) If the devices are constantly taken in and out of a digital camera and placed, say, in a reader, the wear and tear may slightly shorten the life of the device. USB connectors on many new cameras mean fewer reasons to remove your memory card, thereby reducing wear and tear. SmartMedia cards are very thin and are more susceptible to damage than the larger and thicker CompactFlash cards. Both cards are able to withstand extremely rapid increases or decreases in temperature, but sustained temperatures below freezing may temporarily affect the card's performance. Like with most electronic equipment, sustained heat (over 110 degrees F) can cause permanent damage. What do you do if you accidentally erase a photo that you wanted to keep from a memory device? Is there a way to retrieve the image? If you haven't reformatted your card, and you've simply erased a few images, there are downloadable utilities available that can be useful for retrieving files. For a link to these resources, refer to **www.shooting-digital.com.**

Shooting Action

Great action shots can be the most rewarding photography there is—be it the goal at a soccer game, a surfer on the crest of a wave, or a galloping horse. Shooting action is also very difficult. It puts more demands than ever on your shooting skills and equipment. This chapter will help you get the best action shots with your digital camera.

4

Chapter Contents

Terry Schmitt

The Zen of Shooting Action

The faster an object moves, the more challenging it becomes to capture the decisive moment. Take a look at the surfer shown in Figure 4.1.

Figure 4.1. This shot by Terry Schmitt was taken with a Canon D-2000, a dated but nonetheless professional digital camera.

It really helps if you learn to position yourself carefully and locate the "sweet spot" where action is more likely to unfold in front of you. In the case of the surfer shot, professional photographer Terry Schmitt actually talked a boat owner into ferrying him into a perfect position between the surfer and the beach. However, you don't always have to go to such extremes!

It also helps to hone your skills at anticipating the right moment. Terry—who has shot news and sports for 35 years for UPI and other news organizations—sums it up very well when he says, "It's best to fish when the fish are biting."

While bobbing around on the boat, for example, Terry ignored the lesser waves and positioned his digital camera only when a big wave was apparent. (Later in the chapter we'll get into anticipating other decisive moments—as well as look at more technical details of Terry's shot.)

Finally, as the scene unfolds and the decisive moment approaches, you'll have to learn to let intuition and impulse take over. Terry and other experienced sports and news photographers I've talked with have trouble finding words to describe exactly what goes on as they follow the action through the viewfinder or on the LCD panel. They say the perfect moment usually lasts only a fraction of a second, and there is not enough time to consciously evaluate and respond. Instead, they describe the feeling of being "in a groove" where the brain, the trigger finger, and the framed scene become one and somehow they just react, Zen-like, without thought and without effort. When they get the shot—which isn't always—they are often exhilarated. There is nothing quite like the feeling of getting it right.

Optimal Digital Camera Settings for Speed

Of course, a big part of capturing fast-moving action depends on adjusting your digital camera's settings correctly.

Your choices include:

- Selecting an appropriate shutter speed
- Increasing (or decreasing) ISO in order to get the shutter speed you need
- Using burst mode (if your camera has it) to capture a rapid sequence of frames
- Decreasing resolution—which, depending on the specifications of your digital camera, may help speed the capture rate
- Selecting an appropriate file format (usually JPEG)

Shutter-release lag, a problem associated with many digital cameras, is something you have little control over but it is also an important consideration when shooting anything that moves. We went into great detail on this subject in the previous chapter, showing you how to determine how much, if any, lag there is between the time you press the shutter release and the time the shutter is actually released. We also showed you ways to overcome, to a degree, the difficulties associated with a long shutter-release lag.

Shutter Speed

Shutter speed is the most obvious setting you have to pay attention to. The faster the shutter speed is, the more likely you are to capture a sharp image rather than a blurred one. For the surfer shot, Terry set his camera to shutter priority mode and chose a shutter speed of 1/1000th of a second, which was plenty fast enough to stop the wave and the surfer. The exact shutter speed you use will depend on the speed of the object you are photographing, the focal length of your lens, the direction the action is moving, and your distance from it.

Note: Your chances of stopping a fast-moving object are greatly improved if the object—be it a car, a person, or an animal—is heading straight toward you, straight away from you, or diagonally toward or away from you, such as the surfer is in Figure 4.1. It's most difficult to stop action that is moving at a right angle in relationship to the camera. It's also easier to stop action that is far away rather than action that occurs close to the camera.

If your digital camera doesn't give you control over the shutter speed, taking successful fast-moving actions shots is much more hit-and-miss. You'll have better luck if you keep your distance from the speeding object, position yourself so you are either at a diagonal to it or straight on, or use the panning method described later in this chapter. Using a camera's flash is also a good way to stop action. Most flashes operate at over 1/2000th of a second. If you are close enough to the moving object, and the flash is the primary light source, you are effectively making the flash the shutter.

Some digital cameras have a so-called "action" mode. When this mode is selected, the camera automatically chooses a fast shutter speed and corresponding f-stop. This may or may not be useful, depending on the lighting conditions and the other factors mentioned earlier.

Sometimes a slow shutter speed is preferred. We'll get into this in "Panning for Action," later in the chapter.

Increase (or Decrease) ISO

Getting a fast shutter speed—and a correct exposure—is usually easy on a bright, sunlit day. However, what do you do if you are indoors or outside in a low-light situation? If you have an extremely fast lens (i.e., one with a wide aperture) you might still get a proper exposure with a fast shutter speed. However, there is something else you can do to ensure a proper exposure with a fast shutter speed. If your digital camera allows, you can boost the ISO and increase the sensitivity of the sensor. You'll see later in the chapter that Terry did this to get a great indoor basketball shot. Increasing the ISO may give you the shutter speed you need, but keep in mind that there is a price for this added speed. As you increase ISO, "noise" increases and image quality may suffer. Still, the tradeoff is often worth it. In the days of film, sports photographers always chose the faster, albeit grainer films, and left the slower, more fine-grained film to other photographers who were more concerned with image quality than capturing a fast-moving object. Figure 4.2 illustrates this point. The image on the left was shot with an ISO of 200. The f-stop was 3.5 with a corresponding shutter speed of 1/60th of a second, which wasn't enough to stop the action. The image on the right was shot with an ISO of 1600. The f-stop remained the same, but with the higher ISO the shutter speed was 1/500th of a second, which was fast enough. Because these images are printed here so small, it's likely you won't see a quality difference. However, when the image on the right is enlarged, it appears quite 'noisy'.

If you decide to use the panning method described later in the chapter, you may actually want a slow shutter speed. In this case you may actually need to decrease the ISO, or use a neutral density filter or polarizing filter.

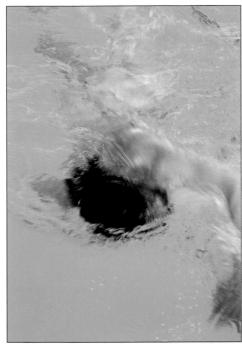

Figure 4.2: Setting a higher ISO gives you a faster shutter speed, which may allow you to stop the action.

Burst Mode

Many digital cameras have a burst mode, which allows you to hold the release button and shoot several frames quickly, one after another. The burst rate will vary depending on the chosen resolution. Anywhere between 3 frames per second (fps) and 8fps at full resolution is typical. Burst sustainability is also an important consideration. Most digital cameras with a burst mode have a buffer that stores images until shooting is complete or the buffer is full. Then the images are processed and files written to memory. Some digital cameras can handle a burst of 3-6 frames without stopping to write images. The more professional the digital camera, the more burst sustainability.

Note: Although the ability to take several shots in rapid succession can improve your odds of getting the right shot, it's no substitute for "feeling the action." Technical Editor Fred Shippey remembers shooting Big 10 college football when 35mm cameras with motor drives first arrived: "Those of us without motors had to learn to wait for the peak of the action. All too often, those with motors just 'blasted away.' We used to kid them and ask, 'Think you got it in there somewhere?' Actually, in many cases the best shot was between two of their images and they missed it!"

Resolution

Many digital cameras offer a choice of resolutions. When you set the camera to the highest setting, you get the maximum quality. However, depending on the digital camera, the higher resolution may take significantly longer to write to memory. Most digital cameras have a buffer so this transfer takes places in the background, enabling you to continue shooting. However, if the buffer is limited, shooting several shots in a sequence will quickly fill it and the camera will become inoperative while the image files are writing to memory. For the sake of speed, consider selecting a lower resolution. This isn't true of all digital cameras, so you'll have to check your camera's specifications. For example, with the Olympus E-20, the burst mode specification is the same regardless of which resolution you choose; it's always 3.6 fps.

File Format

When a fast capture rate is desirable, JPEG is the file format of choice. JPEG files are generally much smaller than TIFF or RAW files and therefore take less time to write to the storage media. They also take up less storage space. (Terry's older professional digital camera saved files only in the RAW format, but it did it very quickly, as do most professional digital cameras.)

Movie Mode

One final thing: Consider using the movie mode of your digital camera as a super-fast burst mode to capture the decisive moment. Most digital cameras offering movie modes are capable of capturing 15 fps, and some go as high as 30 fps for anywhere from 15 to 60 seconds. You can shoot through the peak action, and later use software to grab the single image that captures the moment best. (See the next chapter for ways to grab single frames from minimovies.) Granted, the image resolution is limited to only 340×260 pixels, or less, but if it is a question of getting the shot or not, resolution is not that big a deal.

 Note: LCD previews are great for seeing whether you've got the fast-moving shot. But wait to look until all the peak action has passed. If you spend your time buried in the LCD previewing, you could miss the really great shot that is happening in front of you!

An Ideal Digital Camera for Action Shots

There is no getting around the fact that the individual characteristics and features of a digital camera can make a huge difference in your ability to capture fast-moving action. In Chapter 1 I outlined the make up of an ideal action digital camera. I suggested you look for a digital camera with:
- Shutter speeds of and in excess of 1/1000th of a second.
- Extremely fast response time.
- A burst mode capable of capturing 3 fps or more. (More is better, of course.)

- A fast zoom lens capable of 200mm (equivalent) or longer focal length.
- Fast autofocus with assist.
- Image stabilization to minimize camera or movement shake.
- Higher ISO option settings (1600 ISO, for example) to enable fast shutter speeds.
- Lightweight and sturdy body construction.

Having said all this, a word of caution. Just because a digital camera looks good on paper, specifications don't always paint a complete picture. Take the Canon D-30, for example, which is a great camera by just about any standards. It is used by professionals as well as serious amateurs. If you look at the specifications, you'll agree that it is an ideal action camera. It boasts a burst rate of approximately 3 fps for up to approximately 8 frames in full-resolution mode. However, if you use the camera in the field, you'll quickly find a flaw. You can shoot several frames one after another, no problem. But if you stop shooting and remove your finger completely from the release button for just a moment, the camera begins transferring image files from the buffer to the memory card. During this time, until the writing is complete, you can't shoot. For some photographers this isn't a big deal. For others, critical follow-up shots are missed.

(In all fairness to this groundbreaking digital camera, you can work around this limitation by maintaining constant pressure on the release button between shots. Also, the D-30 has been superseded by the Canon D-60, which doesn't lock up between bursts.)

You may wonder why I didn't include pixel count as part of my wish list. It's true that pixel count is important—you'll want a digital camera with enough resolution for a decent-sized print. But as I have said repeatedly throughout the book, it is only part of the picture. Take for example, the Canon D-2000, the digital camera Terry Schmitt used to take the surfer shot in Figure 4.1 (and others in the chapter). This camera, which is basically the same as the Kodak DCS 620, was a sensation when it was introduced in 1998. It cost over $12,000, and used—get this—a 2 megapixel chip! If we were only going by pixel count, the 2-megapixel resolution would be an automatic turnoff in this day and age of 4 to 14 megapixel cameras. Also, the D-2000's maximum rate of 3 fps may sound slow when compared with newer professional models that boast 8 fps for up to 21 frames in high-resolution mode. However, the D2000 is extremely rugged and responsive, and still compares very favorably to most of the current prosumer and consumer digital cameras.

(By the way, recently I've seen the D-2000 and DCS 620—body only—for under $800. If you own Canon lenses and action photography is your thing, you might consider tracking one down!)

Bottom line: If action photography is your passion, it's worth the time and money to get a digital camera that does the job. Test it if you can. If you have to, buy it; just be sure you can return it within a reasonable time if you aren't satisfied.

Accessories That Make a Difference: From the Kitchen Drawer

Not all accessories need be purchased at a camera store. Some of the most useful accessories are found in kitchen drawers, closets, or at corner hardware stores. An informal polling of many of the professionals who contributed to this book turned up this menagerie of useful odds and ends for digital photography:

Duct tape can be used for just about everything, from holding together a broken camera to attaching a flash.

Wire coat hangers are the modern version of "haywire;" can be used for propping objects or backgrounds in place.

Aluminum foil crumpled up can be used as an interesting background; laid out flat, it can be used as a light reflector. **Compact, metallized "space blankets"** also work.

Zip-lock bags keep digital cameras, lenses, and accessories dry, and prevent condensation when going from heat to cold and vice versa.

Soft Cotton Napkins make lightweight camera covers with some impact protection. Just wrap them around your digital camera or strobes and accessories. No buttons, zippers, or clasps makes access easy and fast. (Shoeshine mitts, like those you find in hotel rooms, also work.)

Leatherman, Swiss Army knife, or similar multi-tool can be used for everything from cutting duct tape to opening hard-to-open battery and memory covers.

Velcro strips and ties can be used to tie cables and cords (**rubber bands** also work).

Tiny screwdriver sets are the only way to open a small electronic apparatus (and void most warranties!).

Panning for Action

Your ability to stop motion depends, in part, on the relative motion between the moving subject and your camera. Panning—moving your camera to "track" the moving subject—can make it easier to "stop" the action. Regardless of what digital camera you use, with the right technique you'll likely be able to make action photos like the one shot by John Isaac, shown in Figure 4.3. It helps if your digital camera offers shutter-speed control, but with a little luck and the right shooting conditions, even the most basic point-and-shoot digital camera will work.

Figure 4.3. John Isaac used a slow shutter speed and panned his digital camera along with the horse to make this shot.

John used an Olympus E-20, a prosumer digital camera that isn't all that well suited for taking fast-action shots. The camera has a top shutter speed of 1/640th of a second (at low quality settings, shutter speeds are higher), a 4-image buffer, and a top ISO of 320. However, for shots like this, it works great.

To get this kind of shot:

1. Select and use a slower speed—less than, say, 1/125th of a second.
2. Focus on the moving object either manually or with your camera's autofocus system.
3. Pan the camera along with the moving object.
4. Keep the moving object in the center of your viewfinder as you release the shutter. The background will blur, but the moving object will remain relatively sharp. (The slower the shutter speed, the more the background blurs.)

Shoot a lot and use your LCD to preview the results. Don't be discouraged if you don't get what you want. Practice will help produce more predictable results.

With a point-and-shoot digital camera, or one with no shutter priority mode, this technique works only if the ambient light is low and your camera automatically selects a slow shutter speed.

Instead of getting a static image—which John might have gotten if he had chosen a shutter speed of, say, 1/500th of a second—he got one that created a feeling of speed, and ultimately one that is more interesting.

Bottom line: Regardless of which digital camera you use, learning to pan will extend your picture-taking abilities. Use a slow shutter speed if you want a blurred, "artistic" background; use a faster shutter speed to reduce background blur.

Composition and Motion

For the bowling shot shown in Figure 4.4, Doug Clark used a Canon G2 prosumer digital camera. Not only did he catch the perfect moment before the bowling ball was released, but he also used the camera's swivel LCD screen to compose the shot in such a way that there was a dynamic tension between the static bowling balls in the foreground and the action in the background. (For most sports, including bowling, tennis, golf, track, and baseball, there is always a moment when the action almost stops. This is often the time to press the shutter release button.)

Doug didn't use a flash and instead left the camera in automatic mode, which produced f/2 and a slow shutter speed of 1/10th of a second—explaining the blur of the bowler.

This shot would have been very difficult to make without the camera's swivel LCD monitor. Doug placed the camera in the return ball well, twisted the LCD screen up so he could first compose and then shoot the frame at just the right moment.

Bottom line: Combining movement with careful composition produces great photos.

Figure 4.4: Doug Clark used the Canon G2's swivel LCD screen to carefully frame the shot, and then waited for the right moment to shoot it.

Software Solutions: Changing a Background and Adding Motion Blur

You can use software to add a sense of motion to an otherwise static shot such as the one shown here.

Here's how I used Photoshop Elements to get a horse that looks like this:

1. I opened the image and renamed the "Background" layer "Rocking Horse".
2. I erased the white background to transparency using the Magic Wand and other selection tools and the Edit ➢ Cut command.
3. I created a new fill Layer from the menu bar. I made the fill black and made sure the fill layer was the bottom-most layer.
4. I made a copy of the "Rocking Horse" layer and named the copy Motion Blur.
5. I selected the layer named Motion Blur and ran the Motion Blur filter using the following values: Angle: 41, Distance: 185 pixels. (The effect of the Motion Blur filter will be unsatisfactory if you have locked your transparency in the Layers palette.)
6. I selected the Eraser tool, and on the Motion Blur layer I selectively erased the effect.

Capturing the Decisive Moment

Every competitive sport has moments when the action accelerates and peaks. Figure 4.5 shows a shot taken by Terry Schmitt during the last few minutes of a tight basketball game between the Golden State Warriors and the Portland Trailblazers. (The Warriors won.)

"At exciting times like this, players abandon themselves," says Terry. "There's more at stake and they throw themselves around a lot more. That's when your chances of getting a great shot are greater."

Terry's also learned to position himself away from the referees who often get between him and his shot. He sits on the floor, shooting up. That way, he can emphasize faces rather than shoulders and arms. Shooting up also provides a more interesting background. Terry generally uses a 70-200 mm zoom lens. Taking into account a multiplier of 1.6, the lens is really more like 112mm-320mm (35mm equivalent).

Figure 4.5: Terry Schmitt knows that most decisive moments occur at predictable times.

Strobes aren't allowed at games, so Terry simply boosted his Canon D-2000's ISO rating from 200 to 1600. This allowed him to set his shutter speed at 1/500th of a second and still shoot with an aperture of f/4.5.

Terry also made the photograph of the pelicans shown in Figure 4.6 with his Canon D-2000 digital camera. For this shot, he used a 300mm lens with a 1.4 teleconverter. With the multiplier effect and the teleconverter factored in, the 35mm equivalent focal length was about 672mm. He selected a shutter speed of 1/2000th of a second (at f/4) and used a monopod to minimize blur. Using the burst mode, he fired four shots off in quick succession and got one that worked.

> **Note:** When you need to hand-hold your camera, you can still avoid the blur that's typically induced; just select a shutter speed greater than the focal length. (The actual focal length, not the 35mm equivalent.) For example, if you're shooting a 300mm lens, select a shutter speed faster than 1/300th of a second.

Although Terry isn't a wildlife photographer, *per se*, he still has the knack—learned from shooting sports—of capturing the decisive moment.

Bottom line: There is always a decisive moment; when you figure that out, you are well on your way to making great action photos.

Figure 4.6: Terry Schmitt photographed these pelicans with his Canon D-2000 in Baja, California.

Focus on Reaction

Quite often in sports photography, the winning basket, touchdown, or goal isn't the most interesting shot. The reaction to the action can often be much more interesting. Figure 4.7, for example, was taken by Terry Schmitt moments after his son Ross kicked a winning soccer goal.

Terry shot this photo with his Canon D-2000 mounted on a monopod with a 672mm (equivalent) lens. He shot it at 1/1000th second.

Bottom line: Terry used a professional digital camera to get this shot, but most of the time reaction shots can be taken with just about any digital camera, as long as you are prepared.

Figure 4.7: The shot here wasn't the goal, but the reaction to the goal. (Photo by Terry Schmitt)

Know Your Camera: Frame and Focus

Your digital camera most likely offers two distinct ways of framing and focusing a shot: a large LCD, used also for previews, and a smaller viewfinder, usually found somewhere near the top of the camera.

You'll quickly learn that each has its pluses and minuses.

Large LCDs are especially useful when they can be swiveled or moved independently of the direction of the lens. Most large LCD displays provide a fairly good real-time representation of what the lens sees. This is critical if you are shooting close-ups and at other times when precise framing is important. They also don't restrict you to favoring one eye or the other, as the smaller viewfinders do. On the minus side, the electronic display often displays a low-resolution version of the scene, which makes accurate focus check nearly impossible. (Image preview is usually played back in a higher resolution.) It's also difficult to view large LCDs in bright-light conditions, but some digital cameras are much better than others at doing this. (Special LCD shades help.) Continuous use of a large LCD for framing and focus also quickly drains battery power.

Viewfinders are familiar vestiges of the film-camera world. Some viewfinders are simply glass windows looking out on a scene independently from the lens. Others are really just small LCD displays that electronically represent a scene just as the lens sees it. Window viewfinders are notoriously inaccurate, unless they are part of a so-called single lens reflex (SLR) system. Most of the time what you see is only an approximation of what you get. The discrepancy is greatest in close-ups. An SLR camera viewfinder, on the other hand, is part of a mirror or prism system that diverts the light passing through the lens to the viewfinder. This gives you a more accurate representation of the scene. With the assistance of a focus screen or pattern, focus check is also possible.

Electronic viewfinders have many of the advantages of the large LCD displays mentioned earlier. They are more accurate than window viewfinders and can display useful information such as a histogram and exposure data. They also display, in real-time, white balance and exposure changes. Because the eye is pressed close against them, bright ambient light isn't an issue. However, electronic viewfinder quality varies greatly between digital cameras, and some are so bad they are nearly useless.

Shooting Digital Minimovies

Many digital cameras offer an option of shooting short digital video clips, which, if you know how to use them, have both practical and fun applications. How does a photographer go from seeing the world in a fraction of a second to a series of frames that capture a duration of time, and even sound? This chapter focuses on this and other related issues such as how to edit and prepare your minimovie for sharing via the Web, e-mail, or DVD.

Chapter Contents

Beyond the Single Frame
General Shooting Tips
Minimovie Case Studies
Editing and Sharing Minimovies
Creating an Animated GIF from Frames
Creating a Collage from Frames
Storyboarding with Frame Grabs

Beyond the Single Frame

For the most part, photographers know light and composition. Digital photographers know how to use shutter speeds, f-stops, ISO, focal length, white balance, and flash proficiently to produce an image that evokes an emotional response. Many digital cameras have an additional feature that gives a digital photographer yet another creative option: the ability to capture duration of time coupled with sound. Figure 5.1 shows an example.

Most consumer digital cameras offer motion as an option, and many prosumer digital cameras do as well. However, it's very rare to find a professional digital camera with the motion option, although this situation is likely to change as the usefulness of this mode becomes apparent. (I remember a day when most professional film cameras didn't come with a built-in pop-up flash—that changed when it became evident that this was a handy feature even for pros.)

Figure 5.1. *There are times when a moving sequence of images captures the emotion of a moment more effectively than a still photograph.*

What's the current difference between the minimovies produced by a digital camera and digital motion produced by a digital video (DV) camcorder? First, NTSC DV camcorders are generally capable of capturing 720 × 480 pixels of data per frame, as compared to most digital cameras, which capture only 320 × 240 pixels. (PAL DV camcorders capture 720 × 576 pixels.) Second, NTSC DV camcorders capture about 30 frames per second (fps), while most digital cameras capture only 15 fps. (PAL DV camcorders capture 24 fps.) Finally, DV camcorders are capable of capturing at least an hour of motion and sound, while most digital cameras are capable of shooting only about 15-30 seconds. (The NTSC or "National Television Standards Committee" format is used in North America and Japan while the PAL or "Phase-alternating line" format is used in most of Europe and South America.)

The distinction between digital cameras and digital camcorders is diminishing and continues to blur. In the future, digital cameras will get closer and closer to matching the specifications of a digital camcorder, in the same way that digital camcorders have gotten better and better at capturing still images. Technology is making it increasingly easier to move between the world of $1/1000^{th}$ of a second to sequences that capture several minutes of motion and sound. (The Sony DSC-F717 digital camera, for example, captures full motion at up to 25 fps, and movie duration is limited only by available memory. The Fuji Finepix 602 captures movies at 30 fps.) Boundaries between digital cameras and digital camcorders WILL continue to blur until someone creates one multipurpose digital camera that does it all. There are already devices on the market that combine a PDA, a cellular phone, and a digital camera, albeit one with very low-resolution capture capabilities—so why not a movie camera, too?

There is something to be said for the current capabilities of digital cameras. Limitations—especially the 15-30 second limit on full motion—can act like training wheels to the budding moviemaker. Limits teach good shooting techniques and force you to think economically. Hand me a DV camcorder with a blank cassette and soon everyone around me is saying, "Stop, too much shooting!" The complaints are even louder later when my friends and family are subjected to viewing my overindulgent work.

As you'll see later in this chapter it's also relatively easy to share minimovies made with a digital camera. Not only can they be viewed instantly (which makes them great for on-the-spot training purposes) but also with just a little image processing they can easily be edited and trimmed to a polite e-mail or Web size. Just about anyone with a computer and Internet connection can then see your work, which may or may not be a blessing.

Let's start with some general shooting tips, follow with examples of minimovies created using digital cameras, and then end with a focus on software solutions.

CHAPTER 5: SHOOTING DIGITAL MINIMOVIES ■

92

Know Your Camera: LCDs

Just about every digital camera comes with a color LCD display, such as the one shown here. They generally range in size from 1.5" to 2.5". Not only does the LCD display a resampled version of your image, but the LCD may also display invaluable information such as a histogram. The histogram is a graphic–and thereby extremely accurate–representation of the tonal values of your image.

LCDs are great at providing instant feedback, but the image shown on the screen shouldn't be used to determine accurate exposure–it's best to use the histogram for that if you have it. (To learn how to read a histogram, ☞ "Reading the Histogram" in Zooming In.) Also, LCDs, with their limited resolution, won't always inform you whether the image is sharp or not. It helps to zoom in on a detail, but ultimately you'll have to view the full image on a larger monitor to know for sure. The LCD is the most power-hungry component of your digital camera system and therefore should be used sparingly if power is an issue. (It does help if you lower the brightness of the LCD.)

LCDs are notoriously hard to view in bright light. That's why I suggest using a sun shield such as Hoodman's LCD Hood for viewing. LCDs are also susceptible to scratches, and you should use care when cleaning them. A washed, 100% cotton t-shirt will work. Hoodman also makes a clear protective overlay that peels and sticks onto the LCD. (More at **shooting-digital.com**.)

For more on using LCDs and viewfinders for framing a shot, ☞ "Know Your Camera: Frame and Focus" in Chapter 4.

General Shooting Tips

I turned to an old friend and award-winning filmmaker, cinematographer Dave Drum, to offer some professional tips that apply to shooting minimovies with a digital camera.

Here's what Dave suggests:

- A movie has to move. This means the subject must move, the camera must move, or—if the camera has the capability—the lens must zoom.
- Use lens zooms sparingly. Overuse is the biggest mistake that beginners make. It is best to walk the camera toward the subject and, if you use the lens to zoom in, remember that the longer the focal length of the lens, the more that camera shake and motion is accentuated. (Not all digital cameras are capable of zooming while shooting a minimovie, so this isn't always an issue.)
- Shoot tight because of the small viewing area.
- Get depth in the shot. Let the background go soft.
- If you move the camera, include something stable in the foreground to establish a relationship to the movement.
- Establish a scene by starting wide. Move in quickly to the meaningful action.
- Direct attention to where you want the viewer to look.
- A good minimovie has a beginning, middle, and end.
- Watch TV commercials. They tell a complete story in about 15 to 30 seconds, which is the same length of the minimovie that many digital cameras are capable of producing.

Dave also says that sound needs to be audible to be effective, and that is not always easy with camera-mounted, limited microphones. Using video-editing software (discussed later in this chapter), it's possible to add a separate audio track to your video, but synchronizing it is difficult. However, there are a couple of ways to capture effective sound in real time as you shoot. You (or someone standing next to the camera) can read a scripted voice-over. Or, if you simply want a music track, you can play it through a stereo as you shoot. (If you're not going to distribute your video, copyrights won't be an issue; if you do plan to distribute it, be sure to obtain permission for the music if it isn't your own, or use something from one of the many public-domain music libraries available.)

Note: Watch the orientation of your digital camera when you shoot full motion. If you shoot with a vertical orientation, your minimovie will play sideways on a monitor. Orientation can be changed later, of course, but you'll need software such as QuickTime Pro to do this.

Minimovie Case Studies

Minimovies have several functions ranging from pure fun—your child bobbing for apples at a birthday party—to practical—showing a student the correct way to roll on a kayak. Here are some examples of real world uses of minimovies created using various models of still digital cameras.

Minimovie Training Clips

Figure 5.2 shows a sequence of frames from a 6-second minimovie created by professional photographer Doug Clark. Doug is not only a photographer, but also an avid kayaker who teaches the sport as well. Knowing how to properly roll a kayak is critical—if you don't get it right, you drown. As a teaching tool, Doug uses the movie mode of his digital camera to film his students rolling a kayak. Then he plays back the movie on the camera's LCD and explains what they did and didn't do right. For this Doug uses a Canon G2 digital camera, which captures up to 30 seconds of full motion video at 320×240 pixel resolution at 15 fps.

Bottom line: Minimovies make great training aids. Sharing can be as simple as viewing them on the digital camera's LCD.

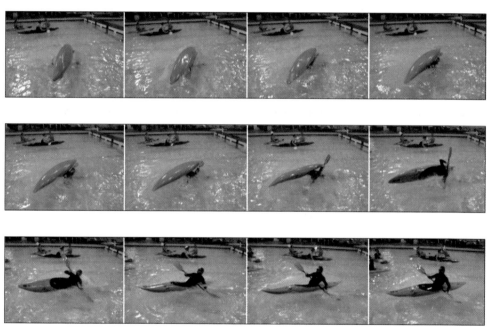

Figure 5.2: Minimovies give instant feedback, and in this example, show a beginning kayaker what he did wrong during a practice roll. (Photos by Doug Clark)

Minimovie Portraits

Artist Tom Mogensen is well known for his figurative painting. Recently, his fascination with movement inspired him to use a digital camera set to movie mode to create a series of minimovie portraits such as the one represented in Figure 5.3.

Figure 5.3: A series of images from "Motion Portraits" by Tom Mogensen. Shot with an Olympus D-340L set to movie mode.

For Tom's "Motion Portraits," as he calls them, Tom identifies a characteristic motion of a person or animal—a twitch of an eye, a particular walk, a hand gesture, etc., and then films it. In the case of his bird Trooper (shown), he focused on a distinctive head movement the bird makes whenever she hears her name. Tom used an Olympus D-340L set to movie mode. He edited the film on his Mac using QuickTime Pro. Some of his "Motion Portraits" are available on the Web at **www.shooting-digital.com.**

Bottom line: Don't think of a "portrait" as necessarily static. Sometimes a minimovie may be the perfect format to capture and share the essence of a person, or a pet!

Minimovie Documentaries

Fred Shippey, the technical editor for this book, also wears a number of hats. For the last 18 years he has served as a member of his local school board and he continues to be very involved with educational issues. Fred used the movie mode of his Minolta DiMAGE X digital camera to document the finals of "Destination ImagiNation," a creative problem-solving program for students in elementary school through high school. He created several minimovies, each up to 35 seconds long, of events ranging from the opening kickoff to valedictorian speeches and awards ceremonies, and then placed the clips on the Web for all to see. See Figure 5.4.

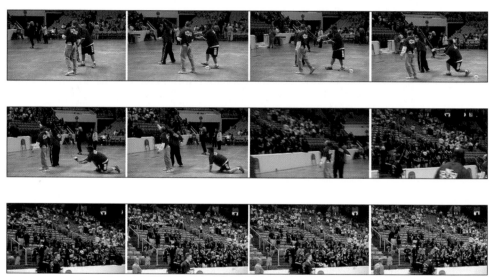

Figure 5.4. This is one of several minimovies created by Fred Shippey (shot with a Minolta DiMAGE X digital camera) for use on a website.

Fred had to make tradeoffs among image quality, file size for downloading, and cross-platform compatibility. He came up with a process described later in the chapter to edit and compress the minimovies down to very reasonable sizes so that most people, even those with a slow Internet connection, could view them.

You can view the clips at **www.destinationimagination.org/d2k.2/video.html**. To view Fred's work you'll need the RealOne Player plug-in, which is available for free download at **www.real.com**.

Bottom line: If you place minimovies on the Web, take some time to make them a manageable file size, viewable by all.

Minimovies Just for Fun

With two daughters, I've photographed my share of birthday parties. It's always difficult to capture that "defining moment" year after year. One year for my daughter Miranda's 6th birthday I tried something different. As Miranda and her friends bobbed for apples, I started as I normally do, camera to my eye, looking for the right moment that included the apples, the child's face, and a successful bite. It suddenly occurred to me after a few moments that a video sequence would be more useful (see Figure 5.5). I was using a Minolta DiMAGE 7i, and it was easy to switch from photo still mode to movie mode. I shot 15 seconds of video and later, using QuickTime Pro, I edited the "footage" down to a very brief 8 seconds that caught the essence of the game. Furthermore, I resized the clip from 320×240 pixels to 160×120 pixels and e-mailed the resulting 150K **.mov** file to the grandparents in Spain.

Bottom line: Don't hesitate to shoot motion when appropriate. When preparing for e-mailing, reduce the duration and the size of the minimovie.

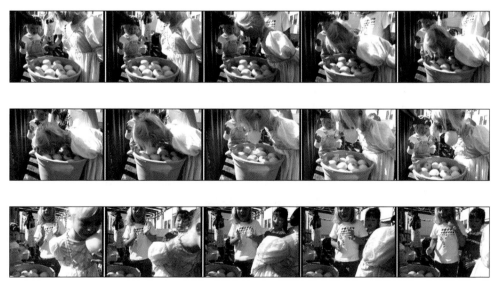

Figure 5.5: Sequences from a 15-second minimovie shot with a Minolta DiMAGE 7i digital camera. Later, the sequence was edited and resized and sent via e-mail to the grandparents in Spain.

Accessories That Make a Difference: Batteries

It's hard to believe that once upon a time cameras worked without batteries. Now it's come to this: A digital camera without batteries is just an expensive decorative ornament hanging around your neck.

Many digital cameras use the common AA-size battery. A standard-size battery such as this makes life easier in some ways, and more complicated in others. AA batteries are readily available, but there are several types to choose from. It's generally recommended that you use the rechargeable nickel-metal hydride (NiMH) batteries and avoid standard alkaline batteries except in an emergency. A four-pack of NiMH batteries generally runs for $10-$18. Chargers range in price from $20-$40, depending on brand and charging speed.

If your camera comes with a proprietary battery, it is probably a rechargeable lithium ion (LiIon) battery, and you are set: there isn't much to do except buy a spare and make sure you charge the battery regularly.

Both the NiMH and the LiIon rechargeable batteries are relatively maintenance free and don't suffer from "memory" associated with the older type of nickel cadmium (NiCd) batteries. They also don't contain toxic metals like the NiCads do. Depending on the brand and usage, you should easily get anywhere from 400-600 charges from these types of batteries before they lose their effectiveness. Both the NiMH and LiIon batteries are susceptible to impact. Don't drop them or let them bang around in your camera bag.

To keep your digital camera properly powered, it's critical that you establish a battery maintenance procedure. If your camera uses AA batteries:

1. Acquire at least two sets of rechargeable NiMH batteries.
2. Keep one set in the charger at all times. (Most chargers turn off automatically when the batteries are fully charged; if not, remove your batteries when they are charged.)
3. Don't wait to recharge until the set in the camera is dead. Swap sets regularly. (The amount of time you'll get from a battery will depend on the make of your digital camera and how much you use the power-draining LCD or auto-focus mode.)
4. Carry a set of non-rechargeable Lithium-ion digital camera batteries as well. These are your life raft, only to be used when the previous procedure isn't followed correctly. These batteries generally are expensive, but they have a long shelf life. You can get four AA-Lithium-ion digital camera batteries for $10-$20 and they have about twice as much power as the rechargeable ones. (My Olympus E-10 takes either four AA batteries or two CR-V3 Lithium-ion batteries that cost around $10 each. I generally carry a pair of these batteries and use them only as a backup.)

Finally, don't throw used up batteries into the trash. Take them to community recycling centers or to retail outlets such as Target.

Editing and Sharing Minimovies

It's easy to shoot a minimovie and share your work on the camera's LCD or use the video out to plug your digital camera into a TV monitor. It's a bit more difficult if you want to edit your minimovie, make a CD or a DVD, or reduce the file size so you can send it via e-mail or share it on the Web. Again, all you budding moviemakers out there will need to know this stuff soon enough anyway, when you start using a digital video camera. Making minimovies produced by a digital camera is a good place to start.

There are some digital cameras, such as the Sony F717, that allow you to perform limited file editing inside the camera itself. However, most of the time you'll need to transfer your minimovie file to a computer and use special software to really do the job right.

It would be very easy if there were just one cross-platform software application that did everything. But unfortunately, there isn't. The type of software you use depends largely on what you want to do:

- Edit the duration of your movie
- Incorporate your movie into other movies and/or add text and titles
- Compress efficiently for e-mail and the Web
- Convert file formats
- Create DVDs

The software you use also depends on:

- The native file format generated by your digital camera (most are .avi, .mov, or .mpg)
- The platform used for editing and producing (Mac, Windows, or Linux)
- The platform and/or plug-ins used for viewing

Software pitfalls and shortcomings abound. Nothing illustrates this point better than this: Neither Apple's iMovie 2 (Mac only), nor Microsoft Movie Maker (Windows only)—both widely distributed, free programs—can import most of the .avi, .mov, or .mpg files generated by digital cameras. Both programs require you to convert the files first using another program! (I'll tell you how shortly.)

Also, QuickTime Pro, an inexpensive cross-platform application, is a good program for editing and file conversion but it won't edit an .mpg file. It also won't export to an .rm file to be read by RealOne Player or to a Windows Media File (WMV), two other formats that offer a variety of compression schemes.

There is no way that I can cover all the possible software/platform/format combinations here. (That's another book. Heck, that's several other books!) However, I've chosen a few of the more common tasks you'll likely want to do to your mini-movies, and paired them with some commonly available video- and image-editing applications to give you a sampling of possible solutions:

- **QuickTime** is often bundled with many computer systems and can be downloaded at no cost at **www.Apple.com**. With the free version you can view most minimovie files created by digital cameras. In order to edit minimovies, you'll need to purchase a $29 key for QuickTime Pro that enables the editing and exporting functions of QuickTime.

- **iMovie 2 and iDVD** are two free applications for the Mac platform. Used together, and with QuickTime Pro, you can easily create DVDs for wide audiences.
- **TMPGEnc** is a free file converter for Windows users only (available for download at www.tmpgenc.net/).
- **Helix Producer Basic** is a cross-platform, free application for creating highly compressionable .rm files (available for download at www.realnetworks.com/products/producer/basic.html).
- **Microsoft Movie Maker** is a free video-editing application for the PC that comes bundled with Windows XP.

I haven't included the software packages that come bundled with some digital cameras. If they work for you, that's fine. Use them. I just haven't had good luck with the ones I've tried.

 Note: There are several useful books on editing digital video. I particularly recommend *Digital Video Essentials: Shoot, Transfer, Edit, Share* by Erica Sadun (Sybex, 2002).

Editing Duration and Resizing

One of the most common tasks, even for a movie that is only 30 seconds long, is editing out the unwanted parts. Editing duration is also a good way to reduce the overall file size of a movie to make it more e-mail friendly. Just about any video-editing software will allow you to trim a video clip. However, not all editing software will accept the files generated by digital cameras. (☞ "Converting to Another Format," later in this chapter.)

Here's the basic procedure to use in QuickTime:

1. Open your movie file.
2. In the player window, point your cursor to the duration bar under the image window.
3. Click and slide the two triangle icons relative to each other to select the desirable parts of your movie that you want to keep.
4. From the menu bar, select Edit ➢ Cut to remove the unselected parts of your movie.
5. From the menu bar, select File ➢ Save As, name your new file, and you are finished. (Be sure to select "Make Movie self-contained" in the Save As dialog box if you want to e-mail the movie to others or share it on other systems.)

If editing your minimovie for duration didn't reduce the file size enough, consider reducing the pixel count. Most minimovies are saved at 320 × 240 pixels. Experiment with smaller dimensions.

Here's the basic procedure to use in QuickTime Pro:

1. From the file menu, select Movie ➢ Movie Properties.
2. Choose Video Track from the left pop-up menu.

3.   Click the Adjust button and drag the corners of the player window to resize the movie. The new dimensions are displayed in the Properties window. You can also rotate the movie and change the orientation.

You can also use Export ➤ Options ➤ Size to specify the exact size. You'll see this used shortly.

Combining Clips and Adding a Title

To combine different minimovies, to incorporate clips from your minimovie into a slide show of stills, or to add a title or other text, you'll need a digital video-editing program such as QuickTime Pro, iMovie 2 (Mac only), Microsoft Movie Maker (Windows only), or the "Plus" version of Helix Producer ($200). If you use iMovie 2, remember that you'll need to use a program like QuickTime Pro to convert your .avi, .mov, or .mpg file into a DV stream. (A word of warning: not all digital cameras' .mpg files are supported by QuickTime.) The skills required to edit video clips or add text will vary depending on the program you use and your goals. Refer to the program's user guide for more on this subject.

Converting to Another Format

If ever there was a Tower of Babel, it exists in the world of digital video formats.
*   If your minimovie is saved in the .mpg file format (as many of the Sony digital cameras do) you may be able to view it in QuickTime Pro but not edit it. Use QuickTime Pro to export your .mpg file as an .avi, and then reopen the converted file in QuickTime Pro. Now you'll be able to edit the frames. However, sound—if available—will not survive the conversion.
*   If you want to open your minimovie in Apple's iMovie 2 you must first convert your files to a DV file format. Use QuickTime Pro and under the Export options, choose Movie to DV Stream.
*   To take advantage of the Real Media .rm format (faster downloads, cross-platform readability, etc.), use the free Helix Producer Basic application to convert your .avi or .mov files. To convert the .mpg format to the .rm format, you may be able to use a program such as QuickTime Pro to convert it to .mov, and then open it in Helix Producer Basic.
*   You can use Microsoft Movie Maker to edit and add text to a minimovie, but if you want to create a Video CD you'll need to save your Movie Maker work as an .avi file and then use the free TMPGEnc application to create an MPEG-1 file. (Once you've done that, you can create a video CD using a program such as Roxio CD Creator.)

Preparing for DVD or CD ROM

The DVD format is slowly replacing VHS tapes, and more and more homes have DVD players. Many computers also have the capability to play DVDs. Normally it takes an expensive DVD writer hooked up to your computer to create DVDs for home viewing.

However, a low-cost alternative is to use special software to create a Video CD that is also viewable with some DVD players.

If you have a Mac with a SuperDrive, it is very easy to create a DVD using a combination of QuickTime Pro, iMovie 2, and iDVD software. The disc may not play in all DVD players—but as of this writing, no DVD-writeable disc plays in all players because of media differences and the lack of a single DVD standard.

If you are using a PC, you'll also need a DVD-writeable drive, and you can choose from several software packages including Ulead DVD MovieFactory 2, Ulead DVD Workshop, and Ulead DVD PictureShow 2 (**www.ulead.com**), Nero 5.5 (**www.nero.com**), or Roxio Toast 5 Titanium (**www.roxio.com**).

If you want to use a CD burner drive to create Video CDs, which can be read by many DVD players, you'll need software such as Roxio's Toast Titanium (about $90), which is available for both PC and Mac.

Creating a Minimovie Mask to Avoid Blurry Playback

Regardless of what platform you are working on or which software you choose, you will probably want to create a full-sized frame to place your small minimovie in since most minimovies are only 320 × 240 pixels. Applications like iMovie and iDVD will blow your minimovie up to fill the screen. However, if you view your minimovie blown up to this size it will likely look pretty bad.

If you create a frame, or mask, when the movie is played, it will run at its native 320 × 240 pixel resolution surrounded by a sea of black (or white, depending on the color of mask you make).

Here is what tech editor Fred Shippey does on his Mac to prepare his clips for DVD using a combination of Photoshop (or Photoshop Elements) and QuickTime Pro. Further work can then be done in iMovie and iDVD.

1. To create the mask, use image-processing software such as Photoshop or Photoshop Elements to draw a 640 × 480 pixel (for NTSC) black rectangle with a slightly lighter black 320 × 240 pixel center, and save the mask as a .jpg file (see Figure 5.6).

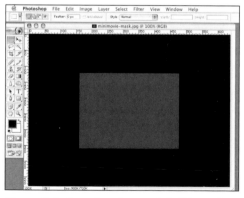

Figure 5.6: Creating the mask in Photoshop.

2. Open your minimovie in QuickTime Pro.

3. Choose File ➢ Import to open the saved mask in another QuickTime Pro player (see Figure.5.7).

Figure 5.7: The mask and the minimovie open in separate QuickTime Pro players.

4. Click the mask clip to select it, choose Edit ➢ Select All, and then choose Edit ➢ Copy.

5. Click the minimovie to select it and then choose Edit ➢ Add Scaled. This will add the mask to the minimovie and make it the same time length as the minimovie clip.

6. Next, select Movie ➢ Get Movie Properties.

7. Select Video Track 2 on the left and Layer on the right. Set the layer to 1, moving the mask to the back (see Figure 5.8).

Figure 5.8: Moving the mask to the back.

8. Select Video Track 1 on the left and Size on the right, and click Adjust. Red crop marks appear around the video. Click on the picture (not the marks) and center the video on the lightened 320 × 240 box. When you are ready, click Done (see Figure 5.9).

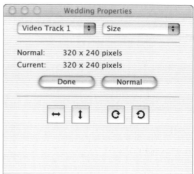

Figure 5.9: Centering the minimovie clip within the frame.

9.   The video may not completely cover the lighter box, but as you can see, the crop marks should line up. When you view the movie, if you used a slightly lighter black for the center area, you won't notice a lighter area when it's played in iMovie or iDVD.

10.   Choose File ➤ Export, and then choose Movie to DV Stream as the Export type (see Figure 5.10).

Figure 5.10: Exporting the movie as a DV stream will allow you to do further editing or burn it to a DVD.

11.   Open the DV stream file in iMovie or iDVD (or other movie-editing or DVD-burning program) as required for further work.

Software Solutions: Grabbing Stills from a Minimovie

There are times when all you need is a single frame or a sequence of frames from your mini-movie.

The latest version of Photoshop Elements, version 2, makes it very easy to import individual frames from your minimovie through a Frame From Video import command. The earlier version of Photoshop Elements doesn't have this command, nor does Photoshop 7. (I'll show you how to import frames with these programs later.)

With Photoshop Elements 2 open, here's the basic procedure for capturing a video frame:

1. Select File ➢ Import ➢ Frame From Video.
2. Browse to your .mov, .aif, or .mpeg file.
3. Play your movie using the controls at the bottom of the dialog box. When you see the frame you want, either select Grab Frame or simply press the Spacebar.

You can select as many frames as you want. Each frame will open in its own window.

If you are working with Photoshop or Photoshop Elements 1.0 you can use the free, cross-platform QuickTime player to grab a frame from just about any minimovie file format (except .mpeg) and paste it into your program. If you are using a Mac, open and then pause the movie in QuickTime, then simply drag and drop the window into an open window in Photoshop or Photoshop Elements 1.0. If you are using a PC, you need to select Edit ➢ Copy from the QuickTime menu. Switch to Photoshop or Photoshop Elements 1.0, and click File ➢ New. The size will match the clipboard. Paste the clip. With QuickTime Pro, you can save the frame you are viewing as a still image by selecting File ➢ Export ➢ Movie to Picture.

Preparing a Minimovie for Use on the Web or With E-Mail

In the previous case study, "Minimovie Documentaries," we saw how Fred Shippey used the movie mode of his Minolta DiMAGE X to document an event. Fred's goal was to produce entertaining and informative mini-documentaries that were small in file size with a minimum tradeoff in quality, as well as viewable on different computer platforms.

These are the steps to follow to achieve Fred's results:

1. Open the minimovie in QuickTime Pro and select File ➢ Export.
2. Select Export: Movie to QuickTime Movie and click Options.
3. Select Video Settings and on the Compression tab, choose Photo-JPEG, Color, and Best Quality. Click OK.
4. Select Size and choose Use custom size, Width: 180, Height: 135. Click OK.
5. Select Filter and make sure it says None. Click OK.
6. Click Save to export the resized minimovie. Figure 5.11 shows the settings at this point.
7. Open RealProducer Basic.

8. A Recording Assistant guides you through the initial setup. This is what the Recording Assistant prompted Fred to do:

- Select your source file.
- Enter any information you want included with the clip.
- Under File Type, select Single Rate.
- Under Target Audience, you are given a choice of connection speeds. Choosing 28K Modem will produce a small, highly compressed file. Choosing 512K DSL/Cable Modem will produce a large file with the highest quality. You will want to experiment with the different settings to see what produces the size/quality tradeoff you want.
- Under Audio, select the appropriate one. Keep in mind that Music will produce a larger file than Voice Only.
- Under Video Quality, start out with Normal Motion Video. Again, experiment.
- Select your Output File destination.

9. Fred then clicked Finish on the next screen and left the Recording Assistant. The main RealProducer Basic screen then appeared, showing all of Fred's earlier selections. (You can change any of your selections on this screen. At this point you also may want to experiment.) Fred clicked Start to save his clip in the RealMedia format (see Figure 5.11).

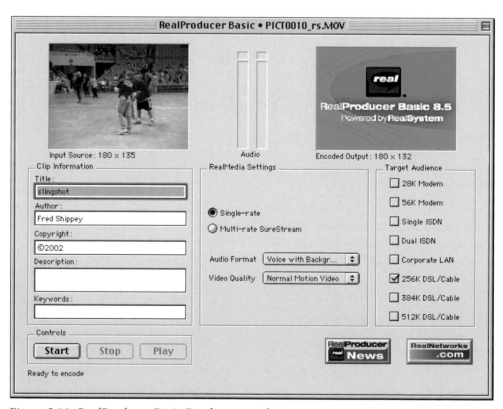

Figure 5.11: RealProducer Basic Ready to encode screen

10. Finally, Fred checked his new file in RealOne Player (see Figure 5.12).

Figure 5.12: The RealOne Player screen.

Creating an Animated GIF from Frames

The GIF file format is commonly recognized by all web browsers, and it also supports animation. You can easily condense your minimovie to just a few frames and save the frames as an animated GIF using a program such as Photoshop or Photoshop Elements. (Animated GIFs don't support sound.)

Figure 5.13 shows three frames from an animated GIF totaling only 65K—much more Web-friendly than the 4.6MB original .mov movie.

Figure 5.13: All it takes is three frames grabbed from a minimovie to make an entertaining animated GIF.

I'll show you how to do this using Photoshop Elements 2, but you can use other GIF animation programs, such as GIF Builder or ImageReady.

First, follow the steps for "Grabbing Stills from a Minimovie," earlier in this chapter, selecting at least three grabs from the beginning, middle, and end of your minimovie. Then:

1. Copy and paste each frame into a single file comprised of three layers.

2. Select File ➤ Save for Web.

3. In the Save for Web window, set your options to the following:
- In the optimized file format box, select GIF.
- In the color reduction algorithm box select Selective.
- In the Dither Algorithm box select Diffusion.

- Under Colors and Dither, it's okay to use the default settings; however, later you may want to change these values to reduce the final file size of your animated GIF.
- Most importantly, check the box next to Animation.

Animation options are found near the bottom of the window. You can choose whether or not you want the animation to loop and you can also choose the frame delay rate.

To test your animation, select Preview In at the bottom of the Save for Web window.

 Note: In my book *Photoshop Elements 2 Solutions* (Sybex, 2002) you can find more detail about using the Save for Web plug-in to create animated GIFs.

Creating a Collage from Frames

A collage is a great way to display a series of grabbed frames from a minimovie. It's especially easy to create one such as the one shown in Figure 5.14 using a batch of frame grabs with the Photoshop Elements Create Photomerge command.

Figure 5.14: You can make a collage from grabbed frames.

To do this, follow the steps for "Grabbing Stills from a Minimovie," earlier in this chapter, and select as many frames as you want using the Frame From Video import command. Then:

1. Save and name each frame (File ➤ Save). Save in the .psd file format.
2. With the saved and named frames open in Photoshop Elements, select File ➤ Create Photomerge. Your files should be listed in the dialog box.
3. Select OK.

Photomerge will attempt to "merge" your grabs automatically but will fail. Instead, you can drag and drop the thumbnails from Photomerge's lightbox and arrange them any way you want in the main work area.

For more on using Photomerge, refer to my book *Photoshop Elements 2 Solutions*.

Storyboarding with Frame Grabs

It's also easy to make a storyboard out of a series of frame grabs from your minimovie. Storyboards are used for a variety of purposes—from advertising to filmmaking—and they show a sequence of events viewable at a glance.

I'll show you how I created the storyboards used to illustrate the case studies in this chapter. This time I'll use both QuickTime Pro and Photoshop Elements. I started with QuickTime Pro.

1. With my movie open, I selected File ➤ Export.
2. In the Save Exported File As dialog box I selected Export: Movie to Image Sequence.
3. I clicked the Options button to the right of the Export command, which brought up another dialog box.
4. In the Options dialog box, I selected Format: Tiff and Frames per second: 6. (If you have a long minimovie, you may want to change this to a higher number to reduce the number of frames grabbed.)
5. I clicked Save and QuickTime Pro did the rest, saving a batch of frames to a designated location.

Remember, this works only if you are using QuickTime Pro, not the free QuickTime player.

Next, in Photoshop Elements, I did the following:

1. Chose File Print Layouts ➤ Contact Sheet.
2. In the Contact Sheet dialog box, I selected Choose and navigated to the folder containing the frames generated by QuickTime Pro.
3. I chose a document size of 8 × 10 inches at 200 dpi. (The size depends on what you want to do with the document.)
4. In the Thumbnails section, I selected Across first and Column: 4, Rows: 5. (Again, these settings will vary depending on your needs.)
5. I deselected Use Filename and then clicked OK.
6. After Photoshop Elements was finished, I used the Crop tool to crop extra white area away from the sequence of images.

Shooting Digital on the Road

Whether you take your digital camera with you for a long Sunday drive, or on a 747 to Asia, you'll have similar concerns. For example, how do you pack your precious digital camera safely? How much digital storage should you bring along? How do you back up the shots you've taken? What kind of batteries and power supplies should you bring? What can go wrong with your digital camera? How do you fix it when something goes wrong? This chapter will answer these questions and give you on-the-road travel shooting tips as well.

Chapter Contents

Bruce Dale

Packing Digital for the Road

Packing for a trip is always a challenge. Not only do you need to balance your equipment needs with size and weight considerations, but you also need to pack everything in such a way that the bump and thump of life on the road doesn't turn your valuable equipment into useless junk. See Figure 6.1.

Figure 6.1: Shown here is the Tamrac Double Decker Model 5685 Digital Photo Camera Bag, a versatile bag which accommodates a wide range of digital cameras, extra lenses, batteries, and other accessories. The lower compartment can be separated from the bag and used to store battery chargers and adapters.

Here is an at-a-glance "laundry list" of photographic equipment that may be useful for you. The list is loosely organized in order of importance. Following the list is a look at the luggage and packing lists of several professional photographers who spend a great deal of the year shooting digital images on the road.

As you plan your trip, consider taking the following:

- One or more digital cameras
- Enough camera memory card capacity (the exact amount will depend on the resolution of your digital camera, the file format you save your images in, and whether or not you are bringing a method for backing up data)
- External data backup device (laptop, digital wallet-type memory, etc.)
- Extra batteries and multi-voltage battery charger
- Portable tripod or monopod
- Filters (polarizing, neutral density, UV, etc.)

- Compressed air and/or wipes
- External flash (not an issue if your digital camera's onboard strobe has proven to be all you need)

When you pack camera equipment, be sure there is adequate padding between items. Many camera bags come with padded compartments, but the extra padding often adds bulk and weight. Consider a more lightweight bag and wrap each piece of your equipment individually with soft cloth.

Now let's play voyeur and look into the bags of three professional photographers, to see what they carry with them when they travel. Obviously, your needs will vary and may not be as extensive as a professional who makes a living shooting digital on the road.

Chester Simpson

A professional photographer for 25 years, Chester recently switched over completely to digital. When I talked with him he had returned from a trip to the Middle East, Hong Kong, and Bolivia. This man is always moving! His travel bag includes Canon EOS-D30 and EOS-D60 professional digital camera bodies with lenses and UV filters, plastic zip-lock backs for lenses and cameras (especially when he is going to the desert, where sand easily ruins lenses and digital cameras), a plastic garbage bag for the camera if it rains, a Gitzo travel tripod with a ball head, two Canon 550 EX external flash units that are radio controlled with plenty of Energizer E2 photo batteries, Lithium batteries, a power strip with surge protection, travel converter plugs, and a charger for the Canon camera batteries. He also carries an Apple Powerbook G3, with a CD burner, and eight CD-R discs, and two CD-R/W discs, plus all cables.

Chester is particularly proud of his Storm Case carry-on luggage container. Not only does all of his equipment fit into it, but also it qualifies as hand-carry luggage so it never leaves his side. The luggage is hard plastic, waterproof, dustproof, and crushproof, with wheels and a handle. (I've included a link to the manufacturer on **www.shooting-digital.com.**)

You might also be interested in hearing some of Chester's non-camera related baggage: two paper copies of his credit cards and passport. One copy is hidden in his camera bag and the other is hidden in the pocket of a pair of his packed pants. He also carries phone numbers of the American embassies in all of the countries he plans to visit, and ten Energy bars, aspirin, antacid pills, a toothbrush, a small tube of toothpaste, a bottle of water, an inflatable neck pillow for sleeping on the plane, a small windup clock, a magazine or small paperback book, a set of ear plugs, and finally, $500 in cash stashed in various spots inside his camera bag and on his body.

John Isaac

John has traveled the world for 25 years as a photographer for the United Nations. Now he travels the world as a freelancer shooting exclusively digital. He uses an Olympus E-20 digital camera as his primary camera, and a smaller, lighter, Olympus Camedia 5050 digital camera as well. He carries a small portable tripod, two 1GB IBM Microdrive storage cards, two 256MB cards, and four 128MB smart media cards. For backup he carries an Apple iBook plus a small, portable EZQuest 48GB hard drive. John doesn't take filters with him, but he always carries compressed air and wipes, as well as one external flash, the Olympus FL-40. He carries several AA batteries and a rechargeable battery pack for the E-20 that provides power for several days of shooting and viewing. He also carries electrical adapters for both digital cameras, which he uses when he is loading all the memory card data from the digital camera to his laptop. (Using plug-in current saves battery life.) Finally, he carries both telephoto and wide-angle attachment lenses.

Bruce Avera Hunter

Bruce is a professional photographer who lives in the Mid-Atlantic region and spends a lot of his time exploring various South Pacific islands and coastal regions above and below the water. (His underwater shot of a shark taken in the Sea of Cortez is shown in Chapter 11.) In addition to the items on the general list provided earlier, Bruce adds a self-altered backpack with a built-in PVC tube to hold an opened umbrella, so he can shoot in the rain. He also takes with him a plastic shading hood for the LCD monitor on his camera, and a plastic bag large enough to hold all of his gear in case of rain. Other items include: a mini tripod, a solar charger for AA batteries, model and property release forms, a mini light reflector, a flashlight to "paint" or spot fill, a mini water spray bottle for creating flower, plant, and spider web droplets, a multi-tool like a Leatherman, several plastic zip-lock bags, a lens brush, a pen and pad of paper, a lighter, a first aid kit, aspirin, business cards, sunscreen, insect repellant, and chapstick. Finally, handyman Bruce also brings a roll of duct tape and a folded wire coat hanger, with which he says he can make countless things.

Note: Having had a couple of Swiss army knifes confiscated by airport security, I'd suggest packing pocketknives and multi-tools in checked baggage. You probably won't have much luck with a lighter in your carry-on luggage either.

Know Your Camera: What Goes Wrong with Digital Cameras

Digital cameras are filled with complex electronic circuitry, and yet, remarkably, they rarely fail on their own. When they do, it is usually within the first few days of use. According to repair services we contacted across the country, most of the damage that repair technicians see is a result of dropping, banging, or otherwise putting the digital camera in harm's way. Opening the memory card cover while data is being written to it also ranks as a leading cause of camera damage. Most of the repairs have to do with built-in strobes or LCDs failing. Following these repairs come repairs to mechanical parts such as shutters.

What can you do to increase the life of your digital camera?
- Avoid prolonged exposure to extreme heat or humidity, which can cause permanent damage. On the other hand, exposure to extreme cold may hinder the performance of your digital camera, but rarely does it causes permanent damage. However, condensation caused from moving from extreme cold to heat, or vice versa, is serious if the moisture doesn't have a chance to dry. Moving between cold and heat incrementally will reduce the chance of condensation.
- Protect your digital camera from dust and sand. Use plastic zip-lock bags or garbage bags. Keep your lens covered until you are ready to shoot. If you are using a high-end digital camera with interchangeable lenses, be extremely careful when changing lenses not to let sand or dust contaminate the exposed sensor.
- Avoid contact with water, especially salt water. Actually, immersion in clean, fresh water doesn't automatically mean the end of a digital camera. Dry the camera quickly with a blow dryer or other forced heat source. Spilling a soft drink on your camera, however, usually means the end of it, regardless of any attempts to save it.
- Watch for corroded batteries. Corrosion can spread to other electronic parts of the camera.
- Keep the camera clean with a soft cloth. Use compressed air, or a Q-tip dipped in alcohol to clean it more thoroughly. (If you use an SLR digital camera, don't use compressed air to clean the sensor, which can ruin it. Check your camera manual for cleaning instructions.)

Pack your digital camera carefully. Surround it with soft cloth or special foam. Invest in a padded camera bag with cushioned compartments. What do you do if your digital camera suddenly fails?
- Check and replace depleted batteries.
- Clean the battery terminals with Q-tips or the eraser end of a pencil.
- Turn the digital camera on and off (and say a prayer in between).
- Remove the memory card, and then put it back in.
- Replace the memory card.
- Call tech support. Sure, waiting on the phone for a human to answer can be frustrating. But believe it or not, patience often pays off. If the problem persists and is covered by the manufacturer's warranty, send the digital camera in for repairs. If it's not covered, think twice before spending good money on an expensive repair. Take a look at eBay or other online auction sites and see what your digital camera is really worth. You may decide that this is a good time to upgrade.

Storage and Archiving on the Road

A huge concern for traveling digital photographers is how to make external backups of digital images. Digital cameras with memory cards full of precious memories can be lost or stolen. Memory cards can become corrupted or damaged and data lost.

There are many easy—and increasingly inexpensive—ways to back up data generated by digital cameras.

- Digital "wallets" are relatively small storage devices that either accept data directly from the digital camera via a USB connection or accept media cards directly (☞ "Accessories That Make a Difference: Backup Devices").

- Lightweight laptops, which can transfer data directly from a digital camera to a hard drive via a cable, card reader, or built-in PCMCIA card slot with an appropriate memory card adapter. Ideally, the laptop is equipped with a CD-R/W drive to provide a way to make yet another copy of the digital data.

- So-called "disc" digital cameras—most notably, the Sony Mavica CD series that burn digital data directly to mini CDs. (The main drawback to this type of camera is recording speed, which is often slow.)

- Transferring card data from one card to another. Some digital cameras, most notably Olympus and Fuji models, have two slots so you can actually transfer data from one card, such as a compact flash card, to another card, such as a smart media card. This makes it possible to make multiple copies of your images. For example, you can keep one copy with you and send a copy on another card home via the mail.

Another increasingly viable option for ensuring that your images make it safely home is to send them home or to friends via the Internet or e-mail. It helps if you carry a laptop with dial-up capabilities, but this isn't always necessary. Cyber cafés around the world are adding digital camera memory card readers to their computer systems. This means you can pop into a cyber café in Kona, Hawaii, place your memory card into a reader, and via the Internet send your digital images to any of a number places, including your own e-mail address. Most cruise ships also offer this capability. As the digital infrastructure continues to increase around the world, it'll get easier and easier to upload your digital images to online photo services such as **ofoto.com** and **shutterfly.com**, where they are not only safely stored but available for viewing or printing by anyone you designate. This type of "online backup" is obviously limited by available bandwidth. It takes time to send large image files, and you may want to edit your selection to a few "keepers"—images that deserve extra protection or attention.

Accessories That Make a Difference: Backup Devices

Backing up your digital image data is always important, but even more so when you are on the road. There are many off-the-shelf devices available that make it easy—and affordable—to transfer and save valuable data from your digital camera. These devices, which range in price from $100 to $500, are called everything from "digital wallets" to "picture pads" to "mini hard drive card readers." Some connect directly to your digital camera via a USB or FireWire cable, while others allow you to slip your camera's memory card into the device, transfer the files, and then return the memory card to your digital camera.

Backup devices offer a wide range of options and your choice is likely determined by a combination of price, features, storage capacity, and compatibility with your digital camera system. You can be sure that as digital cameras continue to proliferate, demand for these devices will drive their cost dramatically down, with even more features and increased ease of use.

At this time, the most inexpensive devices are simply mini hard drives. Some connect only via a USB cable, and others, such as the Interactive Media KanguruMedia X-change, accept only the most commonly used memory cards. On the other end of the spectrum are devices such as the Delkin eFilm PicturePAD, which provides 20GB or more storage capability and runs on battery or AC power. These small devices not only accept standard memory cards but also include an LCD panel that allows you to view transferred photos. A USB or FireWire connection makes it easy to transfer backups to a personal computer.

Another form of backup that shouldn't be discounted is memory cards themselves. Some digital cameras, such as Olympus and Fuji models, have multiple media slots so you can transfer data from one card to another, thereby making a simple and inexpensive backup system.

It's important to remember when choosing a backup device that peace of mind is an important consideration and well worth paying for. With some backup devices, you have to take it on faith that your images have successfully transferred. There is no feedback loop. Having an LCD panel on the device, or a means to connect the device to an external monitor or a TV to ensure that your valuable photos are safe, is a desired feature.

Another thing to keep in mind: These devices are susceptible to damage. They can be lost. They can break. There is no substitute for building redundancy into any backup system.

Shooting Digital Candids

A favorite "souvenir" of any trip is images of people interacting naturally and candidly with their environment. Figure 6.2 is a wonderful example of this kind of image. It was taken in Peru by professional photographer Morton Beebe with a Sony DSC-F707 prosumer digital camera. (Morton also shot film of the same scene with a professional camera).

Figure 6.2: This candid image was shot in Peru with a Sony DSC-F707 digital camera. (Photo by Morton Beebe)

There is a common misconception about candid photographs that they have to be taken on the sly, secretly and spy-like. In fact, often the best candids show people at ease and comfortable—not necessary unaware of the photographer.

To get the shot of the Peruvian people, direct descendents of the Incas, Morton and his wife brought and shared food and created a quick but special relationship. Morton made no attempt at all to hide his cameras and in fact, showed the Peruvians images he had taken with the digital camera. In the past, Morton shared Polaroids, but carting the bulky camera was a nuisance. Sometimes, in the absence of a Polaroid, Morton promised his subjects he'd send them a print. Using the LCD on his digital camera to share images has turned out to be very useful. "I think most of the time people just want to know that you aren't catching them in a compromising position," Morton says. "Sure, a print would be nice to leave behind, but just showing them the LCD is often satisfying enough."

Morton, whose background is photojournalism, does nothing to pose or interfere with the people he is photographing. He doesn't use reflectors. He is especially sensitive to the people he photographs close up. Often, he has his wife ask if it is all right to use the images for publication. Morton also travels with 3 x 5 inch cards containing model releases in German, Spanish, and French.

Note: When do you need a model release? If you think you will ever publish or otherwise make public a shot you have taken of a person, you may want to consider having them sign a model release. A model release is not critical if the person you photograph is depicted in a public place, such as on the street or in a public market. It is also not as critical if the usage is editorial (such as for a newspaper or magazine, or for educational purposes). A model release is essential if you photograph someone in the privacy of their own home. Model releases are always necessary if the person or persons are recognizable and you use the image in an ad or otherwise commercial application. For a sample model release go to **www.shooting-digital.com.**

Of course, Morton agrees that there are times when it's reasonable to shoot surreptitiously. In public markets, for example, he doesn't attempt to engage his subjects. Instead, he steps back out of immediate view and uses a long focal length to capture candid man-on-the-street shots. But you don't have to step back and use long focal lengths to get these kinds of shots. You can wade into the middle of a crowd and adjust your digital camera's LCD to allow you to frame the shot without placing your eye to the eyepiece and drawing attention—assuming, of course, your digital camera has a swivelable LCD. It's also easy to take photos on the sly with a digital camera because many digital cameras are also extremely silent when the shutter is released.

Morton reminds photographers to show respect for local customs and not shoot if anyone objects. This can also keep *you* from getting shot—literally. To elaborate a little more on Morton's suggestions, don't shoot the following without permission:

- Other people's children
- Religious services
- People drinking in public
- People using or buying or selling drugs (I got beat up once for doing this inadvertently)
- Military personnel in action

Note: Here's a handy tip from professional photographer Morton Beebe: if your digital camera has a movie mode with sound capabilities, shoot a sequence of a person agreeing to the usage of their image. Have them provide additional information such as their address, phone number, or e-mail address for follow up.

From a technical point of view, when Morton Beebe shoots candids he generally sets his digital camera to automatic everything. He also selects JPEG as the file format of choice and always chooses the best quality setting. Although JPEG doesn't provide the same image quality as TIFF or RAW, JPEGs write quickly to memory cards and compress to a smaller file size. Also, candid shots, by their very nature, won't suffer from less than optimal image quality. Capturing the fleeting emotional moment is more important. Morton often uses a wide-angle attachment lens—used to get the fur seal shot shown in Figure 6.6—with a multiplier of 0.7. The attachment lens screws into the barrel of the existing lens and effectively extends the camera's capabilities from a 35mm equivalent of 38 mm to one of about 28mm, with little noticeable loss in quality. Morton travels with a laptop and at the end of a day of shooting he transfers files from the camera to an external hard drive.

Bottom line: Use your LCD preview openly to develop trust between you and your subject. Conversely, use the LCD monitor to get shots on the sly without drawing attention to yourself.

A Digital Road Trip

Figures 6.3, 6.4, and 6.5 were taken on a single road trip by photographer Bruce Dale. He and his wife logged over 15,000 miles in a Ford pickup truck as they crossed from their home in Washington, D.C. to the West and back.

Bruce is a 30-year National Geographic Magazine veteran who has photographed in 75 countries. The images shown here were shot using a Panasonic Lumix digital camera, a camera the company asked him to test. Bruce says about the shot shown in Figure 6.3: "I shot this at dusk on a tripod just before darkness. In these kinds of shots the tripod is critical to maintain image sharpness, but I often frame the image before I put the camera on the tripod. That way the tripod—which is rigid and more difficult to move—doesn't determine my composition. It's also my experience when shooting shots like this to wait a little bit later than the point when my eyes say it is perfect. When my eyes tell me the sky is dark enough—but not too dark—I find that the camera sees something quite different."

Figure 6.3: This photograph was shot by Bruce Dale with a Panasonic Lumix digital camera.

Figure 6.4: Bruce spotted this 1959 Chevrolet in Holbrook, Arizona, parked in front of the Wigwam Motel on old Highway 66. After getting permission from the owner, he held the Lumix about a half inch above the ground and carefully composed and shot the scene. (Photograph by Bruce Dale)

Figure 6.5: Bruce says: "This is a fun little picture I like sharing with others. The owners of a rock shop along old Highway 66 built this dinosaur to attract attention. It worked." (Photograph by Bruce Dale)

The Lumix is a 4-megapixel prosumer digital camera that provides a moderate measure of user control. For other assignments Bruce uses higher-end, professional digital cameras. However, by looking at the images he created with the Lumix, it becomes quite clear what I've been saying throughout the book—it's the creative eye that matters most, not the equipment. (You can see more images of Bruce's road trip at **www.brucedale.com.**)

Bruce has been involved in different aspects of digital photography since the '80s, but it's only recently that he has switched almost completely to shooting digital. He acknowledges the advantages and flexibility of shooting digital—from the preview capabilities to shifting color balance and quality on-the-fly—but he admits that digital cameras haven't fundamentally changed the way he shoots.

"I plan on the unexpected," he says. "I go off in one direction, with a particular shot in mind, but then something unexpected and spontaneous presents itself and that becomes THE shot."

Bottom line: For a photographer like Bruce Dale, it's not the digital camera that matters so much. It's the eye!

Shooting in the Cold

When Morton Beebe stepped off the ship in Antarctica he stepped into a blizzard. It was 10 degrees below zero. Freezing cold, he slipped and landed in a pile of fur seal droppings. A few moments later he turned his digital camera toward the source of his misery, and got the shot shown in Figure 6.6.

Figure 6.6: Photo taken in Antarctica by Morton Beebe with a Sony DSC-F707.

Forty-five years earlier, Morton had also been in Antarctica, stationed there as a young sailor. He had a camera then too, but it was a film camera and to keep the mechanical parts from jamming in the freezing cold he had to take the camera apart and remove all the oil and replace it with graphite. He documented his first experience in Antarctica in a book titled *Operation Deep Freeze, Antarctica*, which was published in 1958.

What a difference four and a half decades make, at least from a technical point of view. Not only did Morton's digital camera perform flawlessly in the cold, it was so much easier to use. He didn't have to replace film, which is an especially trying task with heavy mittens on. Replacing a memory card can be awkward, but it is doable, he notes. Since Morton left his camera's settings at automatic and his auto focus on, he didn't need to fiddle with tiny knobs or dials. He suggests the following when shooting in extreme cold:

- Keep the camera warm inside your jacket until you are ready to shoot. Cold zaps energy out of your batteries. (Cold can also hinder the performance of microdrives and other memory storage devices.)
- Use two pairs of gloves, with the just the tips of the inner glove cut to make it easier to change memory cards. Thin, high-tech gloves are also good; they are available in most winter sport shops. If possible, avoid prolonged contact between frozen metal parts and bare fingers. Prying flesh from frozen metal is painful. This also applies to noses and cheeks.
- Keep the lens covered until you are ready to shoot.
- Avoid condensation on your lens and in your camera by letting the camera warm incrementally as you go indoors. You can also seal it in a plastic bag, which prevents the condensation from forming. (Of course, as you can see in Figure 6.7, condensation on the lens can actually be used creatively!)
- Brush snow off of the camera before entering a warm room. Keep falling snow off your camera by putting it into a zip-lock bag with holes cut out for the lens and viewfinder.
- To prevent fogging, avoid breathing on a lens or viewfinder.

Bottom line: When it comes to shooting in the cold, digital cameras don't share may of the drawbacks associated with film cameras of the past.

Figure 6.7: No, this wasn't shot with a diffusion filter. Andrew Tarnowka brought his Olympus E-10 in from the frigid air of Krakow, Poland, to a cozy café, and photographed his daughter Sabina through the resulting condensation. It's a nice effect. But probably not so good for the camera!

Shooting in Heat and Humidity

Literally a few days after Morton Beebe left Antarctica, he was in Peru, in the Amazon Manu rain forest facing completely different shooting conditions. One of the shots he took is shown in Figure 6.8.

Figure 6.8. Shot in the Amazon Manu rain forest with a Sony DSC-F707 digital camera. (Photo by Morton Beebe)

Once again, conditions that used to plague Morton as a film photographer aren't as big an issue with a digital camera. In humid conditions, film quickly deteriorates, but as long as your digital camera is exposed to heat and humidity for only a few days, there shouldn't be a problem.

> **Note:** Although airport security x-rays can damage film, digital cameras are safe. However, at security checkpoints you'll often need to power up your camera for inspection. Make sure your batteries are charged.

In extreme heat, many digital cameras actually shut down automatically to protect sensitive electronic circuitry. Most of the time, once the temperature drops, the digital camera resumes working with no lasting effects. (Sometimes it's not the camera that shuts down, but the rechargeable batteries that have built-in heat protection.) Condensation can also be a consideration in the heat, especially if you go from the heat of the day to the cool air of a restaurant or hotel. Digital cameras should also be protected as best as possible from the dust that often accompanies heat. Don't leave digital cameras in the direct sun. Morton suggests carrying a spare digital camera, if your budget allows. Redundancy is always the best insurance.

Bottom line: Heat may temporarily cause your digital camera to shut down. But the effect lasts only until the camera cools. More attention should be paid to avoiding dust and condensation.

Using the Movie Mode

When my traveling friend Kate Grady told me about the wild traffic in Taipei, Taiwan, I didn't believe her. She then shot the mini-movie sequence shown in Figure 6.9 with her Sony digital camera and e-mailed it to me. Ok, now I believe her.

Figure 6.9: Sometimes the movie mode of a digital camera is what it takes to capture the hustle and bustle of a foreign city. (Quicktime movie by Kate Grady)

Bottom line: Use the movie mode of your digital camera when it is appropriate.

Software Solutions: Changing the Quality of Light

As pointed out elsewhere in this book, morning and evening light are ideal for shooting. At these times, the sun is angled to the horizon and the shadows are long and dramatic. Sunset light is especially pleasing when the light passes through a thick layer of particulates, such as smog, moisture, or dust. Midday light, on the other hand, is much more difficult to work with. Depending on the time of year and the place, the light is harsh, and shadows are short and intense.

What do you do if you can't shoot when the conditions are perfect? You can always use software to change the quality of light later.

For example, I thought the following photo might benefit from a warmer, more golden sunset light. Here's what I did using Photoshop Elements:

1. I opened the image and made a new layer called **Sunset Light**. I set my layer Opacity to 56 percent and the Mode to Color Burn.
2. I selected an appropriate color for my warm tint. I did this by clicking the foreground color selection box in the toolbox. This brought up the Adobe Color Picker, the default color picker. Here I chose a color with the following RGB values: R = 255, Green = 204, and Blue = 102.
3. I selected the Gradient tool from the toolbox. I chose the following settings from the options bar: Gradient Picker: Foreground to Transparent; Type of Gradient: Linear Gradient; Mode: Normal; Opacity: 100 percent. Then, with the empty **Sunset Light** layer selected, I applied the Linear Gradient tool to the image. I did this by holding the Shift key and dragging the cursor from the bottom of the image window half way up, just past

the top of the row of buildings. Holding the Shift key while I did this constrained the angle to 45 degrees. (I used the Linear Gradient tool to apply the warm tint, but you can also apply the tint selectively by using the Airbrush or Paintbrush tools. Just be sure to apply the color to a layer of its own, using the color values from step 2 and the **Sunset Light** layer specifications from step 1.)

4. After I applied the warm tint, I noticed that the sky looked too light for the late hour I was trying to imitate. To darken the sky, I created a Levels adjustment layer and adjusted the entire image so the background darkened appropriately. I then selected the Gradient tool and kept the same settings as described in step 3. However, I clicked the Default Colors icon to set the colors in the color selection box to their default colors in the toolbox, and I reset my foreground and background colors to black and white. I then used the Gradient tool on the adjustment layer to create a mask that prevented the levels adjustment from affecting the foreground.

Here's the new image, now bathed in sunset light. (For more details on this procedure, refer to my book, *Photoshop Elements 2 Solutions*.)

Shooting Interiors and Exteriors

Digital cameras are used by a wide range of professionals—from architects to real estate agents—to document both the insides and the outsides of buildings large and small. Whether you're making a great travel shot of a high rise in Kuala Lumpur, or you just want to document the contents of your home for insurance purposes, it will benefit you to know how pros use light and texture, and how to select the best angle to get the most revealing shot.

7

Chapter Contents

A Different Approach
Choosing Light and Location
Maximizing Image Quality
Playing with Scale
Adding Motion
Considering Keystoning
Composing the Shot
Interior and Exterior Light
Mixing Interior and Exterior Light
Attention to Detail

A Different Approach

As we've seen in earlier chapters, when the object you are photographing moves, shooting it tests both your reflexes and the capabilities of a digital camera. Buildings and their contents usually don't move, but shooting them presents a whole new set of considerations that require a different approach. (Much of what is written here also applies to shooting landscapes, the subject of the next chapter.)

Figure 7.1: The Point Cabrillo lighthouse has been in this location for nearly a hundred years. With only a few camera positions to choose from, photographer Chris Wahlberg was at the mercy of the sun and the elements. This photo was shot with a Nikon Coolpix 990.

For example, generally speaking, when shooting either the interior or exterior of a building:

- You have only a limited choice of viewpoints with slight variations in distance and height, as illustrated in Figure 7.1 with a photograph by Chris Wahlberg. (If you tried to go around and shoot from the other side of the lighthouse, you'd be in the water!) Complicating matters even more is the fact that many digital cameras aren't equipped with super-wide-angle lenses.

- Outdoors, you are at the mercy of the elements. Buildings may not move, but the world around them does and you'll have to factor in the position of the sun, which varies from hour to hour, day to day. You'll also have to take into consideration the weather, which can dampen the best-laid plans.

- Regardless of which digital camera you use, you will likely want to maximize the resolution and quality of its output by choosing an appropriate file format, selecting the highest resolution, and minimizing the chance of camera movement.

- Indoors, you'll often want to balance ambient light with daylight to bring out a particular mood or sense of place, or know how to use software later to merge two differently exposed shots.

- Indoors or outdoors, you will face—and need to compensate for—complex lighting situations that may fool even the most sophisticated metering systems.
- You'll also want to set your white balance correctly and avoid the consequences of trying to fix color imbalances later.

Let's address these problems and come up with solutions.

Note: The first photograph ever taken was in 1826 of a roof and surrounding buildings in the south of France by Joseph Nicéphore Niépce. Exposure time: 8 hours!

Choosing Light and Location

The direction and quality of light, combined with camera position, are critical considerations when shooting interiors and exteriors—and, as you will see in the following chapter, landscapes. It doesn't matter what kind of digital camera you are using—consumer, prosumer, or professional—you'll get a more interesting shot if you choose light and location carefully.

Look at the image on the left in Figure 7.2. Not only did I take the shot at the wrong time of day—the sun was nearly behind the building—but I shot it with little consideration to camera angle or position. If you look at the image on the right in Figure 7.2 you'll see a much better shot. To get it, I came back at a different time of day and shot the same building from a different position.

Figure 7.2. Here the light and positioning are all wrong (left). Same building but taken at a different time of day and from a different position (right).

Now look at Figure 7.3, taken by professional photographer Chester Simpson. Chester carefully chose the time of day, waiting for the dramatic late afternoon light to fade just enough so the building's interior lights would create an interesting mood when contrasted with the outside lights and the dusky sky. Chester mounted his prosumer/professional digital camera—a Canon EOS-D30—on a tripod and metered the exposure using the camera's manual exposure mode. He left the ISO at its normal setting of 100, and chose f/8 to maximize his depth of field. He tried a range of shutter speeds, from 5 seconds to 10 seconds, finally settling on 9 seconds based on the histogram readout displayed in the camera's LCD. To maximize the quality, Chester saved the image data in the RAW file format.

Figure 7.3: Attention to light and position will dramatically improve just about any shot. (Photo by Chester Simpson)

Light

The quality of outdoor light varies from hour to hour, and sometimes even more quickly than that. Early morning and evening light tends to be soft, and brings out textures and contours of any surface. When the sun is straight overhead, the light is strong, contrasty, and unflattering. Not only does the quality of light vary throughout the day, but also it varies from one day to the next, depending on the season and the weather. It will also vary depending on where you are located in the world. The Parisian light for example, even in the summer, never seems as strong and contrasty as the winter noon light in Los Angeles.

The direction of light is also critical when shooting outdoors. If the sun is directly behind you and shines on the subject, it will cover the subject evenly. With this kind of lighting it is easier to make a proper exposure, which is especially important considering the limited dynamic range of most digital cameras. If the light comes from the left or right of you, it'll emphasize the shape of the object, as well as give it dimension and depth, but it may also add problematic shadows. In this case, getting the proper exposure is a little more difficult. (We will get into proper exposure in more detail later in the chapter.) If the light is coming from directly in front of you, you'll create a silhouette, which is dramatic but doesn't reveal many details of your subject.

Even when you aren't shooting, take time to observe the way natural light acts on the buildings and landscape around you. Think of your observations as an exercise that will make you a better photographer.

As for interior lighting, the quality of light is just as varied and ultimately just as important as it is when you are shooting in natural outdoor light. One distinct advantage of shooting digital over shooting film is the ability to change white balance settings from picture to picture to match different light sources such as tungsten or fluorescent. With film you had to carefully match film to light or filter to avoid strong color casts, and you couldn't evaluate the results until the film was processed. The power of digital photography gives you much more freedom to use existing light rather than set up extensive lights of your own. We'll look more closely at white balance and interior lighting later in the chapter.

Location

Choosing the right location to shoot requires exploration. Don't settle for the obvious vantage point. Walk around. Consider adjacent buildings as a means to gain height and varying perspectives. When I used to work for a construction company that required work-in-progress photo documentation, I'd carry a small ladder with me. Even the smallest added height often helped make my shots more interesting. Another thing I learned from that experience: wear comfortable shoes and clothing! Often the best shot required that I crawl or pull myself into an awkward position. I also found it very useful to have someone with me to keep a watchful eye out for errant traffic or oblivious pedestrians, thereby allowing me to concentrate on making the good shot.

Later in the chapter you'll read how photographer Leonard Koren carefully crafts his shots, paying special attention to scale, perspective, and relationships between a building and its surroundings.

Note: Most digital cameras lack the capability to shoot very wide-angle shots. When shooting large buildings or tightly cramped interiors it can be especially difficult to get the shot you need. Consider shooting a sequence of adjacent, overlapping images and using so-called "stitching" software to piece the shots together and create wider angles of view. Some digital cameras have a "panoramic" mode to assist you in lining up your sequenced shots. For more on this, Chapter 9.

Maximizing Image Quality

Image quality is always important, regardless of what you shoot. But when you are shooting interiors and exteriors—and other shots such as landscapes, where nuance and intricate detail make the shot—it's especially important to do what you can to maximize image quality.

Regardless of what kind of digital camera you use, there are several things you can do to ensure the best possible image quality.

Pixel Resolution and File Format Settings

The single most effective way of controlling the quality of your image is through your digital camera's pixel resolution and file format settings.

All prosumer and professional digital cameras provide various file format options ranging from non-compressed TIFFs to RAW to JPEG, with a selection of compression choices. Consumer digital cameras may or may not provide these options, depending on the model, and at this time no Sony digital camera provides a RAW format option.

If your camera supports it, you will always get the maximum flexibility and quality from the RAW data format. This format stores data that comes directly off the sensor and it requires special imaging software to view and process. (RAW is discussed in more detail in the following chapter and in Zooming In.)

The TIFF file format, if your camera supports it, is your next best option. TIFF files are larger than RAW or JPEG files, but there is no compression to produce compression artifacts.

The JPEG file format is the most commonly used file format. JPEG compresses data by throwing away information that isn't important to the eye. Most digital cameras offer a choice of JPEG compression settings ranging from low to high. A high compression means a smaller file size but lower quality. Low compression means less compression and therefore higher image quality. For most purposes a low compressed JPEG is perfectly adequate. (To learn more about file formats, ∂ "Know Your Camera: File Formats" in Chapter 8.)

With most prosumer and professional digital cameras, and many consumer digital cameras, you can reduce the actual pixel resolution as well. The Sony DSC-F 717 camera, for example, has a maximum resolution of 2560 × 1920 pixels. You can also set the camera to make images of 2048 × 1536 pixels, 1280 × 960 pixels, or 640 × 480 pixels. (There is also the option of changing the aspect ratio.) Most of these settings will create a smaller file size, but limits your output options.

Remember, quality doesn't suffer significantly when you reduce the resolution of an image using a computer and imaging software. However, it's another thing to try to *boost* resolution later. You'll never match the quality of an image that was originally shot using a higher pixel resolution.

Note: Your choice of file format and pixel resolution will determine approximately how many image files will fit on a memory card. Refer to your camera's manual for a breakdown of these numbers.

Check Your Settings

Many times I've picked up someone else's digital camera and observed that the pixel resolution and/or file format settings were unintentionally set wrong. One time the owner of a Nikon Coolpix 5000 had set his file format to JPEG, which, considering he was shooting mostly candids, was a perfectly valid choice. But he had not paid attention to the JPEG compression settings, which were set to the lowest quality. Since the photographer had plenty of storage capacity, there really wasn't anything gained by creating a smaller file size with the tradeoff in image quality.

Another time I noticed that a photographer had set his image resolution to less than the capability of the camera. He was shooting a Canon EOS-D60, which has a maximum pixel resolution of 3072 × 2048. He had set it to the medium setting, or 2048 × 1360 pixels. When I asked him why he had done this he confessed that he had been fooling around with his settings and just forgot to change it back.

I know there are times when reducing pixel resolution might be tempting—for example, if your images are destined for screen viewing only, when capture speed is more important than the highest resolution, or if you have only a limited amount of space left on your memory card and a high JPEG compression setting alone isn't enough. However, this reduction should be a conscious decision, not an inadvertent mistake.

Take a moment to familiarize yourself with your digital camera's settings. The actual method of changing file format and resolution settings will vary from model to model, so check your camera's manual. On some digital cameras, you must navigate through the display menu to find the settings, as shown in Figure 7.4. With other digital cameras, a simple—and sometimes inadvertent—push of a button is all it takes to change either the file format or resolution settings.

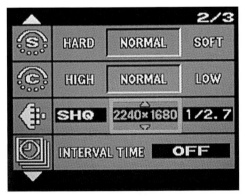

Figure 7.4: On some digital cameras the quality settings are found by accessing a menu, such as the one shown here.

Sharpness Settings

Many prosumer and professional digital cameras offer a variety of "sharpness" settings. Consumer-level digital cameras do not. These settings are accessed via the camera's menu display, usually along with settings for contrast and color saturation. Sometimes the sharpness values are expressed numerically, other times with terms such as Hard, Normal, or Soft. It's important to understand that these sharpness settings have nothing whatsoever to do with the optics of a camera, or with the resolution—only with the processing of the data that comes off the sensor.

When you select more sharpening, image processing enhances areas of detail by increasing the contrast of edges. While this may increase the appearance of sharpness, it really doesn't make an image "sharper," *per se*. In fact, increasing "sharpness" too much also sharpens the image noise from the sensor and actually can make an image look coarse or rough.

Many pros set sharpness to its lowest value or turn it off altogether, and then use imaging software later to sharpen when necessary. Many image-processing programs, such as Adobe's Photoshop or Photoshop Elements or nik multimedia, Inc.'s nik Sharpener Pro!, give you much more control over the sharpening process than your camera ever will.

If you are saving your data in the RAW format, sharpness settings are not so critical. You control sharpening later in imaging software.

Color Space

Another option offered by some prosumer and most professional (but not consumer) digital cameras is choice of color space. Photographic systems typically can't reproduce the whole spectrum of colors seen by the human eye. The range of colors that can be displayed or printed by a system is called the *color gamut* of that system.

Most of us deal in the RGB (Red, Green, Blue) color space rather than in the CMYK (Cyan, Magenta, Yellow, Black) color space, and these two spaces have very different color gamuts. The subsets of the RGB color space that most of us are exposed to are Adobe 98 RGB and sRGB. sRGB was developed by Hewlett-Packard and Microsoft to represent the range of colors that can be displayed and printed by consumer computer systems. This range is used by default in most digital cameras, especially consumer digital cameras.

How can choice of color space settings affect quality? I'm going to get very simplistic here. sRGB, for example, represents a narrower range of colors than Adobe 98 RGB. This narrow range is actually beneficial if the destination of your final image is the Web or a PC monitor, because sRGB more accurately represents the reproducible colors for that particular medium. However, if you want the widest range of colors, then you should choose Adobe 98 RGB.

If you look at your EXIF data in imaging software, often you'll be able see what color space, if any, was applied to an image. Again, if you save your data in the RAW format, you can apply the appropriate color space later, in imaging software.

Proper Exposure

Another way to maximize quality is by getting the correct exposure. Getting the right exposure depends on several interconnected factors, including the quality and direction of light and the capabilities of the digital camera you're using. If light is evenly distributed on your subject, as it often is in the early morning and late afternoon, even the simplest autoexposure system will likely do a good job of making the proper exposure.

However, if your subject consists of a large range of light and dark areas, even the most sophisticated metering and exposure systems won't help.

What exactly is correct exposure, anyway? Correct exposure is a relationship between f-stop, shutter speed, and the sensitivity of the sensor onboard your digital camera. If too much light strikes the sensor via an incorrect f-stop or shutter speed, then the capacity of the sensor is overwhelmed and the image is overexposed. If not enough light strikes the sensor, then little or no detail is recorded.

Dynamic range is another important concept to understand in the context of correct exposure. For example, if the light-sensitive element—film or sensor—has a wide exposure latitude (i.e., a large dynamic range) then precise exposure isn't as critical. Many of the newer print films on the market have a wide latitude, while slide film has traditionally had a very narrow latitude. It's always been more difficult to make a proper exposure using slide film. At this time, electronic sensors act more like slide film because they capture a narrow range of tones, thus making careful exposure—and shooting under even light—especially important. This statement holds true for the most inexpensive consumer digital cameras as well as the professional models.

What can you do to get the best possible exposure using your digital camera? With the understanding that exposure is a huge topic in and of itself, and keeping in mind that exposure systems vary from digital camera to digital camera, here are few suggestions:

- Choose shooting situations where the light is distributed evenly on your subject. With this kind of lighting, relying on the auto exposure system of most digital cameras is perfectly acceptable.

- Use the LCD preview as a *rough* guide to ensure that you've captured the important details. The LCD displays a low-resolution version of the image and never precisely represents the true brightness range of a scene.

- If available, use your camera's histogram capabilities to determine exposure. Some digital cameras display the histogram before you shoot, so you can adjust your exposure accordingly; others display a histogram only after the shot has been taken. Consumer digital cameras often don't have histogram capabilities. (For more on interpreting a histogram, ↩ "Reading the Histogram" in Zooming In.)

- Use a gray card to take an exposure reading, and use that reading to make an "average" exposure. Gray cards, which are 18% gray, are commonly available at camera stores. This method works especially well if there is a wide range of light and dark tones and it is difficult to find a mid-tone to make an exposure from.

- If possible, "bracket" exposures 1/3 of an f-stop on either side of an "average" exposure, as determined either by your automatic exposure system or by using manual exposure controls. Many prosumer and professional digital cameras actually provide an option to automatically bracket. You merely set the bracket range and the camera shoots a burst of 3 or more frames, each at a different exposure. You'll have to consult your digital camera manual to see if bracketing is possible.

- Consider using imaging software to modify and extend the tonal range of an image. This works, but only to a point. You can't bring out details in a part of an image that doesn't have any. (However, if you use software to merge two shots of the same image taken with difference exposures, you can actually greatly extend the tonal range of an image. I'll show you examples of this later in the chapter and in the next chapter.)

- If possible, change the ISO rating. Most digital cameras are preset to shoot at 80-200 ISO. Most prosumer and professional cameras allow changing this setting. Increase the ISO if you want to capture dark scenes and maintain a reasonably fast shutter speed or a smaller aperture setting to maintain depth of field. Just like going to a faster film, increasing the digital camera ISO increases the electronic noise, which may or may not be acceptable. If you have any doubts, take a series of shots using different ISO ratings and pick the best shot later. (Some professional digital cameras offer ISO bracketing, which works much like the exposure bracketing described earlier.)

- Fool the camera's automatic metering system by aiming your camera at a darker or lighter part of a scene, and then press the shutter release button partway. On many, but not all, digital cameras, this will lock the exposure and focus. Then, swing the camera back to frame the desired image and press the shutter release button the rest of the way. Some digital cameras also have an auto exposure lock (AEL), which essentially does the same thing. You can see how this method was used in Figure 7.5. On the left, the automatic metering system is properly exposed for the top part of the image, but the rest of the image is too dark. In the middle shot, the camera was swung down so that the bright part of the image wasn't in the frame, and the exposure was locked by pressing the shutter release button partway and holding it. Then the camera was swung back into position and the shutter release button pressed the rest of the way, resulting in the image on the right. Now the important details in the shadow areas are revealed.

Figure 7.5: You can fool the camera's automatic metering system (left) by aiming the lens at a darker or lighter part of a scene (middle), pressing the shutter release button partway, then reframing the image before pressing the shutter release button the rest of the way (right).

Setting White Balance

White balance settings can have a tremendous effect on the quality of your image. Most everyone knows what happens when you mistakenly use film balanced for outdoor light to shoot indoors under fluorescent light. You get a yucky green colorcast. With a digital camera, instead of matching film to a light source you simply set the camera's white balance to reproduce colors naturally. Most prosumer and professional digital cameras offer several white balance options, while consumer digital cameras are more limited. For a detailed discussion on how to use white balance, ✑ "Know Your Camera: Adjusting White Balance" in Chapter 11. Additional white balance information is found in the Zooming In section at the end of the book.

> **Note:** There are a lot of misconceptions surrounding white balance. Changing white balance settings does nothing to the RAW data that comes off the sensor. White balance settings are applied only in the image-processing stage of image capture. If you save your data in the RAW format, you can actually apply any white balance setting you want later using imaging software. If you use the TIFF or JPEG file format, your camera's white balance settings are very important because these settings are applied directly to the image. You can alter a color cast later in imaging software, but it takes a lot of work and the results are not always satisfactory.

Other Quality Considerations

Image resolution and file format aren't the only controls you have over the quality of your image. Other important things to pay attention to are:

- Focus. Take time to frame and focus your shot carefully. Many auto focus systems require a moment to properly adjust and focus. It's also very helpful to know exactly what part of the image frame your autofocus system is using to determine focus. Most systems are center-weighted by default, meaning objects in the center of the frame will be sharp. Some systems give you a choice. You can set an autofocus point to the left or the right of center, where it will remain until you change your settings. Consult your camera manual for more information.

- Lens sharpness. You can't change the inherent quality of a lens; however, there is usually an optimal f-stop that provides the best sharpness. For most lenses the optimal f-stop is two to three stops narrower than the widest aperture. For example, if the widest aperture of your lens is f/2.8, then f/5.6 would be the optimal f-stop. (Of course, this assumes you are using a digital camera that allows you to choose your f-stop.)

- Camera movement. Faster shutter speeds help minimize blur caused by camera movement. However, if you want a narrow f-stop to maximize the sharpness of a shot, or if you wanted increased depth of field, a faster shutter speed may not be possible. A tripod is useful to help minimize movement caused by a shaky hand or the mechanics of the camera itself. Use a shutter release cable if possible, or the camera's self-timer mode. This will further reduce the chance of camera movement caused by the pressure of your finger on the shutter release button.

Know Your Camera: The Sensor Inside

The heart of a digital camera is its electronic sensor, such as the pair shown here.

Digital camera specifications almost always start with a sensor's pixel count, expressed as a total number of pixels (i.e., 4 megapixels or 4 million pixels) or by giving the width and height of the image (i.e., 2240 pixels x 1680 pixels). Often two numbers are cited: the actual total number of pixels, and the effective number of pixels. The reason for this discrepancy has to do with the fact that many times, pixels on the perimeter of the sensor are used not for collecting light, but for other purposes like sensor calibration. Sometimes pixels on the perimeter are purposely turned off to achieve a particular aspect ratio.

The physical dimension of a digital camera's sensor is often noted next, usually as a diagonal. The most commonly used sensors range in size from 1/2-inch diagonal to 2-inch diagonal—the same size as 35mm film. The actual number of pixels can be almost independent of sensor size. You can have a small sensor and a large number of very small pixels or a large sensor with fewer large pixels. As you might expect, the larger pixels capture more light and give the sensor greater sensitivity. The physical size of the sensor—not the number of pixels—determines such things as focal length equivalents and, to a degree, the depth of field. Size can also be a factor in final image quality, but not necessarily.

A sensor is also identified as a *charge-coupled device* (CCD) or a *complementary metal-oxide semiconductor* (CMOS). The two types of chips require different manufacturing technologies. Most of the differences don't affect you as a photographer or a consumer, but some of them can. CCDs are generally more expensive to produce, and usually physically smaller because of the expense. CMOS chips are generally cheaper to make, because they're made using the same manufacturing process as other computer chips. CMOS chips consume less power and therefore run cooler than CCDs. CMOS chips suffered from image quality issues in the past but recent innovations have changed that, and several of the professional-level digital cameras now boast CMOS chips that are physically the same size as 35mm film. Sensors, be they CCDs or CMOS, are not all created equal. In the Zooming In section of the book, I'll illustrate this by focusing on two different sensor technologies, one created by Foveon and the other by Fuji.

There is a lot more to sensors than just the pixel count. In the future it will be other features, such as a sensor's dynamic range, or low light sensitivity, that will capture our imagination and make us reach for our pocketbooks to buy the latest digital camera.

Playing with Scale

The brain tricks us all the time. Close objects always appear larger than faraway ones, regardless of their actual relative sizes. You can play with this flaw in our visual perception system to have fun with scale, as photographer Doug Clark did using a Canon G2 prosumer digital camera to make the shot shown in Figure 7.6.

Bottom line: Photography is a visual language. Know the rules of perspective and scale and you'll expand your vocabulary and command over the medium.

Figure 7.6: Close objects always appear larger, a fact that can be used to trick the mind. (Photo by Doug Clark)

Adding Motion

Playing with scale isn't the only way to make a shot interesting. By adding motion, as shown in Figure 7.7, you can also enhance an otherwise staid shot. Bruce Avera Hunter took this shot on assignment for a TV production company using a Nikon Coolpix 990 prosumer digital camera. He placed the camera on a tripod and angled it in such a way that it would capture the taillights of passing cars. He used the camera's shutter-preferred exposure mode, turned the flash off, and set the shutter speed to 8 seconds—which is why the blur of the moving cars is so pronounced. Because the camera was stable on the tripod, the monument, which didn't move, appears sharp. The camera automatically set the f-stop to f/7.8, resulting in the correct exposure.

Although using a digital camera with selective control over the shutter speed is desirable, even a simple digital camera with only automatic exposure can be used to make this kind of shot provided it is night or a very low-light situation. The key is to place the camera on a tripod so the stationary parts of the image remain sharp. Motion blur can be created in a daytime shot as well. However, since most digital cameras will select a wide aperture over a slow shutter speed, control over the shutter speed is essential in order to get a shot like this during the day.

Bottom line: Spice up just about any shot of an immobile object by using a slow shutter speed to capture surrounding motion.

Figure 7.7: Careful positioning of the camera and a slow shutter speed produced this artistic shot of the Lincoln Memorial. (Photo by Bruce Avera Hunter with a Nikon Coolpix 990)

Considering Keystoning

Look at the photograph in Figure 7.8 taken by Doug Salin with his Olympus 3000Z. What you see is a building with sides that appear to converge rather than remain parallel. This is an effect called *keystoning*, and it occurs when the plane of the camera and the plane of the building are not parallel to each other.

Sophisticated 4 × 5 view cameras have backs that tilt and swing to compensate for keystoning, and if you are using a professional digital camera with interchangeable lenses, you can buy expensive perspective lenses that correct this type of distortion as well.

> **Note:** Some digital cameras, such as the Nikon Coolpix 4500, have built-in software perspective correction. Expect more of this type of onboard image correction to be available in digital cameras as software and hardware technologies improve.

Figure 7.8: Keystoning refers to an image where lines that are actually parallel appear to converge. (Photo by Doug Salin)

There are other ways to deal with this problem:

- You can avoid keystoning by positioning your camera so that it is parallel with the plane of the building you are shooting. (You may need to climb an adjacent building or carry a ladder with you to get this perspective.)
- Fix the keystoning later in software. (☞ "Software Solutions: Fixing Keystoning," later this chapter.)
- Don't worry about it. Use keystoning for effect, making a more dramatic image such as the one shown in Figure 7.9. After all, the eye expects to see some perspective distortion.

Figure 7.9: Architect Andrew Tarnowka shot this dramatic shot of the world's tallest building, the Petronas Towers in Kuala Lumpur, with his Olympus E-10. He didn't worry about keystoning.

Bottom line: Keystoning is considered a serious issue for some, and not for others. Most importantly, you can control keystoning if you wish through careful shooting, or later, using imaging software.

Software Solutions: Fixing Keystoning

Using Photoshop's Transform ➤ Perspective command, this is what Doug Salin did to fix his image shown Figure 7.8, which suffers from keystoning. (You can do basically the same thing with Photoshop Elements.)

1. He copied the background layer containing the building (Layer ➤ Duplicate Layer).
2. After duplicating the layer, he made sure all of his image fit on the screen and was visible by double-clicking on the Hand tool.
3. He then selected View ➤ Show ➤ Grid to give him a series of 90-degree vertical references. The grid makes it easier to determine when the sides of the building are straight.
4. He selected the Perspective command (Edit ➤ Transform ➤ Perspective). He didn't change any of the default choices in the Transform options bar.
5. To adjust the perspective he needed some empty space around the edges of his image, so he expanded his image window by dragging the lower right corner of the image window down and to the right. He then placed the pointer on the bounding box handle in the upper right corner of his image and clicked and dragged it outward until the perspective was correct, as confirmed by the vertical grid lines. By expanding his image window first, he was able to see the Perspective control bounding boxes even as he dragged them beyond the edges of his image.
6. When he was finished, he clicked the OK button in the options bar.

For a more detailed explanation of a similar procedure, with screenshots, refer to my book *Photoshop Elements 2 Solutions.*

Figure 7.10: Artist Leonard Koren made this shot with a Sony DSC-F717, after taking time to carefully compose and observe.

Composing the Shot

Figure 7.10 shows a photograph taken by Leonard Koren, a San Francisco artist who writes books about design and aesthetics. He used a Sony DSC-F717 prosumer digital camera. The shot was taken in late fall and Leonard acknowledges that the light was less than perfect. He would have preferred the sun to shine on the front of the Sentenal Building (the old building in the center of the photo), not on the side. This would have emphasized the building more and set it apart from its surroundings. In this case, it wouldn't help to come back at a different time of day—the sun would not be in the right position until another time of year. Leonard relied instead on careful composition to get the results he wanted. He positioned himself in the center of busy Columbus Avenue, using a friend to monitor traffic. He turned the camera to a vertical orientation and placed the vertical axis of the Sentenal Building square in the middle of the shot. He zoomed out just enough to catch the edge of another classic San Francisco building, the Transamerica Pyramid, and framed the old building with the new one. Because he placed the old building in the center of the frame, it wasn't dominated or overwhelmed by the much bigger one. He framed the shot so the streets running on each side of the Sentenal became visual guides, leading the eye naturally to the front of the building.

Leonard left the camera settings at automatic but his first shot, which he viewed on the LCD screen, was badly underexposed. The exposure was weighted toward the sky, which resulted in the building being too dark. Leonard then tilted his camera down toward the ground, took an exposure from the street and shadow area and then held the shutter release halfway down to lock the new exposure settings. Then he tilted the camera back to the original position and made another, correctly exposed shot.

Figure 7.11 shows another urban landscape taken by Leonard just a few minutes later. This time the light was perfect on both buildings. By composing the shot the way he did, Leonard used the evenly distributed light to give both buildings equal weight and emphasis. The articulated facade of both buildings—bricks for one, windows for another—adds another common visual element that contributes to the success of this image.

Bottom line: Obviously nothing can beat having both good light and perfect composition. But careful composition can make up for less-than-perfect light.

Figure 7.11: A beautiful urban landscape by Leonard Koren that benefits from perfect light and careful composition.

Accessories That Make a Difference: Tripods

Tripods (or "sticks," as they are sometimes called) are used in low-light situations or to minimize camera movement whenever sharpness is especially important. They are also used when shooting sequences of images that will be later stitched together into a single panoramic. Tripods with reversible center poles can also be used for extreme close-up photography by mounting the camera between the tripod legs and close to the base. Monopods, as shown below right, which have only one pole instead of three legs, are especially useful for shooting action because they stabilize the vertical axis of the camera and yet are quickly responsive to a wide range of movement, and they are quick and easy to reposition.

 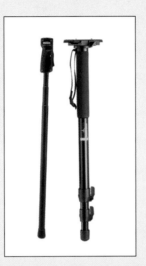

Tripods are not created equal. Not only is there a great difference in the weight and stability of tripods, but the features of the head that actually holds the camera vary greatly as well. Generally tripods are chosen according to the size and weight of a camera—larger cameras require heavier, more stable tripods. Use will also determine the type of tripod you select. Lightweight, collapsible tripods are preferable when travel is an issue. Of course budget is always a consideration. You can buy tripods that are both lightweight and extremely stable, but at a higher cost.

Specifications will never tell the whole story about a tripod. Be sure to try one before buying. From personal experience, I can tell you that a bad tripod is almost as useless as none at all.

How easy is it to open? How fast can you adjust the legs? Are they stable? Mount your camera. Was that easy? How easily does the head rotate into a desirable position? Can you shoot horizontal as well as vertical? Can you reach all the controls of your camera or are some of them blocked by the tripod controls? How well do the legs grip the ground? Many tripods have retractable sharp tips that prevent the tripod from slipping on some surfaces. You can actually stabilize a less than perfect tripod by using a sandbag or another heavy object suspended between the legs.

Keep in mind that ease of use is probably the most important single consideration.

Interior and Exterior Light

To get the shot shown in Figure 7.12 of a model home in Half Moon Bay, CA, professional photographer Doug Salin relied only on the exterior sunlight streaming in through the windows. He placed his Olympus C-3000Z on a tripod, set it to aperture priority, and adjusted the aperture to f/9, which resulted in a shutter speed of 1/10th of a second. The slow shutter speed made the use of the tripod essential. The focal length was slightly wider than normal, his ISO was 100, and he left his white balance settings to automatic.

Figure 7.12: Doug Salin shot this model home using natural daylight only.

 Note: When you photograph someone's private property and want to reproduce the image for commercial purposes, you'll first need to obtain a property release. A sample form is available at **www.shooting-digital.com**.

Just about anyone with a moderately good quality digital camera can make a decent shot with similar conditions. What makes this shot (and Doug's talent) special is the careful attention to composition and detail. For example, notice how inviting the room is. Your eye can move comfortably through different layers of interest. There are objects on the left, in the middle and on the right. The light from the windows adds another layer of interest, as does the reflection on the wood floor. Doug aimed the camera straight into the living room, at waist level, thereby putting emphasis on the content of the room rather than the ceiling or the floor. He cautions photographers who are trying to convey visual information about a room or space to avoid dramatic up or down angles of the camera, which can confuse viewers and take their eyes away from the substance of the shot. Doug also advises photographers to be prepared to move things around to make a balanced shot. He says there is almost always something—a lamp, a chair, a table—that can be removed or repositioned to help make a better picture.

Why did Doug use a camera that might be considered consumer-level, rather than the professional digital camera he often rents for other jobs? In this case, a high-quality JPEG was all he needed. The picture was used in a real estate brochure and ran on 1/4 of a page.

Now look at Figure 7.13, shot a few days later by Doug when the room was more complete. This shot was taken with the same camera, in basically the same position. However, it was early evening and instead of daylight Doug used the ambient lights of the house. Again, he set his white balance to automatic, so the color balance was automatically corrected. The effects are different from the shot that relied on daylight, but equally as successful.

Bottom line: Often you don't need expensive or complicated lighting to make a room warm and inviting. Use a tripod and focus on careful composition instead.

Figure 7.13: The same room a few days later, shot using existing indoor light. (Photo by Doug Salin)

Mixing Interior and Exterior Light

If you look at Figure 7.14 you'll see a common problem associated with shooting interiors. In the shot on the left, taken by professional photographer Richard Anderson, the interior is exposed properly but the light streaming in from the windows is so strong that the windows are overexposed. In the shot on the right, also taken by Richard, the windows are exposed properly but the rest of the room is too dark. (In Doug Salin's similar daylight shot shown in Figure 7.12, the light from the windows was muted and not so intense.)

Figure 7.14: In the shot on the left, the window light is too bright. In the shot on the right, the room is too dark. (Photos by Richard Anderson)

In order to balance the interior and exterior lights, you have a few choices. You can use auxiliary lighting equipment to boost the amount of light in the room to match the intensity of the exterior light. However, lighting a room this way—especially a large room—can be difficult and require more than a basic knowledge of lighting techniques.

You can place light-diffusion material over the windows to reduce the amount of light coming in from the window. Or you can do what Richard often does: use a computer and imaging software to blend two shots taken with different exposures to make one. This technique actually dates back to the early days, when photographic film had a very limited dynamic range. Multiple negatives, taken at different exposures, were often used to make a final print.

Figure 7.15 shows the results of a fairly simple Photoshop technique that Richard uses. Now the light from the windows is correct, and so is the light in the room. (If you want Richard's Photoshop step-by-step procedure, go to the Zooming In section.)

Figure 7.15: This perfectly exposed image was produced by blending the two shots with Photoshop. (Photo by Richard Anderson)

From a shooting point of view, to make this method work, Richard suggests:

1. Always use a tripod and don't move the camera between shots.
2. Set your camera to manual focus, if you can.
3. Use aperture priority or manual exposure modes. Don't change your f-stop between exposures. Use the shutter speed to adjust for exposure differences.
4. Use the same white balance setting.
5. Make one exposure based on the window light. (Use the spot meter function of your camera if you have one, or an external light meter to meter the exposure.)
6. Make another exposure based on the ambient light in the room.

When making your exposures, be extra careful not to bump or move the camera even slightly. The method works best if the shots are exactly the same except for exposure differences.

Bottom line: Extend the dynamic range of just about any digital camera by making two images with different exposures and using imaging software to blend them into one.

Attention to Detail

Often you'll want to focus on the contents of an interior. Figure 7.16 shows a closeup photo of a couch shot by Doug Salin. Once again, Doug used an Olympus C-3000Z mounted on a tripod. He used the aperture priority mode, and set his f-stop to f/9, which resulted in a shutter speed of 1/2 second. By stopping his f-stop down like this, Doug got more depth of field in the foreground. He relied on ambient light, and left his white balance set to auto. Doug selected a longer than normal focal length purposely, to compress the image and help draw the eye to the couch. This made the background go slightly out of focus, which also helped emphasize the shapes and details of the couch. Note that Doug didn't attempt to photograph the entire couch. Instead, he focused on one compelling area of it. By moving in close like this, Doug produced an intimate shot, one that shows more detail than it would have otherwise.

Bottom line: Details often reveal more about the whole than a shot of the whole.

Figure 7.16: Doug Salin focused on just one area of the couch, and by doing so made an image of intimate beauty.

Shooting Beautiful Landscapes

A successful landscape—be it a dramatic waterfall or a sublime country scene—is a combination of composition, content, and craft. This chapter continues where the previous one left off—focusing on ways to get the optimal quality from your digital camera while capturing breathtaking views of the magnificent world around you.

Chapter Contents

What Makes a Good Landscape?

A good landscape, whether shot with a digital or film camera, is much more than just a pretty snapshot taken of nature. Ansel Adams, one of the masters of landscape and nature photography, was often asked what makes his work special. I remember him pointing to one of his prints and asking the viewer to note the detail in the shadowy bark, or the detail in the glittering sunlit leaf. Capturing details like this was no accident, and Adams was a great craftsman who went to great lengths and spent countless hours in the darkroom pulling more quality out of a negative and a print than most people would ever have dreamed possible. Of course, craft isn't the only thing that makes an Adams print—or for that matter, any landscape photograph—work. Successful landscapes such as the one shown in Figure 8.1, taken by John Isaac with an Olympus E-20 prosumer digital camera, are carefully composed and well thought out.

Can you make a good landscape photograph without special knowledge of craft or composition? Sure. Just set your digital camera to automatic everything, point it at a beautiful scene, and shoot. If you are very lucky you just might get something worth looking at.

Since this book goes beyond using "hit or miss" approaches, let's start with the subject of craft and see how you can pull the best quality out of just about any digital camera—and then we'll focus on some aesthetic considerations as well.

 Note: Infrared shooting techniques can also be used to create dynamic-looking landscapes (☞ "Shooting Beyond Visible Light" in Chapter 11).

Maximizing Image Quality

In the previous chapter we saw how maximizing image quality was especially critical for shots that contain intricate detail and nuance. We saw how setting the correct file format, pixel resolution, and white balance made a difference. We also saw how getting the correct exposure was essential. Although we focused on shooting interiors and exteriors, everything we said in that chapter holds true when you shoot landscapes, the subject of this chapter. Let's expand on these points and other quality-related issues by examining some real-world case studies.

Three Approaches to Correct Exposure

Michael Reichmann is a landscape and nature photographer who has gone completely digital. He is also an eminently curious photographer who is constantly pushing the limits of what his digital camera can do. His website, **www.luminous-landscape.com**, is a constantly updated testimony to his commitment to sharing his exploration and results with others. Take Michael's approach to correct exposure. Through trial and error, Michael has come up with three basic approaches that just about anyone can apply to their own work. Keep in mind that while Michael shoots professional digital cameras, his methods can be adapted to just about any digital camera with basic exposure controls.

Figure 8.1: John Isaac took this beautiful shot in Bryce Canyon with an Olympus E-20 digital camera.

Reading the Histogram

Figure 8.2 shows a relatively simple image—at least simple from an exposure point of view. The light is consistently distributed over the scene, and to make the shot Michael set his Canon EOS-D60 with a 16mm-35mm zoom lens to its aperture priority mode and relied on the camera's automatic exposure system to calculate the proper shutter speed. After exposing shots like this, Michael turns his attention to the LCD, but not merely to look at the displayed image. Michael has learned that although LCDs are great for confirming correct framing, for determining exposure they are often misleading. LCDs show an approximation of the actual image data, and can't be counted on for a critical analysis. Instead, Michael uses a histogram that is displayed along with the image in the LCD to make sure his exposure is correct. If the histogram shows an even distribution of tonal values, then Michael is satisfied and considers himself done.

Figure 8.2: Michael Reichmann used a Canon D-60 and the histogram to make this Yellowstone landscape.

A histogram is graphical representation of the range of tonal values in a captured image. It's an extremely accurate way of knowing at a glance whether you've captured a wide enough range of values. If the graph is weighted too much to one side or the other, chances are that your exposure is off. Reading a histogram is relatively easy to do, once you know what to look for. In the Zooming In appendix of this book, I've included examples of several histograms and corresponding images to show you what to look for.

All professional digital cameras such as the ones used by Michael offer a histogram option, and most prosumer digital cameras do as well. If you discover that your digital camera doesn't offer a histogram option, then this first approach to proper exposure obviously won't work for you. However, you can still use Michael's second and third approach, which don't require the use of a histogram.

Bracketing the Heck Out of the Exposure

Michael's next approach applies to more difficult images such as the one shown in Figure 8.3. This stormy-day shot posed a rapidly changing light situation and Michael didn't have the luxury of spending time examining his histogram to make sure he got the exposure exactly right. Instead, with his camera mounted on a tripod, he set it to shoot three sequential images, each with a slightly different exposure: a regular exposure and then two others 1/3 of an f-stop on either side of the first exposure. Bracketing an exposure like this is one of Michael's favorites techniques. Unlike film, which has a price attached to each shot, the cost is the same whether you shoot just one or several frames. Michael's Canon D-60 also has a nifty feature: it automatically shoots a sequence of frames at different exposure values determined by the shooter. If Michael has any doubts about the bracketing, he even brackets the bracket! It's not unusual for him to end up with several images ranging from two f-stops under to two f-stops over. "Hey, it doesn't cost me anything extra," Michael exclaims. The only drawback to this technique comes later, when Michael has to spend time in his hotel room sitting at his laptop, weeding out the unusable exposures.

Figure 8.3: Michael Reichmann used a Canon D-60 and bracketed his exposure to make this stormy landscape.

Some, but not all, prosumer cameras have automatic bracketing like Michael's Canon D-60. Since most digital cameras don't have this feature, it's most likely you'll need to use the more common +/- exposure controls. Some cameras have these controls easily accessible as actual buttons located somewhere on the camera. Other digital cameras require that you open the menu controls and select the exposure compensation that way. In any case, using the +/- controls to bracket may seem difficult and cumbersome at first, but the more you do it, the easier it becomes.

In the previous chapter, we saw how a simple point-and-shoot digital camera without exposure compensation controls can be fooled into taking different exposures by aiming the camera at different light and dark areas of an image and locking the exposure before reframing. Of course, this requires a digital camera with exposure lock control. This control is often accessed by pressing a button marked AEL. As long as the button is pressed, the last exposure reading is "locked" until the button is released.

Figure 8.4: The shot on the upper left was exposed properly for the shadow areas, but not the highlights. The shot on the upper right was exposed properly for the highlight areas, but not the shadows. The image on the bottom is a blend of the other two images, now correctly exposed in all areas. (Photos by Michael Reichmann)

Extending Dynamic Range Through Blending Images

There are times when no single exposure can capture the tonal range of an image. This was the case on the upper left in Figure 8.4, which shows an image accurately exposed for the shadow areas but not the highlights. In cases like this, Michael doesn't even try to get it right in a single exposure. Instead, he makes a series of different exposures and uses imaging software (Photoshop) to blend two or more exposed images together.

In the upper right is another shot of the same image, but this time it is exposed for the highlights. Notice that the shadow areas are too dark. Using his software technique, Michael blended the two images and came up with the properly exposed image you see on the bottom. (This is the same technique that was used in the previous chapter by architectural photographer Richard Anderson to balance indoor and outdoor light in Figure 7.15.)

As you can see, this is an extremely effective way of extending the dynamic range of a digital camera, but it takes work and practice. If you have a good grasp of imaging software such as Photoshop, it really isn't that difficult, and once you get the hang of it you'll wonder how you ever handled difficult lighting situations before. There are actually several ways to use software to do this. In the Zooming In section of the book I'll take you step by step through the process using Photoshop and one of these methods.

From a shooting point of view, however, it is important to remember a few details. Michael suggests setting your camera to aperture priority mode, if you can. Also set the focus to manual, if you can. Also, use a tripod. Following these suggestions will help minimize the differences between frames. Vary the aperture, and you may inadvertently vary the focus and depth of field. If the focus varies or if the camera shifts, you won't get good results later when you try to blend the images in software.

By the way, in the old days of film, Michael often used a graduated neutral density (ND) filter to make difficult shots like this. This type of filter, which gradually varies the amount of light that passes through the lens, was an effective way to vary the exposure over a single scene. However, the filter needed to be carefully positioned to match the tonal values of any scene. The result was not always perfect. (For a software solution that imitates the effect of the graduated ND filter, with much more control, ↝ "Software Solutions: Fixing Exposure," later in this chapter.)

Saving RAW

As I have said several times in this book, the RAW file format is one key to getting the best quality from your digital camera, assuming of course that your digital camera is capable of saving data in the RAW format in the first place. As I've also said, it's not always necessary to use this format. There are many times when a JPEG or TIFF will work fine. However, landscape photos will almost *always* benefit if you knowledgably use the RAW data format. The RAW format saves ALL the data captured by the sensor—unlike the data in TIFF and JPEG files, which the camera software has already modified. Not only is there more data to work with, but with imaging software *you* maintain control over how that data is interpreted, not the camera.

Getting quality images from the RAW format also depends on your technical capabilities. You'll need some knowledge of computers and imaging software, but the process is really not that difficult, once you are set up. If you are really serious about getting the most out of your digital camera, you should make the effort.

Having said all this, I still want to reassure those who don't want to go down the RAW technical road: you can get very good quality out of the TIFF and JPEG file formats. You just won't get as much as you would with the RAW format.

As Chester Simpson pointed out in Chapter 2, it is helpful to think of the RAW data as your negative. What he meant is that the better you are at "printing" (i.e., image processing), the better the print or image file you'll make. (I'm sure Ansel Adams would have been a big fan of the RAW file format!) The good thing about RAW data is the fact that you can always go back later, and with improved skills and software pull out a better print. (This is analogous to applying the benefit of modern papers and developers to turn-of-the century negatives.)

Having impressed on you the idea of saving your data as RAW, I also caution you not to go only halfway. I have a photographer friend who used to shoot everything in the RAW format, then convert it to a TIFF and *throw away* the RAW file, thinking the original file was no longer necessary. I told him he was essentially throwing away the negative, and he nearly had a fit. Needless to say, he no longer does this.

I'll go into a lot more specific detail about the RAW file format in the Zooming In section of this book, but for now let me give you a simple example that illustrates my point. Look at Figure 8.5. I took this shot with a Nikon D100 and saved it in the NEF format. (Nikon designates RAW data with the .nef extension. Other manufacturers use other extensions.) The file size of the NEF image was 9.6MB. I then shot the same scene again, saving the data as a TIFF file. The TIFF file format is a lossless file format and the quality is generally excellent; however, my file size was over 18MB and the processing speed of my camera was significantly slowed.

I used a software program called MacBibble to open and convert the NEF file into an 8-bit TIFF (☞ the Zooming In section for more on this software). I used MacBibble's default settings. In Photoshop, I placed both images next to each other and observed the differences. At first glance, the differences were slight. However, when I magnified the images to 200% there was a marked difference, as you can see in Figure 8.6. The image on the left is a blowup from the NEF-converted-to-TIFF file; the one on the right is from the original TIFF file generated by the camera. In-camera processing doesn't have the computing power of a desktop computer, and the MacBibble software clearly did a better job of rendering color and minimizing artifacts.

Figure 8.5: This shot was saved in the RAW data format and converted to a TIFF later using MacBibble imaging software.

Figure 8.6: The blowup on the left is from the NEF file, and the one on the right is from the TIFF file.

Bottom line: Get to know the RAW data format. It shows your commitment to quality and will give you many more options for making the best possible image. Also, if you save your image in the RAW file format, you'll have many more options later.

Getting the Maximum Depth of Field

There are many times when you are shooting landscapes that you'll want to get the maximum depth of field possible with your digital camera. In Figure 8.7, for example, I wanted both the delicate green leaves of wild grass in the foreground and the stands of trees in the background to be sharply in focus.

Figure 8.7: By using a wide-angle setting and a small aperture, and focusing midway between the grass and the trees, I got everything in focus.

In order to accomplish this I did the following:

- Set my digital camera on a tripod, minimizing the need for a fast shutter speed. (If you don't have a tripod, consider increasing the ISO setting of your digital camera to produce a faster shutter.)
- Set my camera to aperture priority mode and chose f/22, the smallest possible aperture. (The resulting shutter speed was 1/8th of a second, which is why I used a tripod.)
- Set my zoom lens to its widest position, in this case 36mm (equivalent). (The wider the lens, the greater the resulting depth of field.)
- Focused midway between the grass and the trees.
- Carefully tripped the shutter release button so as to avoid any camera movement.

I choose the smallest aperture because it produces the greatest depth of field with any lens. However, as I have mentioned in other parts of the book, the smallest—or for that matter, the widest—aperture doesn't always produce the sharpest image. Most lenses perform optimally when they are set two or three f-stops down from the widest setting. In this case, depth of field was more important. Frankly, I made up for the less-than-perfect sharpness by sharpening the image slightly later in software.

How did I know where to set my focal point? In the old days of film, lenses came with marks that made it easy to determine the depth of field. Once you set the distance and f-stop there were brackets on either side that told you how much foreground and background would be in focus. Rarely do lenses come with these markings any more. Until you get to know how your optical system responds to any given situation, you might consider picking different spots to focus on and shooting more than one shot. Generally, because of the way optics work, it's better to focus close to the nearest object. If you focus on the object that is farthest away, it's less likely that the foreground will be in focus.

In chapter 2 we saw how difficult it is to get a minimal depth of field with many digital cameras. This problem is directly related to the size of the sensor used in many digital cameras. What worked against us when we wanted selective blurring now works for us when we want increased sharpness. Therefore, with a typical sunny outdoor scene, you may get all the depth of field you need without really trying. Of course, this depends on the size of sensor in your digital camera; the larger the sensor, the less this holds true.

Bottom line: For increased depth of field, use the widest-angle setting, the smallest aperture (if possible), and a tripod, and focus midway between the points you want to appear in focus.

Know Your Camera: File Formats

Your digital camera will likely save image data in one or more of the following file formats: TIFF, JPEG, or RAW. TIFF and JPEG formats use the digital camera's onboard processing chip to create an RGB image from the data off the sensor, while the RAW format leaves the data from the sensor relatively untouched. The most commonly used file format is JPEG, which compresses the RGB information in varying degrees to produce smaller file sizes. The TIFF file format, which is an option for many prosumer and professional digital cameras, doesn't compress data. TIFF files, therefore, tend to be very large.

RAW data can be saved in a variety of proprietary ways. For example, Nikon uses the .nef file extension, Olympus uses .orf, and Canon uses .crw. RAW data files are usually much smaller than TIFFs because they contain only the R *or* G *or* B data for each pixel on the sensor—not the R *and* G *and* B data for each pixel of a TIFF file. Some digital cameras offer a compressed RAW, which further reduces the file size, albeit with a slight loss of quality. For more on the RAW data format, ⌔ Zooming In.

One of the things I look for in a digital camera is the ability to easily move between file formats, or to set JPEG compression variables. Some digital cameras have clearly labeled and easy-to-use controls. Others require you to navigate through a menu, which can be frustrating and time-consuming if the user interface isn't intuitive.

Choosing the proper file format—and compression setting—for a particular shot is one of the most important considerations you can make when shooting digital. Assuming that your digital camera gives you a choice, here are some general guidelines:

JPEG: Use JPEG when file size is an issue, and when speed—both from the processing aspect of the digital camera and the entire workflow standpoint—is important. Also use it when quality isn't the most important consideration, or if your image contains broad expanses of color. (JPEG uses "super-sized" pixels in the compression process, and therefore doesn't always preserve intricate detail very well.) Having said this, it's important to note that, depending on the content of the image, the highest-quality JPEG (i.e., the least compression) often creates an image very close in quality to one saved in the TIFF file format.

TIFF: Use TIFF if RAW is not an option and your image contains a lot of fine detail such as that found in delicate fabric or a willowy tree. TIFF files are very large and take a lot of processing time and storage space.

RAW: Use RAW when quality is critical and you have the time and means to process the results yourself. Consider this musical analogy: When you listen to a symphony, you want the highest possible fidelity to enjoy the nuances and subtleties. Fidelity is less important as the music itself becomes less complex. When you want to see a symphony, think RAW.

It's also important to remember that with many digital cameras there is no reason why you can't save one image as a JPEG, a subsequent one as a TIFF and yet another image as RAW, basing your choice on the content of the shot, or your needs. Some professional digital cameras can actually save a single shot in more than one format simultaneously.

Control Through ISO

In order to the get the shot shown in Figure 8.8 of the moon rising over the Grand Canyon, John Isaac boosted the ISO rating of his Olympus E-20 from its default setting of 80 ISO to 200 ISO. This allowed him to select a small aperture (f/7.1) and still maintain a reasonable shutter speed of 1/4 of a second. (Of course, he used a tripod.) The higher ISO did introduce some added electronic "noise," but the noise is apparent only at great magnification.

Figure 8.8: John Isaac boosted the ISO of his Olympus E-20 to maintain a reasonable shutter speed and a narrow f-stop.

ISO is a measurement of the sensitivity of a sensor, and most digital cameras have an optimum ISO rating of 50-200. Most prosumer and professional digital cameras allow you to boost or decrease the ISO ratings, albeit with some tradeoff in image quality.

Michael Reichmann also used ISO as a "third factor" to get the shot shown in Figure 8.9. (The other two factors are f-stop and shutter speed). He was using a Canon EOS-D60 professional digital camera, and as he saw a flock of geese entering the frame he quickly dialed in ISO 400 on the rear of the D-60. He had been shooting 100 ISO for optimum image quality. But it was still before dawn, and the light was low, so he knew he would need a faster shutter speed and smaller aperture to avoid the birds' images blurring. A speed of 400 allowed him to shoot at 1/60th of a second at f/4.5, which was just enough. The increase in noise due to the higher ISO setting is hardly noticeable, even in a large print of this frame.

Figure 8.9: Michael Reichmann set his ISO to 400 so he could capture the sudden appearance of birds.

Bottom line: ISO can be controlled from shot to shot on many digital cameras and should be considered another important creative option along with f-stop and shutter speed.

Using Neutral Density Filters

Sometimes it's not enough to have control over ISO and f-stop and shutter speed. That's when you need to consider using neutral density filters.

For example, look at the image on the left in Figure 8.10. I wanted to capture the rushing water as a blur using a slow shutter speed. However, the scene was so bright that even when I stopped my aperture down to f/11 my shutter speed was 1/125th of a second—which wasn't slow enough to get the effect I was looking for. I was using a Nikon D-100 that has a lowest ISO setting of 200, which made it all that more difficult. What I did was place a –4 stop neutral density filter over the lens. This filter lowered the amount of light passing through the lens without changing the color values. Now I could shoot at 1/8th of second and get the effect you see on the right. Of course I also used a tripod.

Figure 8.10: Sometimes there is too much light to produce a slow shutter speed even with a lens completely stopped down (left). A neutral density filter made shooting at 1/8th of second possible. Zooming in helps accentuate the blur as well (right).

Neutral density filters are fairly common items at most well stocked camera stores. Depending on the size and density, they range from $20-$70. If your digital camera doesn't have a threaded lens mount, you'll need to buy an adapter. (A polarizing filter can also be used to reduce the amount of light. Typically polarizing filters reduce light by about 2 f-stops.)

Bottom line: You can simulate a lower ISO by using neutral density filters. This will allow you to have more control over f-stop and shutter speeds in bright light situations, if your camera allows it.

Accessories That Make a Difference: External Light Meters

In general, light meters—be they external or built into your digital camera—measure the amount of light present in a scene and, based on the sensitivity of a sensor (ISO), attempt to determine the correct f-stop and shutter speed needed to capture the light.

Most digital cameras' internal light-metering systems are extremely sophisticated, and benefit from decades of refinement passed on from the world of film. However, there are times when an external light meter can be useful. (Shown in the image below, from left to right: Minolta Auto Meter VF, a combination incident, flash, and reflective meter; Sekonic Studio Deluxe II, both a reflective and incident meter, and the Minolta Color Meter IIIf, a combination color and flash meter.)

There are four basic types of external light meters:

Reflective light meters measure the light that is reflected off the surface of an object in a scene. This is the same system used by the internal light-metering systems of most digital cameras. Because most digital camera internal metering systems equal or rival the metering done by an external reflective light meter, these meters have limited value for a digital photographer except in special situations. They are useful, for example, when a digital camera is mounted on a tripod and it is necessary to take multiple readings from different areas of a scene. We saw such a case in Chapter 7. Some external reflective light meters can also be used as spot meters, effectively reading only 1-3% of a scene. This can be useful if you are interested in metering only a tiny portion of scene (i.e., a person's face). If a digital camera isn't equipped with spot-metering capability, an external spot meter might come in handy. External reflective light meters are the most commonly used light meters, and are therefore widely available and competitively priced. Most of them are small enough that they don't add significant weight to any camera bag.

Incident light meters look similar to reflective meters and are similarly priced, but instead of reading the light reflected off an object, they read the light striking a subject. Instead of aiming an incident light meter at an object, you place the meter in front of object, allowing the light to strike the meter in the same manner as the light strikes the subject. Assuming that you can position the meter properly, incident light meters are not as easily fooled as reflective light meters and provide a more accurate reading. Incident meters are useful when shooting highly reflective objects under continuous light sources.

Flash meters are capable of capturing extremely short bursts of light that emit from a flash. (Your built-in flash uses a similar system to determine the correct exposure.) If you are using external strobes for your work, an external flash meter is extremely useful. It is possible to "guesstimate" a rough exposure using a digital camera's LCD playback, but it can be time-consuming and not very accurate.

Color meters measure the color temperature of light and are very useful if precise color rendition is critical, as it is in much catalog work. Once a color temperature is determined, the color value is used to determine the correct white balance setting on the camera (assuming that your digital camera gives you more than an automatic white balance setting).

Composition and Content

Let's look at a few images and attempt to see what makes them "work" from a composition and content point of view.

Start with John Isaac's chapter opening shot in Figure 8.1. Not only is there a beautiful contrast of light and dark, but also the color and texture is especially pleasing. As a general rule of thumb, warmer colors such as the ones in this image evoke a very positive emotional response from a viewer. By framing the shaft of light at the top of the image, John has also made the whole composition dynamic. The eyes focus on the brightest part of the image and then move down the shaft of light.

In Dave Harps' snowy image shown in Figure 8.11 (shot with a Nikon D1X professional digital camera) color isn't a factor, but contrast becomes the dominant draw for the eye. The eye is drawn to the dark dots in the foreground and moves toward the softer horizon.

Figure 8.11: In this image by Dave Harp, the eye is drawn to the contrast between foreground and background.

Figure 8.12, which I shot with my Olympus E-10, illustrates an oft-cited "rule of thirds." Simply stated, the rule of thirds suggests that you divide the image area vertically and horizontally into three equal parts. (I've included ruler marks on the image to show this.) The rule suggests that it is best, if you can, to place the center of interest near one of the four intersecting points (marked with an "x" on the photo). The theory holds that by keeping the center of interest off center, you'll force the viewer's eye to move around and not fixate on one spot.

Figure 8.12: The "rule of thirds" suggests the center of interest be placed near one of the four intersecting points marked with an "x".

Figure 8.13 shows a panorama shot created by Bruce Dale with a Panasonic Digilux digital camera. It's really four sequenced shots stitched together with software. It illustrates a variation on the rule of thirds: the horizon line is not centered, but placed in the upper third of the image area. Centered horizon lines are generally static and add no dynamic tension to the image.

Figure 8.13. By framing the horizon line in the upper third of the image, Bruce Dale achieved a more dynamic image.

Bottom line: There's been plenty written on the subject of composition and content, and it seems everyone has an opinion. I suggest that you spend some time looking carefully at images that work for you. In time, you'll get to know on your own what works and what doesn't, and this will translate into your own work.

Software Solutions: Fixing Exposure

You can use software to simulate the effect of a graduated neutral density filter and improve shots like the one shown on the left. Note how the foreground and background have widely different tonal values.

To improve this shot, I used Photoshop Elements to do the following:

1. I created a Level Adjustments Layer.
2. I then used Adjustments to darken the image. Now the upper part of the image is okay, but the lower areas are too dark.
3. With the Adjustment Layer selected, I selected the Gradient Tool from the toolbar. With the Gradient Tool set to Foreground to Transparent, and with black filled in the Foreground Color Swatch at the bottom of the Toolbar, I held the Shift key and dragged my cursor from the bottom of the image halfway up. This effectively created a graduated "mask" that blocked the effect of the Level's adjustment from the bottom portion of the image.
4. I then used the Eraser tool to erase areas of the mask that didn't match up perfectly. This resulted in the improved shot shown on the right.

Shooting Panoramas and Virtual Reality

With just a little help from special software, you can extend the capabilities of your digital camera to create stunning panoramas and enticing virtual reality (VR) images. This chapter shows you how to shoot—and create— images that are not only more beautiful, but also have practical applications in the commercial world as well.

Chapter Contents

Scott Highton

Panoramas and Object Movies

Look at Figure 9.1. It's not what it seems. This panorama is actually comprised of several images "stitched" together using a computer and special software. Because of the limitations of the digital camera's optical system, it would have been nearly impossible to make this in a single shot. Panoramas like this can be printed, or with an extended angle of view and more software help, they can be turned into interactive virtual reality (VR) movies viewable on a computer monitor and distributed via the Web or on a CD.

Figure 9.1: This panorama made by Scott Highton using a Nikon Coolpix 990 is comprised of four adjacent images, "stitched" together using Photoshop Elements' 2 Photomerge plug-in.

If you look at Figure 9.2 you'll see another example where software was used to extend the capabilities of a digital camera. This is part of an object movie, although you can't experience the full effect here on the printed page. While panoramic images show the view from a particular location looking outward in all directions, object movies are created by shooting with your digital camera pointed toward an object while the object is rotated through many angles. This yields a group of images that, once assembled into an interactive sequence, enables a viewer to interactively rotate the object on their computer screen simply by dragging their mouse. The effect is one of being able to virtually pick up an object and move it around in your hands, viewing it from any side. Object movies are often used by online retailers to sell products on websites such as eBay.

Figure 9.2: This object movie was also created by Scott Highton. To get the full interactive effect you need to view it on a monitor, which you can do by going to **www.shooting-digital.com**.

Let's see what it takes in terms of software and shooting to create these and other similar types of images.

Note: I turned to my colleague and friend, Scott Highton, a professional photographer and world-renowned expert on this subject, to gather and present most of the tips and techniques that follow. Scott is working on a book titled *Virtual Reality Photography,* which will be published in the near future. In the meantime his website, **www.vrphotography.com,** contains a plethora of information on this subject.

Shooting Simple Panoramas

It's relatively easy to shoot and stitch a simple panorama comprised of two or three images. Some digital cameras even offer a panoramic shooting mode that guides you through the process and includes basic stitching software.

Inexpensive, off-the-shelf software is also available to stitch the images together. Some of these products include:

- Photoshop Elements (with its Photomerge feature) from Adobe, **www.adobe.com**
- PhotoVista Panorama from iSeeMedia, **www.iseemedia.com**
- PanaVue ImageAssembler (Windows Only), **www.panavue.com**

Note: For a comprehensive guide to using Photoshop Elements to create panoramas, please refer to my book, *Photoshop Elements 2 Solutions.*

You can create these simple panoramas by shooting a series of overlapping images with a hand-held digital camera. However, for the best results—or if you want to expand your panoramas to include 360° views and use them for virtual reality— you'll need to adopt some good shooting practices.

The following general tips will ensure that your panoramas are as good as they can be.

Use a tripod

Using a tripod minimizes camera movement during an exposure. It makes you think a little more about your composition, subject, and framing before you shoot, so the results are more considered. But most importantly, when shooting panoramic images for stitching, the tripod allows you to maintain consistent alignment between the images, thus improving the stitch process. (☞ "Accessories That Make a Difference: Tripods" in Chapter 7 to learn more about what to look for in a tripod.)

Use consistent exposure, focus, and focal length

If possible, turn off the autoexposure and autofocus mechanisms of your camera, or switch them to manual control. While some consumer cameras may not let you do this, they may have exposure lock and focus lock features that you can use instead. The stitching software looks for matching pixel patterns and blends the images based on these. So it is important for every image in a sequence to have the same exposure, focus, and size, or the blends will not work well. Exposure changes between shots will result in light or dark banding in the stitched image. Focus and focal length (zooming) differences will also result in stitching errors, where subjects along the seams don't blend properly. It is best to choose a focal length you like before you start taking pictures (usually the widest possible) and keep your finger off the zoom control while shooting.

Furthermore, you'll want to turn off your camera's auto white balance setting and use a preset such as "bright daylight" or "cloudy" or "shade" instead. (☞ "Know Your Camera: Adjusting White Balance" in Chapter 11 to learn how to do this.)

The good news is that even if your camera does *not* allow override of white balance, most digital cameras will at least maintain fairly consistent settings within a scene. However, if the camera is shut off and then turned back on during the sequence (this can happen if you pause too long between shots and the camera's auto shutoff feature engages), then the camera will likely reset its white balance to whatever it deems best for the light it's restarted under. This change can result in color banding in the stitched panorama. Once you've started shooting a panoramic sequence, try to complete it without delay.

Keep the camera level

Avoid tilting your camera up or down as you shoot, as this causes vertical lines to converge in your images and makes it difficult for the stitching software to match and blend the images properly. If you center the horizon in the middle of your viewfinder, then any vertical lines in your scene will remain straight up and down, and will match properly when you pan and shoot the next image in your panoramic sequence.

Turn the camera vertically to increase your field of view

It's common to take pictures while holding the camera horizontally. However, if you rotate your camera 90° into a vertical or portrait orientation, you'll have a larger view vertically (up and down) than you would if you held the camera horizontally. If you want more vertical coverage in your panorama, shoot your sequences with your camera oriented vertically. To increase your horizontal field of view, simply shoot as many adjacent shots as you can. For example, compare the two panoramas shown in Figure 9.3. The top image was shot with the camera in its normal landscape orientation, and the bottom image was shot with it in portrait orientation.

Figure 9.3: You can extend the vertical field of view of a panorama by shooting your camera in portrait mode. The top image shows an image shot with normal landscape orientation; the bottom shows it shot with portrait orientation. (Photos by Scott Highton)

To mount your camera on a tripod in portrait (vertical) orientation, you will probably require a right angle adapter plate or a specialized VR tripod head. Commercial products such as these are available from many photo manufacturers, including:

- Bogen/Manfrotto (**www.manfrotto.com**)
- Kaidan (**www.kaidan.com**)
- Peace River Studios (**www.peaceriverstudios.com**)
- SLIK (**www.slik.com**)

Alternatively, if you're handy with tools, you can make a right angle bracket by bending a piece of aluminum (or other metal), drilling a few holes in appropriate spots, and adding a couple of screws or bolts to attach everything to your tripod.

Pan the camera an equal amount between shots

You will need to pan your camera a specific angle between shots depending upon the focal length of the lens (or the focal setting of the zoom lens) you are using. It is best to try to keep this pan increment as consistent as possible between shots. Specialized panoramic tripod heads have preset click stops built into them at varying increments. This feature makes shooting easier, particularly when creating 360° panoramas. However, this is not critical when you are combining only two or three images. Simply look through the viewfinder as you pan the camera between shots, and stop when you still have 1/3 to 1/2 of the previous image in your frame. Shoot the next image, and then repeat as many times as needed in order to get the horizontal coverage you desire. Pan from left to right as you shoot.

Be consistent

Getting good results requires consistently good technique and attention to detail. We all make mistakes, and in photography, there are a lot to make. It's hard to diagnose what mistakes you need to correct if you constantly change things without keeping track of what you did or when you did it. Keep a small notebook in your camera bag and use it to jot notes about your location, your camera, exposure and lens settings for special shots, plus the number of images you shoot for each panorama. These will come in handy when you are trying to stitch the images later on. They will also help you isolate problems when they do arise, and help you figure out what to do to prevent those problems in the future. Once you find a combination of camera settings and techniques that work best for the kinds of images you create, remain consistent in their use in order to get consistent results. You can even buy notebooks specifically designed for panoramic and virtual reality photography at **www.vrphotography.com**.

Avoid Filters

Don't use filters, especially polarizing filters, when shooting images for panoramas or VR. Filters can cause slight vignetting or fading on the edges of the image, which will result in noticeable banding when images are stitched together. Stitching images that were taken with a polarizing filter can also result in unwanted banding because the filters can produce varying results depending on the position of the camera to light rays.

Shoot from left to right

Keep in mind that almost all stitching programs stitch images from left to right, so it is a good idea to shoot your panorama sequences from left to right as well. This practice will result in a more automated workflow when you are importing your digital files from your camera, as the files will be in a numeric sequence that matches the stitching sequence. It's not a disaster if you don't do this, but you'll find that using stitching software will be much easier if you shoot from left to right.

Allow the frames to overlap

It is important to allow 1/3 to 1/2 of the frame as seen through the viewfinder or LCD to overlap between shots. The stitching software looks for matching pixel patterns between images and then blends them together across the overlap area, forming a visually seamless combined image. This can be done repeatedly for many images, and can even be extended to compose a full 360° view. If you do not have sufficient overlap between each image however, the stitcher will be unable to match the pixel patterns properly, and the image blends will not align well.

Having too much overlap between images can be problematic, too, as it requires you not only to take more pictures than necessary, but also slows down the stitching process when your computer has to process far more information than is necessary. If you wind up with more than 50% overlap between your images, consider trying to stitch every *other* image together, rather than every image in your panorama sequence.

Note: One of the great advantages of combining multiple images into a single panorama is that you can get a higher level of detail and greater resolution from the same camera than you can by simply using a wide-angle lens adapter or the "panorama" mode on most point-and-shoot cameras. Let's say that your digital camera records 2 megapixels of data in each photograph you capture. When you add a wide-angle adapter to your lens, you are not only degrading the quality of the optics you are using, but you are also compressing more visual information into the frame, resulting in less detail in the recorded image. However, when you shoot multiple pictures with the same 2-megapixel camera and then stitch them together, you are adding pixel data with each picture, rather than compressing the entire view into the same 2 megapixels. For example, stitching three images together, assuming they have 50% overlap, will yield a panoramic image of about 4 megapixels. Mind you, the stitching process can introduce problems of its own at times, but these are minimal to non-existent if you use the good shooting techniques described previously.

Extending Your View

It is possible to extend your field of view to include everything in a scene: 360° horizontally, and a wide angle of view vertically. These sorts of panoramas are commonly used for virtual reality (VR) applications, such as real estate virtual home tours (like the one shown in Figure 9.4), online tourist destinations, promotional websites for hotels, restaurants, and airlines, as well as corporate marketing, training aids, crime scene investigation, education, and interactive games.

Figure 9.4: Part of a 360° panorama, viewed in QuickTime. Kitchen interior, Masco Virtual Showhome, Columbia, MD. The Masco Virtual Showhome project was produced by RDC Interactive Media, Inc., Palo Alto, CA. (Photography by Scott Highton)

Stitching these images together generally requires software specifically designed for VR authoring. The difference is that 360° panoramas will often require anywhere from a half dozen to several dozen source images, and the ends of the resulting panorama need to be wrapped so that the beginning and end are also blended. It is even possible to create 360° panoramas with complete (180°) vertical fields of view, but this requires specific shooting tools and techniques, as well as VR software with spherical or cubic stitching capability.

There are a variety of software applications available. Each has its own requirements for the types of lenses that can be used and how their image sequences should be shot. All of the techniques recommended previously become essential practices when you are creating full 360° panoramas and VR scenes.

Such software applications include:

- Apple's QuickTime VR Authoring Studio (Macintosh only), approximate cost: $395 (**www.apple.com/quicktime/qtvr/**)
- Stitcher from REALVIZ (Mac and Windows), approximate cost: $499 (**www.realviz.com/products/st/**)
- VRPanoWorx and VRWorx from VR Toolbox (Mac and Windows), approximate cost: $149 (**www.vrtoolbox.com**)
- PhotoVista Panorama from iSeeMedia (Windows only), approximate cost: $49 (**www.iseemedia.com**)
- iPIX Builder and Wizard software from Internet Pictures (Mac and Windows) approximate cost: $99, not including licensing fees (**www.ipix.com**)

Once you have assembled a panoramic image, you can either display it as a printed stand-alone photograph, or you can convert it into an interactive VR movie that can be published on the Internet or distributed electronically. These movies are viewed with a variety of Web browser plug-ins or stand-alone media players, such as Apple's popular QuickTime available free for both Mac and Windows at **http://www.apple.com/quicktime/**. Sites offering this content typically include a download link for the appropriate plug-in.

Shooting Tips for 360° Panoramas

As with simple panoramas, alignment and consistency between images are important when shooting full 360° panoramas. The better the alignment and juxtaposition between your source images are, the better the stitched results will be. Remember that you maximize your vertical field of view by rotating your camera to a vertical or portrait orientation.

Pan around the nodal point. For the best image alignment, it is important that your camera be rotated (panned) around the optical center of its lens, or what is known as the *nodal point*, rather than around the point where the camera's tripod socket happens to be located. Panning your camera around the nodal point of its lens means that close and distant subjects maintain their relative positions in your photos, no matter where these subjects are located in your frame.

Stitching software cannot stitch images together properly if the near and far subjects do not maintain their same positions relative to one another in between frames. Nodal point alignment becomes less of an issue the farther your subjects are from the camera, becoming almost insignificant when your nearest subject is greater than 6 feet (2 meters) away from the camera.

Several manufacturers produce custom tripod heads for panoramic VR photography and also provide instructions for aligning the nodal point of your camera and lens. These specialized accessories allow you to both position your camera in a vertical or portrait orientation *and* to adjust its position on the tripod so that it rotates around the optical center of its lens. These manufacturers include Bogen/Manfrotto, Kaidan, and Peace River Studios, cited earlier.

A description of nodal point alignment is also available at www.vrphotography.com.

Use a wider lens and you'll need fewer shots. The wider the focal length of your lens, the fewer overlapping shots you will need to complete the full 360° view. One of the disadvantages of today's non-professional digital cameras is that their built-in lenses do not provide terribly wide coverage, so more images are needed to complete a full 360° stitched view. This is why up until recently, the best panoramic VR images were shot with film cameras, and the film was then digitized for stitching. However, this situation is changing with the introduction of better digital cameras and lenses, allowing for greater fields of view and higher resolutions, along with the commercial availability of multi-row stitching software.

Multiple-Row Panoramas

Unfortunately, with most consumer digital cameras, even shooting with the camera in portrait (vertical) orientation does not always enable you to include everything of interest in the scene. One solution is to use a multi-row stitcher, which allows you to stitch more than one row of source images. This lets you shoot a row of images with the camera level to the horizon, and then add additional rows with the camera tilted upward or downward. In this manner, you can increase the vertical coverage of your panoramas up to and including views directly overhead or below.

In order to shoot multi-row panoramas, you will need a multi-row VR panoramic head for your tripod, as well as multi-row stitching software. Currently, only Kaidan and Manfrotto offer multi-row tripod heads, and RealViz's Stitcher is the only commercial software application that can stitch multi-row panoramas.

Spherical Panoramas

There are other options for creating spherical or cubic (360° × 180°) panoramas. The most notable of these is the iPIX format. Using the iPIX system, the photographer adds a fisheye converter or lens to their camera, which captures a 180° circular image (or hemisphere view) with each shot. The camera is mounted on a rotator unit that allows it to be turned precisely 180° between shots. Only two photographs—one for each opposing hemisphere view—are required for a complete panorama. The iPIX software then digitally aligns these images inside a virtual sphere and outputs a VR movie that the viewer can pan around. The newest versions of iPIX's software also allow for the stitching of three hemispheric images (the camera rotates only 120° between shots) and the larger overlap area improves blending of the seam areas. There are three major drawbacks to the iPIX system, however. It does not capture as much detail in a scene as either single- or multi-row stitching programs; it requires shooting with a special fisheye lens or adapter (not available for all cameras); and there is a fee (called a licensing "key" by iPIX) charged for every panorama created with their proprietary software. Information about the iPIX technology, as well as sales information for their camera and software packages is available from **www.ipix.com**.

A competing software application called Panoweaver allows for spherical and cubic fisheye image stitching (two or three hemisphere images), but without the per-image "key" or license fee that iPIX charges. More information is available at **www.easypano.com**.

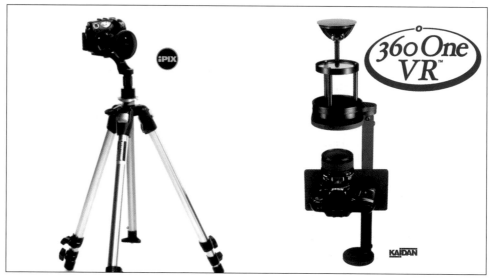

Figure 9.5: Two commercially available 360° solutions. The iPIX system (left) and Kaidan's 360One setup (right).

There are also several specialized one-shot panoramic VR lens systems available that capture full 360° panoramas in a single shot. These systems involve a parabolic mirror that attaches to the lens of a digital camera, resulting in an *annulus* (donut-shaped image) being recorded. Their proprietary software is then used to dewarp the image into a normal 360° panorama, which can be made into a VR movie or printed as flat artwork. The advantage to this system is that you can capture the entire view in a single exposure, which eliminates the problem of objects in the scene possibly moving or changing between frames and causing stitching misalignments. In fact, the stitching process is eliminated with these systems. The disadvantages are that you cannot capture a full spherical view (these systems are limited to anywhere from 30° to 50° above and below the horizon), and the resulting sharpness and resolution are relatively low, since the entire scene is compressed into a single frame recorded by your digital camera. For more information:

- 360One from Kaidan: **www.kaidan.com**
- BeHere system: **www.behere.com**

Object Movies

Interactive object VR movies are a unique feature of Apple's QuickTime VR, although their effect can also be simulated with the use of animated GIFs and a variety of other techniques. They are most often used for the promotion of commercial products on the Internet, such as items for sale in eBay auctions. They are also used extensively in education, online training, advertising, and visual documentation.

Digital cameras are ideally suited for use in object movie VR. Because it may be necessary to shoot a large quantity of images to create object movie sequences, it is far more cost-effective to shoot them digitally than on film. Also, precise alignment of the images between shots is virtually impossible to achieve with traditional film cameras. The alignment consistency that is provided by the fixed sensor inside a digital camera allows for smooth playback when the images are played in rapid sequence.

An object movie is composed of anywhere from less than a dozen to hundreds of images surrounding a subject. Each is taken from a slightly different angle and then all of the images are arranged in a series of linked playback sequences. Most often, an object will be placed on a turntable and photographs will be shot as it is turned in 10° increments.

The more shots you have (the smaller the rotation increment), the smoother the playback of the object sequence will appear in the movie window. However, this increases file size—and therefore also increases the time it will take for your viewers to download the movie. Fewer shots yield a smaller file size, but the playback does not appear as smooth. There is greater movement or "jump" between each frame in the movie because the object is rotated more between each frame.

It is critical to shoot object sequences with your camera mounted on a tripod or other device that keeps the camera in the same position relative to the object, and the object itself mounted on a turntable or rotating platform. (For example, Figure 9.6 shows the setup used to shoot the frames for the object movie shown in Figure 9.2.) The only movement between one frame and the next should be the rotation of the object. If the camera moves between shots, then the movie sequence will appear jittery when played. Remember that you're essentially doing stop-motion animation when you shoot an object sequence, so it's important to keep everything as stable as possible when you shoot.

Figure 9.6: A simple object movie shooting setup: the object is mounted on a turntable, and the camera is on a tripod. (Photo by Scott Highton)

A basic turntable for small objects can be made from a lazy susan, available from many kitchen or department stores. In fact, Rubbermaid makes a plastic one that can be bought for about $5 at many houseware and grocery stores. If you want to build one that is a bit more heavy duty, you can buy a lazy susan mechanism for about $10 at your local hardware store, to which you can mount a piece of wood or other flat surface of your choosing. These can hold and rotate objects weighing hundreds of pounds. Use a protractor to determine degree increments, and mark them on the outer edge of your turntable. Then simply rotate your object on it in prescribed increments as you shoot.

Accessories That Make a Difference: Commercial Rigs for VR Photography

There are a number of sophisticated commercial turntables and rigs available specifically for object VR photography. Their prices range from around $100 to almost $20,000. The most basic of these are manually operated with click-stop increments. The more advanced versions are computer-controlled and feature precision electronic stepper motors. They allow you to shoot multiple level sequences (so you can go above and below the object, as well as seeing it from all sides) and they can be configured for high volume, automated object shooting. For more information, see the Kaidan and Peace River Studios sites mentioned earlier in the chapter or Corybant West at **www.corybantwest.com**.

Once you have captured a series of images for an object, you need to bring them into a computer and sequence them into a movie. These images can be played in sequence as a normal QuickTime or video movie. The result will show an object that rotates in the movie window as the frames are played in rapid sequence.

However, if these images are made into an interactive object movie, the viewer can control the rate and direction of playback simply by moving the mouse cursor in the movie window. If you've photographed the object from multiple levels, then moving the mouse upward or downward changes the view to one from above or below. The viewer can even zoom in or out on the object while it rotates in an interactive object movie.

Fully interactive object movies can be displayed properly only in the QuickTime format. (Other popular media players, such as those provided by Microsoft and RealNetworks, treat these interactive movies as traditional linear movies and simply play their frame sequence from beginning to end.) Integrated QuickTime players and Web browser plug-ins are available at no cost for either Mac or Windows systems from Apple's website at **www.apple.com/quicktime/products/qt/**. (If you post an object movie on your own site, be sure to include a link to the QuickTime download page.)

Object movies can also be displayed quite effectively in linear (rather than interactive) form if they are programmed to loop repeatedly from beginning to end. Figure 9.7 shows how the object movie would appear in the QuickTime viewer. The object rotates continuously and automatically on screen without interactive viewer control. Such sequences can even be assembled as animated GIFs for presentation on websites where no media player other than a basic Web browser is required to view them.

Figure 9.7. An object movie by Scott Highton being viewed in a QuickTime viewer.

Before you start shooting object movies, determine which software application you want to use for their assembly, and then familiarize yourself with how it works. Each one has specific recommendations for image organization, file formats, and general workflow. Make sure you understand those requirements. Interactive object movies can be created with software such as the following:

- Apple's QuickTime VR Authoring Studio (Macintosh only)
  www.apple.com/quicktime/qtvr/
- VRObjectWorx and VRWorx from VRToolbox (Mac and Windows)
  www.vrtoolbox.com
- ImageModeler from RealViz (Mac and Windows)
  www.realviz.com/products/im/index.php
- PhotoVista 3DObjects and Reality Studio from iSeeMedia (Windows only)
  www.iseemedia.com

Non-interactive single row object movies can be authored using the same source images and sequencing them as animated GIFs or other linear movie formats. These can be done with software such as:

- Photoshop, Photoshop Elements, and Premiere from Adobe
- iMovie, Final Cut Pro, and QuickTime Pro from Apple
- Director and Flash from Macromedia

Shooting Tips for Object Movies

Once you have a turntable set up to hold your objects, along with an appropriate tripod or object rig to support your camera, you are ready to start shooting object movies. However, there's a bit more to doing this successfully than simply exposing frame after frame as you rotate the turntable.

Compose the frame carefully

First, choose good perspective, shooting position, and lens focal length. Ideally, you'll want to fill the frame as much as possible with your subject so you capture adequate detail in each image. If you are limited to a fixed-focal-length lens, you will need to adjust your camera distance to frame the image you want. However, with a zoom lens, you can set it to a longer (telephoto) focal length before you distance the camera from the subject in order to fit the frame. Commercial products generally look more natural when photographed with a longer lens from a distance than with a wider lens from close up. The closer your camera is to the subject, the more distorted and unflattering the subject will appear.

Keep in mind that most objects have varying dimensions on each side. You will need to rotate the object on the turntable as you are framing it in your viewfinder to make sure that it still fits the frame throughout the 360° rotation. For example, a model train engine is relatively small and compact when viewed head on. If you fill your frame using this view when you set your camera position, the engine will over-flow the frame when it is turned to a 90° profile. In general, you will want your composition to include the entire object throughout its 360° rotation.

Choose an appropriate background

Background choice is your next important decision. Shooting objects against a black or dark background is often the easiest, because your main worry is how the object itself looks, and uneven or uncontrolled light on the background is less of a problem. Also, postproduction of images with dark backgrounds is often more straightforward than it is with light or white backgrounds, which often require more masking, retouching, and image manipulation. Keep in mind that you may need to retouch *every* frame of your object movie, so any retouching necessary is multiplied by the number of frames you've shot. However, dark backgrounds tend to give a more somber feel to product photos, and may not be the best choice when you're trying to sell or promote a product.

White seems to be the background of choice for commercial products, but it is very difficult to get pure white backgrounds from a digital camera and still expose the object properly. Auto-exposure cameras are often fooled by large expanses of white in a scene, and will try to darken the exposure to keep detail in these highlight areas. Because this is generally the exact opposite of what you want, it's best to use a camera with manual exposure control or exposure lock capability when shooting object movies so you can control your exposure more precisely.

Avoid anything that will cause flicker

Remember that even the slightest change in your camera's position, focus, framing, or exposure settings during the object sequence will result in a flicker or jitter when the images are displayed as a movie. Use a remote release to fire your camera so that the pressure of your finger on the shutter release button doesn't move the camera slightly between frames. Lock your exposure, focus, and white balance settings, and make sure that you don't accidentally touch the zoom control. If you accidentally bump either your tripod or the object turntable while shooting, no matter how lightly, start the sequence over again to be on the safe side. It is usually far more efficient to reshoot the whole thing while you have the chance than it is to try to correct continuity problems in postproduction.

Lighting for Object Movies

Lighting is the final thing to think about before you shoot. You will learn much about what works and what doesn't with every shoot you attempt, but if you start out with a few simple rules of thumb, you should be able to produce pleasing results fairly quickly.

1. Keep it simple. Remember that you need to make the object look good from every angle it rotates through, not just a single one. The simpler you can keep your lighting, the better. As you're setting up and shooting, constantly look through your camera's viewfinder to make sure that your subject looks okay throughout the object's rotation. You want to discover and correct problems with lens flare or uneven lighting before shooting, rather than having to deal with such problems after the fact in postproduction.

    The simplest lighting setup you can use is outdoor sunlight. Try shooting your objects outside in the early morning or late afternoon/early evening when the sun is not too high in the sky. Direct sunlight is a fairly hard light source, and may be a bit too harsh. Sunlight early or late in the day is usually softer than mid-day light because it is more diffused as it comes from a low angle and has to pass through more air and haze in the atmosphere. A slight cloud overcast will also soften it considerably more.

    Put the object on your turntable and walk around it to see which angle gives you the best definition or desired look. Since you can't move your light (the sun), you have to walk around the object rather than rotating the turntable for this step. Once you have your object at the best angle relative to the sun and your camera, then you can position your background. Lock in your framing, composition, exposure, white balance, etc., and begin shooting.

2. Use Fill light when necessary. If the light is still too harsh, consider adding a reflector to bounce additional light into the shadow side of your object. This technique will even out the light somewhat and reduce the contrast between highlight and shadow areas. Your reflector can be a large piece of white artboard (put aluminum foil over it to reflect even more light) or a commercial photo reflector from companies like Visual Departures (Flexfill) **www.visualde-partures.com** or PhotoFlex **www.photoflex.com**. Position this reflector on the opposite side of your object from the sun. Move it in closer to increase the amount of fill light, or move it farther away to decrease it. Experiment until you find an arrangement that works well, and remember that the sun will move slowly across the sky as you shoot, so you may need to subtly adjust the aim of your reflector as the sun moves.

3. Experienced commercial photographers find that soft light is usually better for most product photography, particularly with shiny or reflective subjects. You may find that when you are shooting object movie sequences, it is far easier to get pleasing results with soft lighting than it is with hard light sources such as direct sunlight or your camera's built-in flash unit.

You will find many sources of soft light once you start looking. Any indirect light is usually softer than direct light. Try shooting your object under a covered porch, where the sun is not shining directly on it, or where it is being lit by reflected light off a white wall. (Note that any color painted on the wall will cause the reflected light to take on that color). Shooting indoors with a large window as your primary light source is also an excellent way to get soft lighting. Position your setup with the window to the side of the object, rather than directly in front or in back of it. If the window has direct sunlight coming through it, you can hang up a piece of sheer fabric or gauze to diffuse the light. You can buy fabric samples large enough to cover most windows at your local fabric store. Again, use the purest white fabric you can find so it doesn't filter the color of the light shining through it. If you still need to add fill light into the shadow side of your object, you can again use white artboard, reflectors, or even a small mirror.

Of course, you can always use electronic strobes or studio lighting with soft box attachments, along with a variety of grip or support equipment. If you have these available, you can get fairly precise control of your lighting and make it absolutely repeatable from frame to frame, or even from day to day. For more on this equipment, ↪ "Accessories That Make a Difference: External Artificial Lights" in Chapter 10.

4. Position your lighting off-axis from the camera. Keep in mind that if you use an on-camera flash or other light source directly in line with your camera, your subject will wind up looking flat and lifeless in your pictures. It is tempting to shoot with an on-camera or built-in flash unit, because they are so conveniently provided by the camera manufacturers. But your subject will likely look as though it was rendered as a series of mug shots from a police lineup. It is best to position your primary light source at an angle off to the side of your subject if you can.

5. Separate your background from your subject. Try to position your background some distance away from the object you are photographing. This technique accomplishes several things:
   - The greater distance means that the background will be more out of focus and will be less distracting (remember to focus your lens on the object, not the background).
   - The object will be less likely to cast a shadow on the background (which makes postproduction image retouching easier).
   - You can light the object and the background independently (this requires multiple light sources). In the case of a white background, you can make it considerably brighter by shining more light on it without the extra light spilling onto the object. In the case of a black background, you can better block light shining on the object from spilling onto the background. The increased distance from the object light sources means that less light reaches the background. The background will be rendered darker in the photographs, and will make retouching easier.

Know Your Camera: Lenses

Most consumer and prosumer digital cameras come with non-interchangeable lenses—usually with focal lengths ranging from wide to telephoto. Professional digital cameras offer interchangeable lenses, which are often purchased separately from the camera body itself.

The lens is a critical component of a digital camera. Many of you who already own a digital camera likely made a buying decision based at least partially on the specifications and characteristics of a camera's lens. If you purchased a professional SLR digital camera, lens compatibility with your older film camera lenses may have been a top consideration.

It only takes a few shooting sessions to determine if your optical system meets your needs.

- Does the lens cover a wide enough angle of view? Or are you constantly finding yourself with your back to the wall and still not getting everything you want in the shot? Is the telephoto long enough? Or are the objects you shoot, birds for example, coming out as just tiny specks on the image?
- Most digital cameras boast a "macro" mode for extreme close ups. But "macro" for one lens might mean 6 inches, and for another, 2 inches. If you are shooting rare old coins, the distinction is critical.
- Is the widest aperture of your lens wide enough? Remember, aperture is expressed as f-stop, and the wider the f-stop, the more light passes through the lens to the sensor. This will make a difference in low-light situations without a flash. Also, the wider the aperture, the more control you have over depth of field. Some camera lenses feature f/1.8 as their widest aperture, which is considered very good, but it's not that uncommon to find lenses rated at f/3.5 or even narrower.
- Does your lens stop down enough? If it only stops down to f/8, you won't have the flexibility to shoot in extremely bright circumstances unless the camera features a very fast shutter speed to compensate. (Because of the size of the sensors, increased depth of field isn't usually a problem with digital cameras, regardless of how narrow the aperture is.)
- How easy is it to use the lens? Does it focus quickly in manual-focus mode, assuming you have a manual-focus mode? How does it feel when you zoom from one focal length to another? Is the zoom responsive? Does the lens barrel move quickly and smoothly? Some digital camera lenses offer a motor-controlled zoom; others a mechanical manual zoom. Are you more comfortable with one over the other?
- Is the autofocus system responsive enough for your needs? This is only partially a function of the lens, but involves other electronic components of the camera as well. Depending on what you shoot, an autofocus system that works well in a variety of lighting conditions is extremely important. Some digital cameras, such as the Sony F717, for example, offer very sophisticated "laser" or other type of light assists that can greatly improve performance in low light.
- If your lens has an image stabilization mode, does it work satisfactorily? If it does, you should be free of the restraints imposed by slow shutter speeds.

The actual quality of a lens is more difficult to ascertain. If your images aren't sharp, you can't assume that optics are the reason. Image processing, which occurs after data is captured by the sensor, can also introduce blurriness. In order to know the quality of your lens, you'll need to research the Web for carefully controlled tests conducted by independent camera reviewers. You can, if you wish, purchase targets created specifically for precise resolution testing. These targets contain carefully calibrated test patterns that you photograph using the equipment in question and then visually inspect and analyze the results. These targets are available from a number of vendors, including Eastman Kodak, Sine Patterns, and Edmund Industrial Optics.

If you aren't satisfied with your lens, what can you do? Focal length inadequacies can be worked around, to a point, with add-on lenses and teleconverters. There can be a tradeoff in quality, but that will depend on the actual shooting situation.

With careful shooting techniques and considerations, you can work around the limitations of so-called "slow" lenses—ones whose widest aperture is say, f/3.5 or narrower. This might mean using a slow shutter speed and a tripod, for example. There are also ways to decrease your depth of field, ☞ "Know Your Camera: Controlling Depth of Field" in Chapter 2.

Even some of the best lenses suffer from optical distortions known as barreling and pincushioning. These optical aberrations can often be easily fixed with camera-bundled software such as Olympus's Camedia Master. Check your owner's manual for more information.

There is not much you can do to make a lens more responsive or comfortable, except to learn to live with it and anticipate its shortcomings. There really isn't anything you can do to improve the inherent optical quality of a lens, either, except understand that most lenses, even the bad ones, have a "sweet spot." This spot is the place where a certain focal length, used with a particular f-stop (usually 2-3 stops down from the widest opening), produces the sharpest image.

If you are using a professional SLR digital camera with interchangeable lenses, you can always swap an inadequate lens for one that meets your needs. Just be particularly careful when you remove your lens not to allow dust into the sensor.

Lens maintenance is another important consideration, and one over which you have control. Protect your lens from dust and scratches with a lens cap. You an also use an inexpensive UV filter if your lens has a threaded mount. If you are using interchangeable lenses, be particularly careful when switching lenses not to bump or bang the lens, and store your lenses carefully in shock resistant containers. A small amount of dust on a lens will not affect image quality very much unless you are shooting extremely close up. Oily smudges or fingerprints should be removed immediately, because they produce acids that can permanently etch the lens coating. Cleaning should be done only when needed, and use blown air or a soft brush. If this isn't enough, dampen a lens tissue with lens cleaner and gently rub in a circular motion. The risk here is abrasive particles creating tiny scratches in the coating. Avoid this by rolling or turning the tissue or switching to a new sheet of tissue often.

Shooting Your Stuff

Whether you are selling an antique rocking horse on eBay or a pair of vintage shoes through the want ads, or simply documenting a valuable painting for insurance purposes, digital cameras make it easier than ever to make attractive and informative shots. This chapter will show you several ways to do this, ranging from simple to complex.

10

Chapter Contents

Using Indirect Natural Light

Nothing could be simpler than placing an object that you wish to photograph under indirect natural light and shooting it. This is what professional photographer Robert Birnbach did to produce the beautiful image of a bowl and glass balls shown on the left in Figure 10.1. Robert used a prosumer Nikon Coolpix 990, mounted on a tripod, and positioned the subject on a counter near a window in his San Francisco photo studio. He placed a white foam board to the right of the bowl to bounce back some of the natural window light and fill areas that would have otherwise been too dark. On the right in Figure 10.1 is a diagram of Robert's setup.

 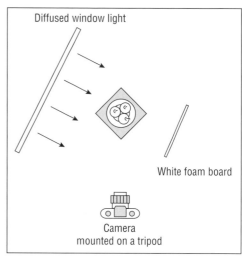

Figure 10.1: A lovely bowl of glass balls, photographed with a Nikon Coolpix 990 by Robert Birnbach. Natural light provided the main illumination and a sheet of white foam board placed to the right provided a fill for the shadow areas.

The critical point here is Robert's use of indirect natural light. Take note of the subtle tonal transitions between the shadows and highlights. If Robert had shot the image in direct sunlight, the light would have produced an extremely contrasty image, with a harsh transition between light and dark areas.

Window light clearly worked well for this shot, but Robert cautions that sometimes even the natural light from a window can be too intense and produce poor results. When this is the case, Robert recommends placing some type of diffusion material over the window itself. He often uses sheer curtains, but a very thin, white bed sheet will work just as well depending on the quality of the light. (Remember that colored fabric will tint the light and affect the color of the shot.)

Although Robert used a tripod to carefully compose the shot of the bowl and glass balls, he wasn't worried that a slow shutter speed might produce blur. Since he wanted a shallow depth of field, he used the camera's aperture priority mode and set the camera to its widest aperture, f/3.8. The resulting shutter speed was a fast 1/411th of a second.

Robert used the Nikon's autofocus system to focus the cameras and the LCD to frame the shot. (The optical viewfinder doesn't accurately reflect what is captured, but the LCD does.). Robert strongly advises anyone shooting digital to fill as much of the frame as possible with the object you are photographing. Filling the frame this way will minimize the need to crop valuable pixels later.

Robert also used the Nikon's automatic white balance mode to make this shot. However, for other shots where precise color is critical, Robert uses custom white balance settings. (For more on white balance, ↺ "Know Your Camera: Adjusting White Balance" in Chapter 11 and "Fine Tuning White Balance" in Zooming In.)

Robert zoomed the Nikon's lens to nearly its maximum focal length (20.9mm, or about 90mm in 35mm equivalent). This, along with the wide aperture, helped produce the limited depth of field that Robert wanted. (Longer focal lengths also flatten perspective, which can be desirable depending on what you are trying to achieve.)

The background for this shot is nothing more than a table top, but Robert uses a variety of backgrounds for his work. He's always on the lookout for potential background material, such as a piece of rusted metal, or a broken piece of shower bubble glass. (You'll see how the bubble glass is used later in the chapter.). Robert insists—and reinforces what I've said throughout this book—that whatever background you use, it should always be simple and not detract from the object you are shooting.

Bottom line: Avoid the cost and hassle of artificial lights; use natural light and get great shots.

Shooting Loose with Software in Mind

It's always preferable to get a perfect shot that requires little or no image processing. In the previous case study, for example, Robert used a tripod and worked slowly and methodically to get a final image that required only minimal cropping. However, with a digital camera, good image-editing software, and some basic image processing skills, you can loosen up your shooting techniques and still get professional-looking results.

For example, you'll be able to use readily available, off-the-shelf programs such as Photoshop, Photoshop Elements, PaintShop Pro, etc, to:

- Alter or replace a distracting background
- Colorize, texturize, or add motion blur to the subject
- Add depth through a drop shadow or other effect
- Remove distracting power cables or wires behind, around, or connected to the object you are shooting

Take the shot shown in Figure 10.2. I shot the rocking horse to use as an example for this book, but I could just as well have been photographing it to put up for bid on eBay. All I did was unroll a few feet of white seamless background paper—available at most photo supply stores—on my kitchen table. I could have just as easily used a white sheet. I didn't set up studio lights because it was a bright sunny day and the light streaming in through the windows was nicely diffused. I didn't bother with a tripod.

Instead, I set my Olympus E-10 digital camera to Program mode and autofocus and fired off a few hand-held shots. I knew the image was destined for my computer and the magic of Photoshop Elements, so I didn't worry about perfectly framing the shot or making the background perfect. I just made sure the exposure was in the ball-park, the focus was sharp, and all of the rocking horse was in the shot.

You can see what I did with software to remove the background and add motion blur to this image in Chapter 4, in the sidebar titled, "Software Solutions: Changing a Background and Adding Motion Blur."

Figure 10.2: This shot was taken with natural light and a simple white background. Since it was destined for software "improvement," framing and background weren't critical.

Note: For a step-by-step tutorial about placing photos on an eBay auction site, go here: http://pages.ebay.com/help/basics/phototut-1.html.

Another example where I shot with imaging software in mind is shown on the left in Figure 10.3. My neighbor, Joe Butler, called and said he needed to scan a large watercolor he'd painted for an exhibition announcement. The watercolor didn't fit on his desktop scanner. Was my scanner big enough, he wondered? I told him to bring the piece over and we'd see what we could do. The painting didn't fit on my scanner either, so I grabbed my Olympus E-10 and took the painting outside to photograph it.

Normally, when I shoot flat art such as this, I take the time to set up a tripod and position a couple of external lights to illuminate the work. To avoid a keystoning effect—where one end of the flat art comes out slightly narrower than the other—I carefully adjust my tripod controls so the camera is square in relationship to the flat art. (I'll describe this process in more detail later in the chapter.)

However, this time, with Joe's work, I simply placed it on a bench, and then framed and focused the camera. I waited until a cloud passed over the sun and fired off several frames under the now-diffused light. To prevent my camera and my body from casting a faint shadow on the work, I couldn't shoot perfectly square to the artwork. You can clearly see the resulting keystoning.

Later, after transferring the photo to my computer and opening it in Photoshop Elements, I used the Transform ➢ Perspective command to plumb the edges and remove the keystoning effect. The result is shown on the right. (This is essentially the same technique used in an earlier chapter to fix a building that suffered from keystoning. ⌒ "Software Solutions: Fixing Keystoning" in Chapter 7.)

Figure 10.3: This photo of a large watercolor painting by Joe Butler was shot with an Olympus E-10 under cloudy skies. On the left, notice the keystoning. On the right, keystoning was fixed using Photoshop Elements' perspective commands.

Bottom line: Shoot loose, but know the limits of what you can and cannot do with imaging software. Also, remember that anything you do later in software just adds to the time required to complete the shot.

Software Solutions: Changing an Object's Color or Texture

It's relatively easy to change an object's color or texture using image-processing software. Software programs such as Photoshop and Photoshop Elements offer several ways to do this.

For example, in order to change the color of the object shown below, professional photographer Peter Figen used Photoshop's Hue/Saturation controls.

I devote much space in my book *Photoshop Elements 2 Solutions* to the methods Peter used and other techniques for changing a product's color and, for that matter, texture.

A Basic Digital Photography Studio

Natural light is great to use for shooting your stuff, but it has its limitations. For one thing, you are at the mercy of the weather and time of day. Also, since light varies from minute to minute, it's nearly impossible to create consistent results from one shot to another.

At some point, if you are shooting a lot of stuff for work or even for fun, it really makes sense to invest in studio lights and other basic photo studio equipment.

In Chapter 2, I demonstrated how a studio's lighting setup can help make great portraits. And in Chapter 9, I showed how studio equipment can help produce "object" movies of products and other inanimate objects. Here are some more things to consider when it comes to photo studio shooting and equipment.

Digital Camera

Robert's opening shot of the bowl and balls was taken with a prosumer digital camera. For all practical purposes the shot could have been made with just about any digital camera, since Robert mostly relied on careful composition and beautiful light and used automatic settings.

However, for more flexibility and ease of use with studio lights, certain features in a digital camera are desirable. I went into detail on this subject (☞ "Matching Your Needs to a Camera" in Chapter 1). In brief, the key features to look for when shooting products and other small objects include: a PC synch outlet for a strobe trip cord, an accurate viewfinder, and macro and zoom lenses.

Studio Lighting

No studio is complete without a set of external lights, be they electronic strobes or continuous source lights. You can get away with two lights, but as you'll see in the following lighting techniques section, ideally you'll have three. (For more on studio lights, ☞ "Accessories That Make a Difference: External Artificial Lights" later in this chapter.)

Note: Your digital camera's built-in strobe has very limited use when it comes to shooting your stuff. Direct light—even if it is diffused—produces a flat, two-dimensional look as well as unwanted shadows. A built-in strobe, however, can be used with a *slave* to trigger an external strobe. (A slave is an electronic sensor that senses a burst of light from one strobe and triggers another strobe.)

Light Diffusion

Studio lights often require some sort of diffusion. Studio umbrellas are commonly used, as well as the specially built soft boxes introduced in Chapter 2 and used throughout this book. Studio lights can also be aimed through translucent, white plexiglass or other similar types of diffusion material. White foam board or commercial reflectors can also be used to bounce strobes or continuous light sources onto an object. (More on techniques later in the chapter.)

Strobe Meters

If you use electronic strobes rather than continuous light sources, it really helps to use a strobe meter to gauge the correct exposure, establish a certain lighting ratio, or ensure the lighting is uniform across the subject. Strobe meters aren't cheap, and start at a few hundred dollars. ("Accessories That Make a Difference: External Light Meters" in Chapter 8.) If a strobe meter is too much of an investment, try exposing by trial and error. Start with a mid-range f-stop, say f/5.6; make a flash exposure, and then use your LCD and/or histogram to view the results. If necessary, adjust the f-stop up or down according to the results. Depending on the amount of ambient light present, your shutter speed will have a minimal effect, if any, on the exposure. If you are using an SLR-type digital camera with a focal plane shutter just make sure you've chosen a shutter speed within the synch range.

Backgrounds

The simplest background is often the best. Stock up on white foam board, or keep your eyes open—as explained earlier in the chapter—for castaway objects that contain an interesting surface. Every professional photo studio is well supplied with rolls of white (or colored) seamless paper, ranging in width from 3 feet to 10 feet, available at camera stores for $30 or less. It's handy to construct a seamless paper holder with a pole and two adjustable light stands. You can also hang the pole and seamless paper from a ceiling, or forego the holder completely and just tape the seamless paper to a wall or drape it over a couple chairs.

Tripods

Non SLR-focal plane digital cameras often have extremely fast strobe-synch speeds. (SLR-focal plane cameras often synch at $1/250^{th}$ of a second or slower.) This makes it possible to shoot without any chance of camera-induced blur and reduces the need for a tripod. However, tripods are useful for other reasons: they facilitate precise framing and enable exposure bracketing while ensuring that one frame to the next is the same.

Supplies

Every professional photographer has a closet full of indispensable consumable supplies that make their shooting go easier. Commonly used supplies include gaffer tape, tacks or pushpins, clothespins, double-sided tape, compressed air, and dulling spray (found at art supply stores) to dull shiny objects and reduce glare.

> **Note:** To achieve the appropriate degree of image quality from your digital camera, review the "Maximizing Image Quality" sections in Chapters 7 and 8.

Accessories That Make a Difference: External Artificial Lights

Built-in digital camera strobes often do not provide enough flexibility for a photo shoot. For more control, you can use external artificial lights, from which you have several options.

Dedicated Strobes

These connect to the camera and use their own power sources. They can be detached and aimed independently from the camera. However, since they are still plugged into your camera, they work with the camera's metering systems to regulate the exact shutter speed, lens aperture, and flash intensity. (A word of warning: a digital camera contains sensitive electronic circuitry and before you connect strobes—especially older ones designed for mechanical sync contacts, or any external electronic equipment—to it, be sure the components are compatible.) Shown below on the left is the Nikon Speedlight SB-80DX, which works with the Nikon D-100 and other Nikon digital cameras. There are also specialized dedicated strobes used for extreme close-ups. They often have medical, scientific, or underwater applications. Shown below on the right is a photo of the Nikon Macro Speedlight attached to the lens of a Nikon D100 digital camera.

Studio Strobes

These don't tie into your camera's metering system and therefore require you to calculate exposure manually, with either a strobe meter or by trial and error. Most of them run on AC power, but battery-powered alternatives exist. Some units include the power as part of the strobe light itself. More common is a power pack that powers up to four strobe heads and is connected by a cable (such as the one shown, top of next page, on the far left).

Studio strobes give you the most power and control of all the external light options, but they are also the most expensive. You'll need a way to trigger the strobes when you release your shutter. This is no problem if your digital camera has a PC synch outlet—many prosumer models and all professional models have one. Just plug in a release cord that connects your camera to your strobes. If your camera doesn't have such an outlet—and most consumer-level digital cameras don't—then you can trigger the strobes via your built-in strobe with a slave attached to the external strobes (in the middle), or use an adaptor that turns the *hot shoe* (the small metal base for camera-synchronized attachments mounted on top of many digital cameras) into a PC synch adaptor (shown on right).

I know, mention the term "studio strobes" and many people hear the ka-ching! of the cash register. Sure, it's easy to spend more on a set of studio strobes than a digital camera, but there are low-cost alternatives as well. Used equipment, for example, is always a good option. Check out eBay, other Internet auction sites, or the bulletin board at your local camera store. Renting equipment as you need it is also a good way to go. I've also noticed more and more companies advertising complete lighting packages—often consisting of three strobes lights, stands, and reflectors for under $300. Because these packages are marketed specially to digital camera users who have a lower power requirement than their film camera counterparts, such packages are priced very competitively. (See **www.shooting-digital.com** for links.)

Continuous Source Lights

Often referred to as flood lights, continuous source lights are an alternative to electronic strobes. I talked in detail about this kind of lighting in Chapter 2, "Shooting Great Portraits." Continuous source lights have many advantages over electronic strobes, and they are often much cheaper. I've also seen floodlight packages such as the one shown below—complete with three lights, reflectors, umbrellas, and stands—for under $200. You don't need a strobe meter to make an accurate exposure, and you can see the effects of the lights in real time. Most of these lights generate heat, which is more of a problem when you are shooting portraits of people. Large continuous source lights, which you'll need for shooting very large objects, draw a lot more power than a strobe with the equivalent output. Again, there are many choices when it comes to purchasing continuous source lights and I recommend you go to **www.shooting-digital.com** for up-to-date information on this subject.

© Akces Media LLC

A Digital Studio in a Box

If the idea of assembling all the needed components of a digital studio sounds daunting, you might want to consider a self-contained studio such as MK Digital Direct's Photo-e-Box shown in Figure 10.4.

With the Photo-e-Box, you are limited to shooting objects that fit on a 10" × 13.5" stage. But this is a perfect size for jewelry, coins, small appliances, and household items. All you do is mount your digital camera to a special bracket (not all digital cameras are supported), power the built-in continuous source lights, position the object, and shoot. It's hard not to take a good picture. The drawbacks? Your images may be sharp and evenly lit, but they lack key emotional impact. For that, you'll need to use your own lighting setup and apply some of the techniques that we will discuss next. (For more on the Photo-e-Box and other models, go to **www.mkdigitaldirect.com**.)

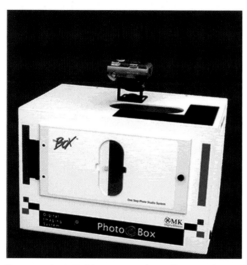

Figure 10.4: Self-contained studios such as the Photo-e-Box make it easier than ever to make consistently good studio shots of your stuff.

Studio Lighting Techniques

Using a studio lighting setup is a sure way to get consistent, professional-looking results. If you apply some of the basic skills that we will discuss here, you'll end up with images that come alive and actually evoke an emotional response from a viewer.

Getting the lighting setup just right can be tricky, but with a digital camera you can instantly see the effect of your efforts and adjust accordingly. People who might have shied away from using studio lights in the past will thrill at how quickly and easily lighting techniques can be mastered, and at how dramatically good lighting will improve their work.

Let's ground ourselves in some basic studio lighting techniques via some actual case studies.

Revealing Shape and Form

Good lighting not only helps reveals surface details but also helps conveys a sense of shape and form. (Shape is an outline of an object, while form is its three-dimensional aspect.)

Most of the objects that you shoot are cube-like (such as a camera, a book, or a computer CPU), spherical (such as a ball, an apple, or an egg), cylindrical (such as a bottle, a table leg, a boot, or a lamp shade) or, mostly likely, a combination of many different shapes (such as a table, a couch, or a razor).

The challenge is to convey 3-dimensional shapes using a 2-dimensional medium.

Shooting a Cube-Like Object

Figure 10.5 is a product shot taken by professional photographer Peter Figen with a professional digital camera, the Kodak DCS 760, at his Los Angeles studio. To give a sense of depth and dimension to this cube-like object, Peter lit it in such a way as to produce three discernable tonal values. The front of the camera is a medium value, the side is a darker value, and the top of the camera is a lighter value.

(By the way, you can also use the basic lighting techniques shown in this example to shoot a spherical object such as a baseball. By varying the intensity of the lights you'll produce the necessary range of highlights and shadows that will reveal the spherical object's shape and form.)

Figure 10.5: This studio shot was taken by Peter Figen.

In order to do this, Peter used three strobes, as shown in Figure 10.6. The strobes on the right and left were encased with an extra small Chimera soft box and placed about 1-2 feet from the subject, and then angled as shown. (Chimera makes a popular line of soft boxes in a variety of sizes.) For the top light, Peter used a slightly larger Chimera soft box and hung it on a boom at a slight angle about 1-2 feet away from the subject. The strobe on the right was set to a lower power than the other two strobes—hence the darker values on the right side of the subject. The strobe on the top, because it was diffused through a larger soft box, was slightly weaker than the strobe on the left. (You can control intensity of light by dialing the strobe power up or down, and to a degree by moving the strobe closer to or farther away from the subject, but this changes the quality of light.) The background is white seamless paper draped over a stand, with the object centered about 3 feet in front of it. The camera was mounted on a tripod and aimed slightly down at the subject.

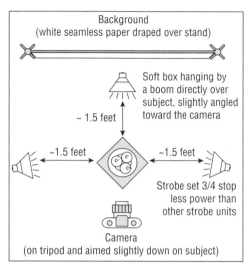

Figure 10.6: The lighting setup for Peter's shot.

Note: A three-light setup roughly like the one diagrammed in Figure 10.6 can be used to successfully photograph just about any object you can imagine. Of course, the devil is in the details. Objects come in different sizes, shapes, and textures. The trick is to vary the lights' angles, relative intensity, diffusion, and distance from the subject until you get it right. The beauty of shooting digital is that you can see the results in near-real time.

Peter suggests this general rule of thumb when it comes to lighting: Small objects are often best lit with small light sources–hence his use of a small light box for the camera shot shown here. If your light source is too large or too close to the subject, then the light striking the subject is flat and produces a low-contrast image. Conversely, if you are shooting large objects, you'll need larger strobes or soft boxes in order to give the shot punch.

The other thing that makes this photo work is the placement of the camera Peter used to take the shot. Peter used a lens with a focal length of about 135mm (35mm equivalent) so that the subject of the shot was slightly compressed. (Peter says there are times when a wide-angle lens will make a shot more dynamic and interesting.) His camera was mounted on a tripod and aimed slightly downward so a hint of the top of the Fuji camera is visible.

This shot was one of many Peter made for a PriceGrabber.com ad and he worked under rigid specifications. Although Peter was instructed to shoot all the products for the ad straight on, the careful lighting and slight angling of the camera resulted in an interesting shot instead of what would otherwise have been a fairly ordinary photo. The shot really accentuates Fuji's industrial design and makes you want to reach out and pick up the camera and touch it. At least it does that for me!

Peter offers a few other tips when shooting products like this. Always keep a can of compressed air for removing dust and lint from the product. Clean off any fingerprints with a clean, soft cotton cloth. It's really difficult to remove fingerprints later, even with Photoshop. If anything on the product rotates (an on/off button, for example), make sure it is in the correct position for the shot. Again, this kind of problem is difficult to fix later with Photoshop.

Bottom line: Control the effects of your lights through angle, distance, size, and relative power output. Experiment and use your digital camera's LCD to see if you got it right.

Shooting a Cylindrical Object

Figure 10.7 on the following page shows a product shot taken by Peter's studio-mate, Wendi Marafino, for a David's Shoes catalog. Wendi used a professional digital studio camera to make the shot—a LightPhase back mounted on a Mamiya RZ medium-format camera. The camera was mounted on a tripod and aimed slightly up at the subject. As with Peter's shot, the background is white seamless paper draped over a stand, with the object centered about 3 feet in front of it.

To give a 3-dimensional look to the photo of the boot, a largely cylindrically shaped object, Wendi used the same three-light setup described previously. However, she moved the two main lights nearly parallel with the boot, as shown below in Figure 10.7. This lighting produced the darker strip that runs down the middle of the boot. The darker core is what produces the sense of roundness. The third soft box is again placed on a boom directly over the subject; this provides a partial fill so that the core shadow is not too exaggerated. (This technique can be applied to wine bottles, coffee pots, etc., with similar results.)

Bottom line: Differently shaped objects require different lighting techniques.

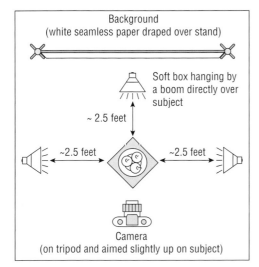

Figure 10.7: The lighting setup for Wendi Marafino's shot, shown on the following page.

Figure 10.7: This studio shot was taken by Wendi Marafino.

Revealing Texture

Good lighting techniques also reveal texture in an object. Take the shot shown on the left in Figure 10.8, again shot by Wendi Marafino for a David's Shoes catalog. Her lighting setup is shown on the right. The camera placement is the same as in Figure 10.7, as are the background and the overhead strobe. But note how the two main lights are placed about 1.5 feet on each side of the bag and angled at about 70 degrees. By angling the light this way, the texture was highlighted. If Wendi had simply aimed the lights directly at the bag, the shape and color of the bag would be illuminated but not the nuances of the leather. This lighting will work equally as well with other objects such as woven baskets and cloth, etc. Wendi adds that some materials, such as dark suede or black velvet, absorb so much of the light that you'll need to use more strobe power to get good results. She also says that sometimes, when the texture is particularly fine and contrasty, moiré patterns can result. There isn't much you can do about this but shoot slightly out of focus or attempt to fix them later in Photoshop, which can be difficult.

Bottom line: Reveal texture by angling your lights. Don't aim the lights directly at the subject.

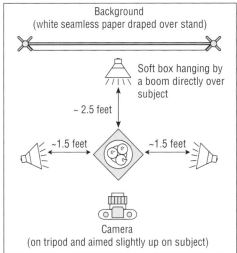

Figure 10.8: Photo by Wendi Marafino (left). The lighting setup for Wendi's shot (right).

Controlling the Quality of Light

Lee-Carraher Photography specializes in shooting gems and jewelry. For 17 years Craig Carraher and Tinnee Lee used film. Recently they have included digital, which has greatly streamlined their work. Often they rent a professional digital camera such as the Nikon D1X. For the shot shown in Figure 10.9, however, they used a prosumer Nikon Coolpix 990 and a set of external strobes. Craig did most of the shooting, while Tinnee handled the lighting and placement of the objects on the background.

Figure 10.9: Craig Carraher took this shot with a Nikon Coolpix 990. ("Equestrians" jewelry is by Ann Marie Fine Jewelry)

The background for Figure 10.9 was a sheet of frosted glass placed above black velvet. Such glass can be purchased from framing shops and black velvet from fabric stores. On other occasions, Lee-Carraher uses frosted glass directly on black high-gloss cardstock, available from art supply stores.

Three external Speedotron 2403 strobes were used: one was placed to the right, one to the left, and one above and behind the subject, shot through a cutout in black paper, creating the soft spotlight effect. (See the diagram shown in Figure 10.10.) Sometimes, to create the spotlight effect, they use a special fiber-optic system, which directs the light precisely where they want. The cutout method is less expensive, but takes more time to set up.

Just as important as the physical placement of the strobes is the way Craig controlled the quality of light coming off the strobes. He didn't use a commercial soft box, which I've often recommended throughout this book. Instead, he created a variation of one, which provided him with greater control over the quality of light. The diffusion material was 1/8" × 16" × 20" near-white translucent plexiglass placed in front of the strobe heads with a custom-built reticulated arm. To vary the quality of light, Craig moves the plexiglass back and forth in relationship to the strobe. For example, if he wants the light source to produce a sharper, more contrasty, less diffused image, he positions it closer to the strobe head, further away from the jewelry. The further away the plexiglass is from strobe and closer to the subject, the more the subject reflects the diffused light of the plexiglass, creating a more diffused look, such as it did for this shot. Craig says he can't get this control with a soft box, because the soft box has a fixed distance between the strobe head and the diffusion material.

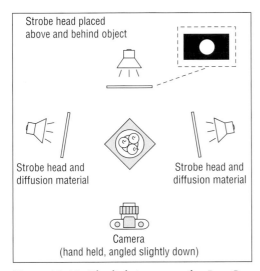

Figure 10.10: The lighting setup for Lee-Carraher's shot.

Since the Coolpix doesn't have a PC-synch connection, the external strobes were triggered using the Coolpix's built-in strobe and a slave. A neutral density filter placed over the camera's built-in flash diminished the effect of the strobe, yet it was enough to trigger the external strobes, which were hooked up to a slave. Furthermore, Craig placed neutral density filters over the studio strobes to reduce their light output. Even at minimum power, the professional strobes were too powerful to produce a proper exposure for the digital camera.

Craig used his camera's manual mode and set his f-stop to 11, as determined by an external strobe meter, and confirmed the setting with the LCD preview display. He set the shutter speed to 1/1000th of a second. With this speed it was possible for him to handhold the camera without fear of camera-induced blur. It also made framing more fluid.

Since the shots were destined for the Web, Craig saved the images in the JPEG file format. He left his white balance set to automatic and his ISO at 100, the camera's lowest setting. In fact, it would have been useful if the camera had been less sensitive. Then Craig wouldn't have had to reduce the power of the strobes with the neutral density filters. (Strobes built especially for the lower power requirements of digital cameras are available. See **www. shooting-digital.com**.)

Bottom line: Control the quality of light by moving diffusion material in and out relative to the light.

The Art of Composition

Placing more than one subject in a shot is a good way to efficiently and economically communicate a larger message. Some online auctions permit you to include only one free photo with your listing, so knowing how to effectively place multiple items in a shot can be very useful.

According to Tinnee, styling is what makes one photo stand out from another. When she works with more than one piece of jewelry, as she did in the jewelry shown in Figure 10.11 and Figure 10.12, Tinnee tries to place them in a way that they interact with each other and create interesting negative space. (By the way, these shots were taken with the same camera and lighting set shown previously in Figure 10.10.) There is no hard and fast rule about how to achieve this interaction, so she experiments until she finds a position that works. Again, the instant feedback of digital cameras makes this experimentation much easier to do.

Figure 10.11: Photo by Craig Carraher, layout by Tinnee Lee. ("Eternity band" rings by Ann Marie Fine Jewelry)

Figure 10.12: Photo by Craig Carraher, layout by Tinnee Lee. (Earrings by Ann Marie Fine Jewelry)

Tinnee acknowledges that it would be much easier just to place items side by side, symmetrically, as many catalog photographers do. The resulting shots impart information about the items displayed, but there is little or no emotion or dynamic tension. With the necklace shown earlier in Figure 10.9, the easiest way to set up the shot would have been to just to make it lie in a straight line or a circle. However, by forming it into an "S" curve, she broke the image plane and made the shot more interesting.

For complicated arrangements that require holding the jewelry in place, Tinnee uses Lectro Stik Wax, available at art supply stores. For heavy objects she uses epoxy, a commonly found commercial adhesive. Normally both the wax and the epoxy can be easily removed by the jeweler. (To see more of the jewelry shown here, go to **www.annmariefinejewelry.com**.)

Bottom line: Lighting is only part of the story. Successful shots of multiple-object images require thoughtful placement.

Note: For those of you who are really serious about the composition and arrangement of objects, I refer you to *Arranging Things: A Rhetoric of Object Placement* (Stonebridge Press, 2003) by Leonard Koren, one of the contributors to this book.

Pushing the Envelope

The basic three-light setup described earlier—one on each side and one in the back—will nearly always give you consistently good results (as long as you also take into consideration other important details such as camera angle, exposure, and focus, etc.).

As you get more comfortable with your basic lighting skills, you may want to try more sophisticated lighting setups. Figure 10.13, shot by Robert Birnbach with a Nikon Coolpix 990, shows one example.

Figure 10.13: This photo was taken by Robert Birnbach with a Nikon Coolpix 990 using some fancy lighting and an unusual background.

Robert used a combination of two electronic strobes and a small tungsten light source covered with a blue filter to balance it to daylight. (His lighting setup is shown in Figure 10.14.) Robert placed one strobe (on the left in the diagram) with a blue gel under the bubbled glass background. Another strobe encased in a small soft box is positioned to the far right side of the bottle. Robert used neutral density filters—as Craig Carraher did in a previous example—to cut the power of the strobes beyond the lowest power setting. The tungsten light is tightly focused as a spot from the top left and creates subtle but important specular highlights on some of the objects inside the bottle.

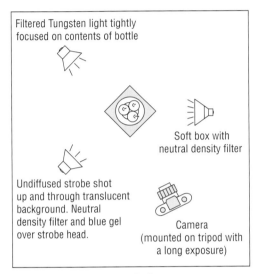

Filtered Tungsten light tightly focused on contents of bottle

Soft box with neutral density filter

Undiffused strobe shot up and through translucent background. Neutral density filter and blue gel over strobe head.

Camera (mounted on tripod with a long exposure)

Figure 10.14: Robert's lighting setup.

Since the tungsten light wasn't nearly as powerful as the strobes, even with the neutral density filters, Robert set his Nikon to manual mode and set the shutter speed to 1 full second. The camera was mounted on a tripod and the room was dark with no modeling lights. He set his f-stop to 8, which gave the strobes a proper exposure. (He used a Sekonic Digital Pro meter to measure both the strobe exposure and ambient tungsten light.) If he hadn't used a long exposure, then the filtered tungsten light wouldn't have made any difference.

Robert's Coolpix 990 doesn't have a PC synch outlet. Instead of doing what Craig did in an earlier example, he used black tape to attach an optical slave directly to the camera's built-in flash. He then connected the optical slave to a synch cord, which plugged into his strobe power packs. Since the built-in flash was fully covered with tape, it didn't add any unwanted light to the shot at all.

Bottom line: Once you start experimenting with your digital camera and studio lights, the possibilities are nearly endless.

Shooting Flat Objects with Lights

Documenting a printed portfolio or other works of art on paper is a common task for digital photographers. If you are shooting individual pieces of flat art, you can lay them on the floor or mount the work to a wall using adhesives, double-sided tape, or other non-destructive methods. If shooting artwork on the floor, watch for shadows cast by you, the camera, power cords, furniture, or lights.

A very effective and easy-to-use lighting and staging setup up is shown in Figure 10.15. Depending on the size of the artwork, you can usually get away with two 500-Watt flood lights (more wattage for larger works). Make sure the light falls evenly across the entire surface. If you choose to diffuse the light, make sure the diffusion material is flame-retardant or be sure to keep it a safe distance from the hot lights. Position lights to either side of the camera, no more than 45 degrees. If there is glare, move the lights closer to the plane of the work so they strike at more of an angle. Try to remove frame glass. If this isn't possible, try varying the angle of the lights to avoid unwanted reflections. A polarizing filter may help to some degree.

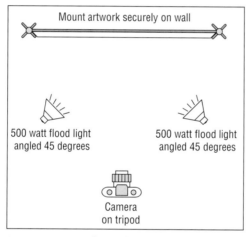

Figure 10.15: A basic lighting setup for shooting flat art.

Keep these points in mind when shooting:

- Secure the artwork carefully so it won't slip or slide.
- Use a tripod.
- Square the artwork by using the controls of the tripod, using the viewfinder frame as reference. (Keystoning will occur if you are angled up or down in relationship to the art. It is more pronounced if you use wide focal lengths.)
- Focus carefully. Your autofocus system may not work if the art contains little contrast. Switch to manual mode if your digital camera has one.
- Traditionally, film photographers used a gray card placed in the scene to determine the correct exposure. You can do this if you want, but with a digital camera you can just as well bracket your exposures until the LCD or the histogram indicates that the exposure is okay.
- If your camera has aperture priority mode, set it to the smallest f-stop for maximum depth of field.

Know Your Camera: Built-in Flash

Built-in flashes are features of nearly all digital cameras. Although they consume camera battery power and are limited in coverage when compared to external studio strobes and dedicated strobes (flashes that attach to the camera), they are invaluable in getting shots that might otherwise have been impossible. Since they are dedicated to the camera, exposure is automatically calculated. Most digital cameras also have indicators to inform you when you are within range. (Of course, a quick look at the LCD will also tell you if your flash was adequate enough.)

Many digital cameras extend the functionality of the built-in strobe by including a red-eye reduction mode, which flashes the strobe (or focus-assist light) several times in rapid succession to dilate a subject's pupils before tripping the shutter. Some digital cameras offer a "slow sync" flash mode, which combines the built-in flash with slow shutter speeds to adequately capture both the subject and the background in low-light situations. You'll have to consult your camera manual for the specific features of your digital camera.

A word of warning: some built-in flashes won't cover the widest focal length, and therefore result in vignetting around the edges of a frame. There is nothing you can do about this except avoid using the flash and the widest focal length setting at the same time.

Many digital cameras have flash exposure compensation capability. This feature allows you to increase or reduce flash output. If it is increased, the subject appears brighter; reducing it darkens the main subject. Many built-in flashes tend toward the "hot" side, so reducing flash output often results in a better-exposed shot.

You can also "customize" the output of your flash by placing diffusion material over it. Try different materials such as tissue or frosted plastic. You can also simply place your finger partly over the strobe to reduce its output and soften the light.

Shooting Past the Boundaries

11

In this chapter we'll move beyond the more clearly defined boundaries of the previous chapters. We'll explore how digital cameras make it possible to do old things in new ways, and we'll see how some photographers are responding to the creative license that comes with shooting digital.

Chapter Contents

Steven Rosenbaum

Shooting Beyond Visible Light

Figure 11.1 and the chapter opener shot show images taken by Steven Rosenbaum using a Minolta DiMAGE 7 prosumer digital camera with a Wratten 87C filter. This filter effectively blocks most visible light and allows infrared radiation to pass through to the digital camera's sensor. As you can see in Steve's photo below, green foliage glowed white and sunny skies turned dark for a spectacular effect.

Figure 11.1: Steven Rosenbaum's infrared shot was taken with a Minolta DiMAGE 7 digital camera.

There is nothing new about infrared photography, but in the past it required special film—as well as a filter—to capture infrared light, and since getting the correct exposure was particularly tricky, the results were often hit or miss.

Many digital cameras are sensitive to infrared light, but not all are. Steve's Minolta obviously is, but the newer DiMAGE 7i and 7Hi are built in such a way that the infrared is blocked. (Most digital camera sensors are covered with an internal IR cut-off filter. This is done to minimize non-visible light from contaminating visible light images. However, these filters vary from model to model and digital cameras that contain ineffective IR cut off filters are the ones best suited for IR photography.) Other popular digital cameras that are "infrared-friendly" include the Sony 707 and 717 (limited to nighttime IR shooting), the Olympus E-10 and E-20, and the Nikon Coolpix 950. There are many more digital cameras on this list. For a fairly comprehensive but not complete list you can also go to **http://cliffshade.com/dpfwiw/ir.htm#testing**.

You can easily check for yourself to see whether your digital camera is sensitive to infrared light. A very simple way to do this is to use a TV, VCR, DVD, or audio remote control and point it at your digital camera in a darkened room. Turn on the camera's LCD viewer. Then, activate the remote device. If you can see a bright point of light in the LCD, then your digital camera is ready for taking these dramatic images.

Besides using an infrared-friendly digital camera, you will also need a filter that covers your lens. There are several filters available that block visible light but transmit infrared, made by various manufactures including Hoya, Tiffin, B+W, and Wratten. Two particularly popular filters are the Hoya R72 and the Wratten 89B. Other filters are available that block the visible wavelengths of light shorter than the infrared in varying amounts. Each produces a slightly different effect depending on the digital camera it is used with, so you will have to exploit your digital camera's endless capacity for experimentation and find one to your liking.

If your digital camera lens has a threaded lens barrel there should be no problem finding a filter at your local camera store or on the Web. If your lens doesn't have a threaded barrel you can buy some gelatin filters and cut them to size, and then tape them in place in front of the lens. You can also use special adapters, but they often cost as much as the filter itself.

Shooting infrared shots is fairly straightforward. Just set your digital camera to autoexposure and autofocus. Since all infrared filters are very dense, you should expect a longer than normal exposure. (Steve's exposure, for Figure 11.1, was 1 second at f/3.5) For this reason a tripod is recommended, but not required. Increasing the ISO can help produce a faster shutter speed but may add electronic noise to the image.

Bottom line: If your digital camera is infrared capable, an entirely new world of photography is open to you.

Shooting Digital Underwater

Digital cameras make it easier than ever to create images that reveal the mysterious underwater world. Figure 11.2, for example, shows an image taken by Bruce Avera Hunter of a whale shark bathed in a majestic cathedral light. Bruce took the shot in the Sea of Cortez with a Nikon Coolpix 990 digital camera cased in an Ikelite underwater housing. He used an attached Ikelite DS-50 strobe positioned about 3 feet off the camera, angled inward about 45 degrees. (An onboard strobe light strikes underwater particles straight on and produces distracting light scatter, therefore it is better to use natural light or an angled externally mounted strobe). Bruce used his camera's automatic exposure and focus settings.

Figure 11.2: This majestic image was taken with a Nikon Coolpix 990 by Bruce Avera Hunter.

Shooting underwater can be tricky. Water acts as a filter and absorbs the different colors of light at different rates, with the longer red wavelengths being absorbed first. The deeper you go, the bluer the remaining light gets. Not only do digital cameras give you instant feedback, but also you can quickly and easily adjust white balance and ISO settings to adapt to the rapidly varying conditions typical of underwater shooting. If you use a memory card with enough capacity, you never face the constant worry of film users—surfacing to carry out the laborious task of removing the camera from an underwater housing and replacing a roll of film.

Traditionally, one of the biggest hurdles to underwater photography was the limited availability and cost of special waterproof equipment. This is not the case with digital cameras. Just about every digital camera manufacturer offers an underwater casing for one or more of their digital cameras. Third-party competition has driven the price down to reasonable levels and these prices will continue to drop as more and more people appreciate the rewards of shooting digital underwater.

Bottom line: Even if you never considered shooting photos underwater with a film camera, think again now that you've gone digital. Digital cameras—combined with some sort of water protection—make it easy to take rewarding photos underwater.

For more information on shooting underwater photos with digital cameras I suggest these two sites:

* New Zealand's Seafriends Marine Conservation and Education Centre: www.seafriends.org.nz/phgraph/index.htm
* Canon's Digital Underwater Photography Guide: http://web.canon.jp/Imaging/uwphoto/page/01-e.html

Accessories That Make a Difference: Underwater Casings

Special underwater casings such as the one Bruce Avera Hunter used to house his Nikon Coolpix 990 are available for just about every digital camera model. Some casings are elaborate and cost $200 and up. They are precision built to fit a very specific digital camera model, and are often rated to several hundred feet below the surface. Other casings are no more than a fancy zip-lock bag and cost as little as $25 and up. Still, they are perfectly adequate for shallow dives, and you can also use them to provide protection in inclement weather or even on river-rafting trips.

Regardless of which housing you use:
* Test it for leaks without the camera inside.
* Prevent fogging of the lens with silica packets or anti-fog fluid on the lens. (Digital cameras get warm, which may increase the humidity within the relatively cool casing.)
* Wipe yourself dry and then thoroughly dry the casing before opening.
* Use fresh water to clean. Saltwater is anathema to electronic equipment.
* If the casing uses flexible O rings, they must be removed and cleaned regularly.
* Remember not to be misled by following only the specifications that use terms such as "waterproof" or "water-resistant." The important specification is the depth rating. Usually the deeper the rating is, the more expensive the housing will be.

Figure 11.3: These three aerial photos were taken by Scott Haefner, with a digital camera mounted to a kite string.

Shooting Digital from the Sky

Digital cameras aren't found only underwater; they are in the sky as well. The three photos shown in Figure 11.3 were taken by photographer Scott Haefner with a digital camera mounted to a kite string.

Scott, whose day job is working for the United States Geological Survey (USGS), spends just about every weekend shooting digital kite photos. He uses an off-the-shelf Nikon Coolpix 5000 mounted to a custom-designed rig, shown in Figure 11.4, hanging from a kite string with the "Picavet"-style suspension device shown in Figure 11.5. Cords run through pulleys at the four points of the cross and through pulleys attached at two points to the kite string, keeping the camera level. The entire camera rig weighs about 2.2 pounds. A model airplane controller with four channels controls the movements of the camera and triggers the shutter release. Although Scott made his own rig, commercial rigs are available (see the note below).

Note: To view more of Scott's kite photographs, go to **scotthaefner.com/kap**. For general information on kite photography, go to **www.fortunecity.com/marina/nelson/479/index.html**.

Kite aerial photography has been around a long time, but digital cameras have revolutionized the sport here in the U.S. as well as in Europe and Japan. Film cameras required frequently bringing the rig down to change rolls—not an easy task. With a large enough memory card, you may not have to bring the rig down at all until you finish shooting for the day. With digital cameras, gone also are the costs associated with taking and developing a bad photo.

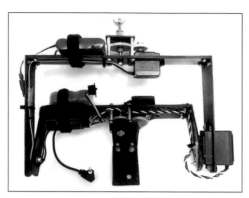

Figure 11.4: This self-built rig is used by Scott to mount his digital camera.

Figure 11.5: Scott's "Picavet"-style suspension cable holds the rig.

To get the shots of the building and the swimming pool, Scott launched his $200 kite (shown in Figure 11.6) about 100 feet in the air, where he caught a strong and stable wind. Then he attached his camera rig to the kite line with the Picavet-style suspension cable setup. He let the kite out another 200-250 feet and started snapping shots with the remote control. (The pool shot was taken at a lower altitude.)

To get the shot of the ocean coastline—the one that looks like it includes the curvature of the earth—Scott used an 8mm (35mm equivalent) fisheye attachment lens zoomed into a 15mm (35mm equivalent) focal length.

For these and many similar shots, Scott sets the focal length of his digital camera to its widest angle, 28mm (35mm equivalent). He uses manual focus set to infinity, sets the camera to aperture priority with matrix metering, and chooses a wide-open aperture to ensure he gets the proper exposure with the fastest shutter speed possible. If the light is very bright, he stops the aperture down a few stops to get a sharper image. He leaves the camera at its default 100 ISO but acknowledges that increasing the ISO during cloudy days would be a good way to maintain a desired shutter speed. He doesn't depend on the automatic white balance mode; instead, he generally uses one of the appropriate presets.

Figure 11.6: Scott Haefner and his kite.

Once the camera is in the air, getting the right shot is tricky and takes practice. Generally Scott can see the camera's orientation from the ground and knows roughly where the lens is pointed. Sometime he uses binoculars to get a better view of his camera dangling in the sky. He doesn't worry about making a bad photo. He uses a 256 MB CompactFlash memory card and, even though he saves his images in the highest quality JPEG format, he can fit over 140 shots on a single card.

Scott has never crashed a kite and rig, but once, when the wind suddenly died, his rig fell into a tree and he spent the good part of an evening untangling it. He's usually more inconvenienced by security guards who ask him to take his rig and go elsewhere.

Night Shots

Night shots are often very dramatic, and with a digital camera they are also relatively easy to get. I'm aware that many people coming from the film world look at shooting in the dark of night with some trepidation. You never know for sure if you got exactly the shot you expected. But with digital cameras, and the instant feedback they provide, you can take more chances and push the boundaries, doing things you might not have otherwise considered doing.

Let's look at a few really different examples to illustrate this point.

Figure 11.7 was taken by Rudy Burger with a Canon D-60 prosumer digital camera. It's a photo of his daughter Mady, taken in a Parisian hotel room at the end of a long, fun-filled day. The only light was a candle, placed near Mady's bed. Knowing that a flash would ruin the idyllic ambience, Rudy placed his camera on a pillow near his daughter, boosted the ISO to 400, and used the camera's self-timer to get the shot. (Most digital cameras have a self-timer and using it in situations like this is a good alternative to a cable release. Not only are cable releases often an expensive accessory, if not used carefully they can potentially jar the camera and introduce motion blur.)

Figure 11.7: Rudy Burger shot this candle lit shot with a Canon D-60 set to self-timer.

Some night shots are more dramatic than others, such as the one shown in Figure 11.8. Chester Simpson was driving to his home in northern Virginia on the night of September 13, 2001 when he saw a perfect overview of the 9/11 damage to the Pentagon building. He pulled off the highway and set up his tripod and mounted his Canon D-30 digital camera. He set the camera to automatic exposure, turned noise reduction on, and boosted his ISO to 400. Seconds before he tripped the shutter, construction workers exposed a smoldering fire and the flames burst into the air. Within minutes the flames were extinguished, but not before Chester got this memorable shot. Shutter speed was 1/4 of a second at f/4.

What I find remarkable, besides the content of the shot itself, is the relatively low amount of noise in Chester's image, especially for such a high ISO and long exposure. Many digital cameras such as Chester's D-30 provide a noise-reduction setting. With some cameras you must activate the setting; with others it is automatically turned on for very slow shutter-speed settings. Generally, noise reduction engages a process called *dark current subtraction* whereby a "dark" frame is shot along with "normal" shot. Then the camera intelligently combines the two frames, and subtracts the noise in the dark frame from the normal frame, producing an image with much less noise.

Figure 11.8: Chester Simpson shot this dramatic shot of the Pentagon damage at night with a Canon D-30.

Here is a checklist of things to keep in mind when shooting most night shots:

- Use a tripod, unless you like (or intentionally want) really wild, blurry shots!
- Use the camera's self-timer or a cable release cord to minimize camera shake.
- Turn off or don't activate the camera's flash. Unless the object you are shooting is within 15-20 feet, it won't do any good anyway.
- Start with your white balance setting set to automatic. Then, if you aren't satisfied with the results, and if your digital camera allows, experiment with different settings.
- Increase the ISO as needed, keeping in mind that the higher the ISO, the more the image degrades. (Noise-reduction methods continue to improve, so one day this will be less of an issue.)
- If your autofocus system doesn't work well in low light—and many don't—switch it off and use the manual mode.
- Start with autoexposure mode. If that doesn't produce a useable image, switch to manual mode if you can, and try different settings until you get it right.

Some digital cameras, such as the Sony 707 and 717, provide a night-shot mode. In this mode you can actually take photos of scenes barely or not at all visible to the naked eye. The Sony cameras, for example, do this by physically moving the infrared blocking filter from in front of the CCD and augmenting the existing IR light with two infrared LEDs on the front of the Carl Zeiss lens. The result is a monochromatic image with a strong green cast. (Think night-vision goggles.)

Bottom line: When shooting digital, don't let the dark intimidate you! Okay, so what if you don't get the shot the first time. Try again with a different setting. You'll be amazed at the world that opens up to you.

Digital Grid Photos

If you're working with a consumer-level digital camera, another boundary you may need to shoot past is your camera's limited resolution. Shots that look fine at a smaller size (print or on-screen) may not look so great when blown up. Figures 11.9 and 11.10 illustrate one creative solution to this problem by the New York photographer and designer, Jorge Colombo. The figures show a series of related digital images carefully arranged in a 4 × 4 grid using Photoshop. Each image is distinct and interesting, but viewed as a whole, all 16 images also add up to make a complete picture.

Jorge's digital grid photos have appeared in many publications including *Smart Money, YM, The New York Times,* and the *Village Voice.*

Jorge uses two relatively low-resolution digital cameras for his professional work: the Fuji MX-2700 and the Fuji FinePix 6800. The Fuji cameras are both small and lightweight and elegantly designed (important for a designer). Jorge takes one or the other camera everywhere he goes.

Theoretically, a single image from this kind of camera wouldn't reproduce well if blown up to the full-page treatment such images often get in a magazine. But Jorge has circumvented this limitation with his grid technique, effectively increasing the resolution simply by including a lot of images on a page.

"I also find it hard to say what I want with just one image," says Jorge, and indeed his work is almost film-like, building a narrative based on a collection of images rather than a single shot.

He doesn't take lights, a makeup crew, or an assistant. It's more casual that way, he explains. "I'm more like a tourist." He rarely plans his shooting sessions, instead going with what presents itself and keeping his eyes and mind open to the unexpected. Most of the time he leaves his digital camera settings at automatic and saves his images as JPEGs. If the exposure or color is off, Jorge fixes it later in Photoshop. "Knowing what software can and cannot do is very important to me," he explains. "It frees me to pay more attention to my shooting and not worry whether everything is perfect."

Jorge comes from the world of film, like many professional photographers, but doesn't care if he ever uses a darkroom again. "I used to find it so frustrating," he says, "when I'd shoot film, and then have to wait to see what I got. It would be like a musician playing a note and having to wait several hours or days before he heard it."

Pushing the musician analogy further, Jorge explains that another reason he is thrilled with shooting digital is cost. "With film, I was like a musician who had to pay five cents for every note. It adds up. And it limits you."

Bottom line: If you perceive a limitation, such as a camera's limited resolution, there usually is a creative way you can work around it.

Figure 11.9: Digital grid photo by Jorge Colombo.

Figure 11.10: "Becky 2002," a digital grid photo by Jorge Colombo.

Software Solutions: Removing Noise and Other Artifacts

Some images produced by digital cameras suffer from electronic noise—tiny flaws in the image. These aberrations are caused in a variety of ways: sensors develop clusters of dead pixels, dust gets on the sensor, or dust and smudges get on the lens. Noise can also be caused by the high ISO settings used to shoot at night. Even high JPEG compression can cause unwanted artifacts, which show up as "blocks" and are especially obvious in flat areas of an image. Whatever the cause, they can often be cleaned up using imaging software. For example, Photoshop (or Photoshop Elements) offers a variety of options for cleaning images. The following before and after images demonstrate how the simple use of a Photoshop Dust & Scratches filter automatically cleaned up an image.

The following is more problematic. The flaw, which was caused by a dirty lens, is too big to effectively use the Photoshop filter. Instead, I used the Clone tool to sample nearby areas and apply them to the flawed area. This method is more time-consuming, but very effective.

There are other alternatives, of course, to Photoshop and Photoshop Elements, including general image-editing programs such as Picture It! and PaintShop Pro. There are also plug-ins for these programs, such as Image Doctor by Alien Skin, that do a very good job of cleaning up images. Another great standalone program that is specifically made for cleaning up images is Digital Ice by Applied Science Fiction.

Know Your Camera: Adjusting White Balance

All digital cameras have white balance control. Prosumer and professional digital cameras provide a variety of ways of customizing this control.

When the white balance is set to automatic—a normal default setting—a digital camera attempts to compensate for the natural variations in the quality of light. For example, if a digital camera discerns too much green in a scene, it attempts to find a balance between the three primary colors (red, green, and blue), resulting in a white object appearing white rather than green. It then goes on to use the calculation as a basis for which to balance the remaining colors in the image. This attempt to balance the light is all done with onboard computing, with various degrees of success. If there are multiple light sources with different color values, the automatic controls have trouble getting it right. In fact, if a scene has multiple color temperature light sources, there is NO perfect white balance setting—only the best compromise (and then a Photoshop fix).

In difficult cases such as this it's useful to operate a digital camera with more control over white balance settings. Nearly all prosumer digital cameras and all professional digital cameras offer specific white balance settings for a variety of lighting conditions. Some cameras express these conditions in the following terms: Incandescent, fluorescent, direct sunlight, flash, cloudy, shade, etc. Other digital cameras express the lighting in terms of the approximate color temperature, ranging (for example) from 3000°K (incandescent) to 8000°K (shady). The two images shown here illustrate this point. They show the same scene, shot with two different white balance settings. The first image was shot with an Auto white balance setting and the second image was set to Shade. Note how much "warmer" the shot on the next page is.

Preset or Custom modes provide a way to customize a white balance setting. This is done by placing a white or gray card in a scene and using it as a target to create a more precise white balance adjustment. (In the Zooming In section of this book, you'll see a very clever and precise way of creating a custom white balance setting using a special lens attachment.)

Some prosumer and professional digital cameras also have a white balance bracket mode that functions much like an exposure bracket mode: A series of 2-3 images is automatically taken with predetermined variations in the white balance setting.

Many professional photographers use custom settings to tweak or fine-tune the color produced by their digital camera. For example, if they are shooting outdoors on a sunny day, instead of setting for daylight (or 5200°K), they set the white balance to Cloudy or Shade (or a higher °K value). This technique produces a deliberate warm cast into an image. Conversely, if they want a cooler cast, they shoot a daylight shot with an Incandescent white balance setting (or a lower °K).

When white balance is inadvertently set wrong, you can fix the mistake later using image-processing software, but only to a degree. Even the simplest color correction can take time, so it's always best to get the white balance right in the first place. Of course, for creative purposes you can set your white balance wrong. But that's another story. (The film analogy to this was photographers purposely shooting tungsten film in daylight conditions, producing a very artsy look.)

If you save your image data in the RAW file format, keep in mind that white balance settings are only a guideline for post-processing software to refer to. If you have capable RAW software, you can actually dial in any white balance or color settings you want, without any loss of data.

Organizing and Sharing Digital Photos

This chapter outlines your options for transferring digital images from the camera into a form easily shared by others, either as hardcopy or purely in electronic form. It also suggests software solutions for organizing your digital images so they don't gather dust in some sort of electronic shoebox.

12

Chapter Contents

Direct to Print
Digital Camera to Computer
Organizing and Managing
    Digital Photos
Sharing Digital Photos

Mikkel Aaland

Direct to Print

Nothing can be simpler than taking your digital camera or memory storage card to a corner photo finishing store and letting someone else do all the work of printing for you. You don't need a computer or a printer of your own. Direct-to-print is about as close as you can get to the old days of dropping off film to be processed and printed.

Some of the vendors who offer these services print digital images on photo paper using traditional chemical processing. Others use high-quality inkjet printers or printers that use heat and dye techniques. Some use methods that are faster than others and sometimes the process is so slow you might as well come back the next day to pick up your prints. Some services also provide a CD, which contains backup copies of your image files so you can erase your memory card and start over.

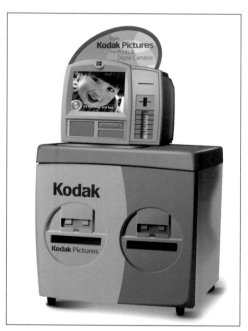

Figure 12.1: An Eastman Kodak Picture Maker Print Station accepts most digital camera memory cards, and your credit card.

Photo kiosks are also popping up everywhere and they offer similar convenience and service. Instead of dropping off your digital images for someone else to do the work, however, kiosks are set up in such a way that you do the work yourself. The Eastman Kodak Picture Maker Print Station (shown in Figure 12.1) is one such kiosk. The kiosk is set up so consumers can zoom/crop, eliminate red-eye, adjust colors, and print up to 8" × 10" photo-quality prints on to top-quality Kodak paper, either through the kiosk itself or at a retailer's digital photo lab. It also allows consumers to write images to a Kodak Picture CD. When the consumer is finished, they will have the option to pay for the entire transaction by credit card. Other similar types of customer-controlled kiosks are made by Agfa, Sony, Fujifilm, and Olympus. Conceivably, as these direct-to-print kiosks proliferate and improve, they will eventually have ATM-like convenience and prints can be created anywhere, from hotel lobbies to airports, to cruise ships, or even to ballparks (along with cash back?!).

Just about all direct-to-print services require you to save your images in the JPEG file format. Most of them accept a wide variety of storage media, including CompactFlash, SmartMedia, Sony Memory Sticks, and other formats, via common PCMCIA adapters. If you are using one of the Sony Cybershot CD digital cameras, you'll need to 'finalize" your images from within the camera before the images can be printed. You'll also find it hard to locate a place that prints anything but standard sizes, including 3" × 5", 5" × 7", 4" × 6", and 8" × 10". If you want larger images, say, poster-sized, or if you want to print extra-wide panorama images, you'll need to turn to other custom print services or do it yourself on a desktop printer.

Note: The simplest way to share digital images is via your camera's built-in LCD. Most digital cameras also have a video-out plug, which makes it easy to connect the camera to a standard television for larger size viewing. Some memory card readers—such as SanDisk's portable Digital Photo Viewer—can also be hooked up directly to a television. (The SanDisk's viewer comes with a remote and can also be programmed to display images as a programmable slide show.)

Direct from Memory Card to Desktop Printer

Most people connect a desktop printer to a personal computer. But with some printers, you don't need a computer at all—just the printer and a source of power. The HP Photosmart line of printers, for example, accepts memory cards so you never have to fuss with transferring images to a computer. With the HP Photosmart 7550 photo printer, shown in Figure 12.2, you can preview, edit, and even enhance your photos using a color LCD and front-panel buttons. These kinds of printers range in price from $149 to $299. Direct photo printers are also offered in a variety of sizes and prices by Epson, Canon, Olympus, and Eastman Kodak, among others. Some printers allow you to connect a digital camera directly, via a dock, or cable and print images without ever removing the memory card from your camera. (Most, but not all, of these direct photo printers also hook up to a computer.)

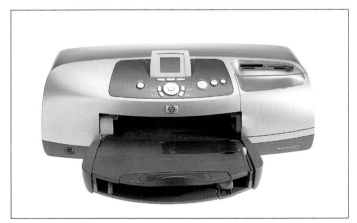

Figure 12.2: The HP Photosmart 7550 photo printer allows you to bypass a computer completely and get prints directly from your digital camera's memory card.

Digital Camera to Computer

To get the most out of digital images, you need to move the image data from your digital camera to a personal computer. Here are two of the most common ways to do that.

Direct from Camera to Computer Using a Connecting Cable

Older digital cameras used a relatively slow serial connection to connect with a computer. Newer digital cameras use a USB port, which is much faster but still takes some time if you are transferring lots of large files. You'll need a cable, which is often supplied with the digital camera. Sometimes, depending on the camera and computer, you'll need special software. However, most of the time digital cameras are recognized as an external drive so no software driver is required. The main advantage of using a connecting cable to transfer your files directly from the camera is that you never have to remove the storage media from the camera, which can put additional strain on the media. You also don't need to invest in an additional card reader, or adapter.

Card Reader

You can also use an external card reader that remains hooked up to your computer via a USB connection. (See Figure 12.3.) These card readers are readily available at both camera and computer stores and usually cost around $30. You must be sure to buy a card reader that accepts the media you are using, although many readers today accept a variety of media types.

Figure 12.3: External card readers such as this one from Lexar transfer data from your digital camera's memory card to a computer.

To use this method, you must remove the media from your camera, place it in the reader, and wait while the computer reads the contents of the memory card. Depending on the installed software and the configuration of your computer, file transfer either starts automatically or occurs when you designate a folder on your hard drive for the image files.

Personally, I've never had trouble with card readers. But I've heard of people using card readers of questionable quality (i.e., cheap!) and running into trouble. Apparently, if you insert, say, a CompactFlash card into a reader, and the slots of the card don't match the pins of the reader perfectly, a pin on the reader can bend or break and damage the card. If a pin breaks off and remains in the compact flash card and you attempt to force the card into your camera, not only will the card be damaged (and any images on it potentially lost), but the camera will be as well.

Another word of warning: think twice before attempting to format a memory card or even delete images from it while it's in a reader and hooked up to a computer. Once again, I haven't encountered a problem doing this, but I've heard from others who have. If you want to be on the safe side, I suggest you format or delete by placing the card back into the camera and using the camera's own software.

Other Connection Options

Many laptops contain a PCMCIA card slot, and with an appropriate adapter you can download data from your memory card this way as well.

Some digital cameras, notably ones by Eastman Kodak, can also be "docked" to a dedicated docking station. The docking station is then connected to the computer and facilitates the transfer of data from camera to computer via a cable.

Note: There is no excuse for not making backups of your digital images. With a CD burner you can make multiple copies and send them to multiple locations for safekeeping. With an Internet connection, you can upload your digital images to online services for safekeeping. I suggest you imagine a fire, or an earthquake, or your child spilling a drink over your hard drive. Now imagine a life without any of those great images stored on your computer. Take a deep breath and make a backup!

Organizing and Managing Digital Photos

Once image files are in the computer, you need to organize the images so you can find them later. Good luck!

There are several approaches to this, including:
- The Big Pot method (also known as the shoebox method)
- Organizing by folder and date
- Using image-management software

The Big Pot Method

This is the easiest and arguably the most useless way to "manage" images. You simply throw everything into one big folder on your hard drive. (If you do this, be sure to set up your digital camera so the image numbering system is sequential; otherwise, you might accidentally write over previously saved images.) You can augment this approach by using batch renaming built into some programs, or by using a shareware utility such as THE Rename available at **www.herve-thouzard.com/therename.phtml**. THE Rename will even rename files based on their EXIF data. (This utility is available for Windows only.) A Mac counterpart is A Better Finder Rename plug-in for $14.95, available at **www.publicspace.net**.

Organizing By Folder and Date

For this method, you simply create a new folder for each time you transfer images from your digital camera to computer. The folder is titled by the transfer day's date. Every year you start a new master folder, where you place your dated folders containing the image files. Files are then opened using image-editing software, or uploaded directly to online photo-finishing services. You can burn a large portion of these files onto a CD and then delete the files from your hard drive to free up space. Or you can simply keep buying new, larger hard drives!

Using Image-Management Software

As your image collection becomes larger and larger and your memory fails you yet one more time, you'll need image-management software.

There are many types of image-management software, ranging from very simple and inexpensive to complex and expensive.

Figure 12.4: The Image Browser from Photoshop Elements 2 is a simple, visual way of keeping track of your images.

At the simplest level are programs that allow you to view a thumbnail version of an image stored in folders on your hard drive. The Image Browser in Photoshop 7 and Photoshop Elements and the visual browser in Paintshop Pro function as this type of image-management system. You can't "search" for a particular image by keyword or even date. You simply navigate through folders until you "see" the image you are looking for. Figure 12.4 shows the Image Browser found in Photoshop Elements 2.

The next level of image-management software organizes digital images in a variety of ways. Not only can you view thumbnails of images by folder, but also, by adding keywords, you can actually search for a group of particular types of images. There are several image-management software applications that do this with various levels of sophistication. Some of them also facilitate the sharing of images by making it easy to create slideshows, web pages, and even hardback photo books. Figure 12.5 shows a screen grab from Apple's iPhoto.

Figure 12.5: With Apple's iPhoto, and other similar image-management software packages, you can visually browse your image files or organize them by topic or searchable keywords.

Examples of this kind of image-management software include:

- Apple iPhoto (Mac only, free, **www.apple.com**)
- Adobe Photoshop Album (WIN only, $49.99, **www.adobe.com**)
- Ulead Photo Explorer (WIN only, $29.95, **www.ulead.com/pex/runme.htm**)
- ACDSee (WIN only, $49.45, **www.acdsystems.com/English/Products/ACDSee/index.htm**)
- Picasa (WIN only, $29.99, **www.picasa.net**)
- JASC Paintshop Photo Album (WIN only, $49.00, **www.jasc.com**)
- iMatch (WIN only, $49.95, **www.photools.com**)

More expensive and therefore more sophisticated image-management programs allow you to customize search criteria, search EXIF data, and much, much more. Some of these applications include complete photo studio management capabilities, a feature that is of particular interest to professional photographers. A screen shot from the popular Extensis Portfolio software is shown in Figure 12.6.

Figure 12.6: A screen shot from Extensis Portfolio asset-management software.

Examples of this type of digital asset-management software include the following (most of the prices shown here are for single-use licenses only):

- ThumbsPlus (WIN only, $79.95, www.cerious.com)
- FotoStation (WIN & Mac, $99, www.fotostation.com)
- Cumulus by Canto (WIN & Mac, $99.95, www.canto.com)
- Extensis Portfolio (WIN & Mac, $ 199.95, www.extensis.com/assetman/)
- DigitalPro2 (WIN only, $259, www.moose395.net/digitalpro/index.html)
- StockView by HindSight (WIN & Mac, $495, www.hindsightltd.com/stockview/stockview.html)
- fotoshow pro by S4media (Server Based Program. $2,500, www.fotoshowpro.com/)

Sharing Digital Photos

There are several ways to share digital files once you've transferred them to a personal computer. You can:

- Use a desktop printer and make your own custom prints.
- Upload the digital files to an online print service such as **Ofoto.com or Shutterfly.com** and let them do it for you.
- E-mail a file or files to friends around the globe, either pasted inside the note or as an attached file.
- Create a slide show and publish the slide show to a CD or DVD.
- Create a slide show executable (.exe) file and e-mail it to friends and relatives or clients.
- Publish the images on a personal website.
- Display photos on a digital photo frame.
- Upload image files to an FTP site for others to retrieve.
- Turn them over to a professional offset printing press (i.e., for a magazine, book, or some other type of publication).

    Let's look at some of the various options in more detail.

Desktop Printing

Photographic quality desktop printers are as common as personal computers. Some are so inexpensive that they are given away with the purchase of a digital camera or computer. However, there is nothing inexpensive about operating a desktop printer. Ink and photo-quality paper costs add up. Valuable time is often required to prepare digital images for optimal printing results.

Still, the convenience of having a printer at your command 24/7 is a compelling enough reason to own and use one. If you know what you are doing and you use a good enough printer, ink, and media, you can get results that rival any commercial alternative. The Epson 2200, which is especially popular among professional photographers, is shown in Figure 12.7.

Figure 12.7: The popular photo-quality Epson 2200 inkjet printer.

Getting the Most From a Desktop Printer

To get the most from your desktop printer, you'll want to use image-processing programs such as Photoshop or Photoshop Elements.

Knowing that this topic is big enough for several books on the subject, here are a few things to consider:

- If necessary, use software such as Photoshop, Photoshop Elements, or Genuine Fractals, to boost resolution to match print size using software. (Genuine Fractals, WIN & Mac, from $150, www.lizardtech.com)

- Use image-processing software or nik Sharpener Pro! to sharpen digital images to the specifications of a printer. (nik Sharpener Pro!, WIN & Mac, from $79.00, www.nikmultimedia.com/usa/maincontent/index.shtml)

- Take into account the aspect-ratio effect of the digital camera's chip and how it affects print size. (See the following note.)

Note: 35mm film cameras have an aspect ratio of 3:2, which means you won't get any cropping if you make a 4" x 6" print, which also has an aspect ratio of 3:2. Many digital cameras have an aspect ratio of 4:3, and if you try to make a 4" x 6" print you'll get a picture with two sides having white borders. If you want borderless prints, you'll need to crop your digital images using imaging software to match the digital file with the print-size aspect ratio. Some digital cameras offer a choice of either 4:3 or 3:2 aspect ratio. Check your manual.

- If you resort to color-management techniques and build profiles for your devices, be sure to turn off color management in your printer driver. Some color printers use a built-in technology called *print image matching* (PIM), which can be disabled.

- Be sure to use the manufacturer's recommended ink and paper(s) and tell your printer the type of paper you're using.

- Follow the manufacturer's advice for print preservation to avoid fading, and remember that some papers are more archival than others.

> **Note:** A particularly good book on the subject of desktop printing is *Mastering Digital Printing: The Photographer's and Artist's Guide to High-Quality Digital Output* by Harald Johnson (Muska & Lipman, 2002). An excellent book on color management is *Real World Color Management* by Bruce Fraser, et al. (Peachpit Press, 2003).

Using Online Photo Services

Desktop inkjet printing may be convenient, but it is not really cost-effective when compared to online services.

When using online services, you simply upload your images to their website and order prints to be produced on real photographic paper and delivered to your doorstep overnight or in a few days. After you place your images online, anyone you designate, anywhere in the world, can go online, view your digital image, and with a single click of the mouse and a few keystrokes order their own prints in a variety of sizes. Now when people ask you for a print, you can point them toward the online service and have them order their own.

Many of the online services offer other options such as photo mugs, photo t-shirts, calendars, and mouse pads made from your images.

There are several online services to choose from, including **ofoto.com**, **shutterfly.com**, and **snapfish.com**. **walmart.com** also offers a wide variety of photo online services for a very reasonable price.

> **Note:** If your printer can't handle poster-sized images or panorama formats, or if you need a large quantity of same-shot prints, go to **www.andromeda.com/people/ddyer/photo/albums.html** for a list of several online services that specialize in this type of work. This site also rates and compares many of the more popular online print services mentioned earlier.

E-Mailing Your Digital Photos

Sending images via e-mail is one of the easiest ways to share your digital images with others. However, with digital cameras producing larger and larger files, e-mailing digital photos without reducing the actual number of pixels and/or using a higher amount of JPEG compression to make them a "polite" file size can cause problems. Not only do some ISPs choke on large files—and spit them back to you unsent—some of your best friends may become irate as they wait impatiently for your digital file to download via their dial-up modem. Do yourself and your recipients a favor. Either learn to resize and recompress the images yourself using imaging software such as Photoshop or Photoshop Elements, or let a program do it for you. Photoshop Elements, for example, has an Attach to E-Mail command that will resize an image automatically and attach it to an e-mail as a compressed JPEG. Some other image-management software programs such as Photoshop Album, Ulead Photo Explorer, and Picasa, mentioned earlier, will also do it for you. Also, some digital cameras will automatically create an "e-mail sized" JPEG image as well as a full-sized version.

Creating Slide Shows

There are many ways to both create and share digital slide shows. Software applications that make this easy include:

- Apple iPhoto (Mac only, free, **www.apple.com**)
- Adobe Photoshop Album (WIN only, $49.99, **www.adobe.com**)
- ThumbsPlus (WIN only, $79.95, **www.cerious.com**)
- ACDSee (WIN only, $49.45, **www.acdsystems.com/English/Products/ACDSee/index.htm**)
- Ulead DVD PictureShow 2 ($49/95, **www.ulead.com/dps/runme.htm**)
- PhotoShow (WIN & Mac, $29.99, **www.simplestar.com**)
- Extensis Portfolio (WIN & Mac, $ 199.95, **www.extensis.com/assetman**)

Once the slide show is created, it can be viewed on projected large-scale digital projectors or distributed via CDs and DVDs. If you keep the file size down, you can even send a slide show as an e-mail attachment.

Posting to Personal Websites

One of the most inexpensive and effective ways of distributing your digital photos is via the Web. You can create your own website or place your images on many of the special sites set up to share images to a community of interested viewers.

Making a website need not be difficult. Several programs are available that automate the entire process.

Programs that do this include:

- Adobe Photoshop and Photoshop Elements (WIN & Mac, $690 and $99, respectively, **www.adobe.com**)
- Express Thumbnail Creator (WIN only, $39.95, **www.express-soft.com**)
- Extensis Portfolio (WIN & Mac, $199.95, **www.extensis.com/assetman**)

> **Note:** Adding a copyright symbol or watermark to your digital image won't prevent your images from being ripped off by unscrupulous people. But it will help keep honest people honest and give them a way to track you down for permission. Keep in mind that by adding a copyright symbol to your digital file, some print services may refuse to print your image.

Offset Printing

The ultimate destination for just about any serious photographer is the printed page, as in a magazine, brochure, or book like this one. This kind of printing is usually done on expensive offset printers and it requires digital images to be converted from RGB or sRGB (common color spaces produced by digital cameras) to CMYK.

Most of the time, the conversion is done by the printer or by someone between the photographer and the printer. However, if you want to ensure the best quality printing possible of your work, it's in your interest to learn something about the process and, if possible or appropriate, do the conversion yourself. (For this book, I did the conversion—with lots of help from the printer and my photographer friend Peter Figen.) It's not that someone else can't do a good job, but no one knows how your images should look as well as you do.

Conversion to CMYK is VERY dependent on the device (printing press) you use and requires an understanding of the particular press that will be used. You should work with your printer to ensure that the conversion to CMYK produces the best possible results, but remember that printing ink on paper will never be as good as a high-quality photographic print on photographic paper.

FTPing Your Digital Photos

Professional printers and many high-end photo processing services often use FTP sites to receive large image files. FTP, which stands for *file transfer protocol*, is a process that transfers data and program files between computers much more quickly and smoothly than e-mail transfers. File size is usually not a factor, which makes FTPing popular for anyone who works with large graphic or image files.

You can use an Internet browser such as Explorer or Navigator or special FTP software to upload and download files to and from an FTP site with your personal computer. Usually, you must go through a login procedure to access an FTP site.

Programs specifically dedicated to transferring data to and from a FTP site include:

- FTP Voyager (WIN only, $39.99, **www.ftpvoyager.com**)
- Powerdesk Pro (WIN only, $39.95, **www.v-com.com/product/pd_ind.html**)
- Fetch (Mac only, $25, **http://fetchsoftworks.com**)
- CuteFTP (WIN only, $39.95, **www.cuteftp.com**)

Setting up an FTP host site is not easy, but there are alternatives if you want a way to post large images and make them available to others. For example, .mac is a service (**www.mac.com**) that provides you with up to 100MB of online storage space for a nominal annual fee. You can direct friends or clients to the site, and with a password, they have access to designated files. Other sites that provide this kind of service include Yahoo! Briefcase (**http://briefcase.yahoo.com**) and my docs online (**www.mydocsonline.com**).

Digital Frames

Digital frames are actually very simple computers with a built-in flat screen that come in various sizes and quality. They are a great way to share constantly updated digital images with computer-less relatives. Also avoided is the hassle of making and sending hardcopy.

Some digital frames, such as the Digital Photo Receiver by Ceiva shown in Figure 12.8, are connected to an AC power outlet and a telephone jack. The Ceiva frame automatically dials up a server at predetermined times and downloads new images that you've placed on a Ceiva website (**www.ceiva.com**). There is a monthly subscription charge to cover storage and transmission costs.

Figure 12.8: The Ceiva Digital Photo Receiver digital frame with a resolution of 640 x 480 pixels.

Other digital frames such as the Pacific Digital Memory Frame (**www.pacificdigi-talcorp.com**) don't require a subscription fee. Images are transferred to the frame via a USB cable. The mother of all digital frames at this time is the Digi-frame 1710, a 17-inch flat-screen frame with a built-in 10GB hard drive and an Ethernet connection so that images can be added or subtracted remotely (**www.digi-frame.com**). See Figure 12.9. At a list price of $3,000, it is not necessarily meant for Grandpa's wall, but rather for corporate offices and galleries.

Figure 12.9: The 17-inch Digi-frame 1710 is an ultimate digital frame.

Note: For a slightly different approach to displaying your digital photographs, Radio Shack offers a variety of voice-recording photo frames that allow you to add a personal message, behind-the-scenes information, description, shot location, or humorous anecdotes to your photo.

Zooming In

An In Depth Look at Digital Technologies and Procedures

Throughout most of the book, we have focused on shooting techniques and strategies for perfecting your shots. Along the way, we touched on some technical topics that deserve a little more attention and elaboration. Understanding these technologies isn't strictly necessary for you to take good digital photos, but the information provided in this appendix can help you get more out of your digital camera, so let's zoom in and take a closer look.

Chapter Contents

RAW Data Revealed

RAW data has been called the holy grail of digital photography. Understand it, and you understand many of the underlying concepts of digital photography. RAW data is also referred to as the "negative" of a digital image, from which the JPEG and TIFF files are derived, much like a print is derived from a negative in traditional photography.

As I've said throughout the book, the ability to save RAW data is an option in most prosumer and professional digital cameras. Most consumer-level cameras save images in an RGB processed file format.

Not all RAW data is alike. RAW files are generated differently from manufacturer to manufacturer and from digital camera to digital camera. Unlike JPEG and TIFF files, which can be read by just about any imaging software, RAW data files require special software—which is becoming less and less of an issue as more RAW data support emerges. ⌇ "Software for Processing RAW Data," later in this appendix.

I've also said that saving RAW data doesn't automatically translate into getting the best quality image. In fact, if you don't process RAW data properly, you'll end up with an image that is inferior to what a camera can do if left to use its own onboard processors.

Saving RAW data does guarantee flexibility, however. All of the image data produced by the sensor is kept intact. As your skills increase and RAW data imaging software improves, you can always go back to the original data and try again. Like negatives, RAW data files should be saved and archived carefully.

To reveal RAW data more fully—and to illustrate how it is typically processed—I turned to Jack Holm, a former professor at the Rochester Institute of Technology (RIT), and currently a senior scientist at Hewlett Packard. He has worked and published extensively on issues related to the optimal processing of RAW data, be it processing done inside the camera or later, on a computer, via special imaging software.

Look at one of Jack's photos, shown on the left in Figure ZI.1. This figure shows what image data looks like after it comes off the sensor and before it goes through any extensive post-capture processing. Note that the image is monochrome and contains no color. This is "RAW" data.

The image on the right in Figure ZI.1 is a magnification of the image. Each one of the square boxes represents a gray-scale tonal value of only one color (red, green, or blue). Remember from Chapter 1 that sensors don't see "color" *per se* but each pixel is covered with a red, green, or blue filter and is limited to registering the tonal value of that color. What you see here is a patchwork of intermixed red, green, and blue tonal information.

The process that follows is truly amazing, and takes huge computations and sophisticated algorithms to do successfully. For the purpose of this demonstration, Jack used special research imaging software, running on a desktop computer. These are the steps typically required to process an image (not necessarily in order):

- The patchwork of monochrome data is reassembled into red, green, and blue channels.

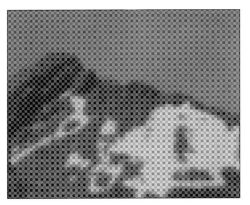

Figure ZI.1: RAW data direct from the image sensor. (Photo by Jack Holm) An enlargement of the image shown in Figure ZI.1, showing a patchwork of intermixed color tonal information.

- In a process called *de-mosaicing*, information gaps between pixels are interpolated and filled in. Remember from Chapter 1 that in a typical image sensor, each pixel is capable of registering only one color. If that color isn't present, then nothing is recorded. Interpolation makes an educated guess based on adjacent pixels to determine what color should be filled in. (With the Foveon sensor, described in "Sensors Expanded," later in this appendix, each pixel can register several colors so these gaps don't exist—making this processing step unnecessary.)
- Sharpening and noise filtering are applied to the image data. An optical blur filter is also used in front of the sensor to prevent aliasing due to high frequency patterns, which cause the moiré patterns and color fringing.
- White balance is determined and applied. (Data that isn't deemed useful is discarded.)
- Color space is expanded from the 12 bits per pixel generated by most sensors to 16 bits of color per pixel. (At the end of the process, images are typically saved in either 16 bits per color channel or 8 bits per channel. The more bits per channel, the more color information is retained.)

If you were to stop the process at this point, you might see an image that looks somewhat like the one shown on the left in Figure ZI.2. De-mosaicing has been applied, but the color is extremely unsaturated. This is the color as seen by the camera, and it is also known as a "device" color.

Figure ZI.2: Color separated into three channels and the image de-mosaiced. A color transformation converts the device color into scene color. One more color transformation remains. (Photos by Jack Holm)

RAW data typically goes through two other basic color transformations before it is saved in its final format. After the RAW data is transformed to device color as described previously, the device color is transformed into "scene" color as shown on the right in Figure ZI.2.

Scene color is then transformed into "picture" color, which you see in Figure ZI.3. It's also at this point that color depth is often (but not always) reduced and a file format is applied, be it JPEG or TIFF.

Why are these color transformations necessary? The human visual system doesn't see or process color the same way the camera (or "device") does. The transformations are attempts to convert the red, green, and blue data into a form that more closely duplicates what we might see if we viewed the scene directly.

Although Jack applied the image processing to this image using software on his desktop computer, in-camera processing follows a very similar procedure to assemble RAW data and produce a ready-to-view file. Of course, when the camera does the work, you have little or no control over the various steps. Before you shoot, you can set various parameters such as sharpening, white balance, color space, and final file format, but you have no control over the step-by-step process once the image has been taken. You are also stuck with the results and can't revert to the original RAW file and start over. The results are only as good as the capabilities of the camera. (Early digital cameras did a poor job of pixel interpolation and the results were lots of images with lots of color fringing. New digital cameras do a much better job.)

Figure ZI.3: Final image ready for viewing. (Photo by Jack Holm)

Processing Compared

Let's look at some more of Jack's work to understand how different techniques for processing of RAW data can make a big difference in how an image turns out.

The image shown in Figure ZI.4 is another one of Jack's shots, originally saved in the RAW file format.

Figure ZI.4: This photograph will look very different depending on the type of processing used. (Photo by Jack Holm)

To the left in Figure ZI.5 is an enlarged view of the same image, processed using a method that simulates the in-camera processing used by many of the earlier consumer digital cameras. See how the highlights are blown out and data is "clipped" or missing? Once the processing is complete, and you have an image like this, there isn't much you can do to fix it—even in Photoshop.

Now look to the left in Figure ZI.5. You'll see the same area of the same image, but this time Jack has applied proprietary image-processing to the RAW data. See what I am talking about? There is no clipping and detail remains in most of the highlights. Processing technique makes a huge difference.

Figure ZI.5: On the left is a close-up showing the result of inadequate processing. Note the lack of details in the highlights. On the right is a close-up showing how sophisticated processing takes the same data and does a better job of rendering it.

Software for Processing RAW Data

In order to take advantage of the RAW data format, you need a personal computer and special software. And, course, a digital camera that can save RAW files.

At this time, most of the major digital camera manufacturers offer an application that interprets their proprietary RAW data, some better than others. These include:

- NikonCapture for the .NEF file format (**www.nikon.com**)
- Olympus Camedia software for the .ORF file format (**www.olympus.com**)
- Canon FileViewer for the .CRW file format (**www.canon.com**)
- Fujifilm RAW File Converter for the .RAF file format (**www.fujifilm.com**)
- Eastman Kodak DCS Photo Desk and File Format plug-in for Photoshop for the .DCR file format (**www.kodak.com**)
- Minolta DiMAGE Image Viewer for the .MRM file format (**www.minolta.com**)

You won't find Sony software listed here because at this time Sony digital cameras don't offer RAW capture.

You can also use applications and plug-ins from third-party sources to process RAW data. Many of the vendors in the following list provide 15- to 30-day free trials available from their websites. As well as the products listed on the next page, many image-management programs noted in Chapter 12 also offer limited RAW file support.

Some of these products include:

- Bibble for Nikon, Canon, Kodak, Olympus, and Fujifilm files. Available for Mac and Windows as a Photoshop Plug-in or a stand-alone application. Free trial download. (www.Bibblelabs.com)
- Adobe Camera Raw plug-in for Photoshop 7.01. Supports Nikon, Canon, Fujifilm, Minolta, and Olympus files. Mac and Windows. (www.adobe.com/products/photoshop/cameraraw.html)
- BreezeBrowser for Canon files. Windows only. Free trial. (www.breezesys.com)
- YarcPlus for Canon files. Windows only. Free trial. (www.yarcplus.com)
- Capture One for Canon and Nikon files. Mac and Windows. 30-day free trial. (www.phaseone.com/en)
- SharpRaw for Canon, Fujifilm, Kodak, Minolta, Nikon, and Olympus files. (www.logicaldesigns.com)

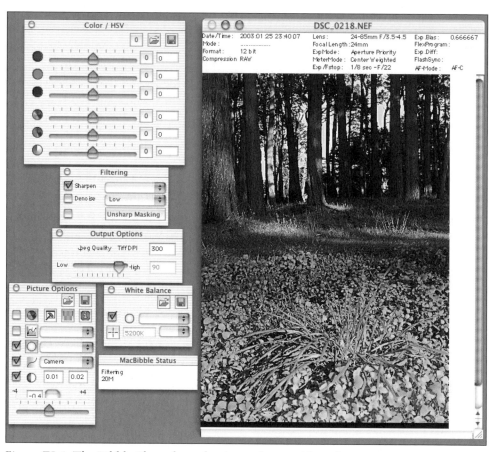

Figure ZI.6: The Bibble Photoshop plug-in workspace. Note the many options.

Most of these programs offer many options for processing RAW data, as well as batch conversion capabilities. Figure ZI.6, for example, shows a screen shot of the Bibble Photoshop plug-in workspace. Note the controls for white balance, sharpening, color, and file format. If you don't get what you want the first time, just enter new values and try again. Your original data remains unchanged.

Keep in mind that off-the-shelf products are constantly being updated and improved. Support for various manufacturers' RAW formats is always constantly expanding. I recommend that you check out the websites listed above for the most up-to-date information on the latest releases.

> **Note:** Not all RAW data is lossless. Some manufacturers offer a compressed RAW file, which reduces the file size but can slightly degrade the image. Other manufacturers may offer "scene" data in the form of a TIFF RGB file, sometimes calling it RAW. Scene data can be viewed without special RAW software, and has already been white balanced. However, once white balancing has been performed, re-adjusting it will cause loss of highlight information.

Reading the Histogram

Your digital camera's LCD is great for providing quick confirmation that you got the shot you wanted. It can also be used for framing a shot. However, it is less useful when it comes to making sure you got the perfect exposure, and that is where the histogram comes in.

Histograms are graphical representations of a range of 256 gray-scale values, with 0 equaling black and 255 equaling white. Histograms are usually displayed over an image in the camera's LCD, at your discretion. Histograms are features of most prosumer and all professional digital cameras and are rarely found in consumer-level digital cameras. Obviously, a histogram is most useful when you are shooting static shots that can be repeated, such as landscapes and still lifes. If you are trying to capture a fleeting moment, it's not useful to use a histogram because the odds are against you getting another chance at the shot. Also, a histogram is most useful when you can override automatic exposure controls and fine-tune exposure.

Let's look at three examples and see how a histogram can be useful in determining proper exposure. I used Photoshop Elements to generate the histograms.

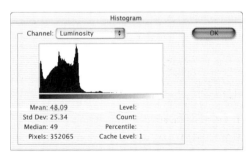

Figure ZI.7: This histogram (left) shows the values for an image that is probably too dark. The histogram data is confirmed on the right.

Look at the histogram in Figure ZI.7. The values are all clumped to the far left of the graph. This is a sign that there is a dominant distribution of the darker values. This is confirmed by the image itself, shown on the right in Figure ZI.7. Assuming that the lighting conditions remain the same, opening the aperture or decreasing the shutter speed will help the next shot.

Figure ZI.8 shows an opposite problem. Now the values are distributed toward the lighter tonal values, telling us that the shot is over exposed. Again, this is confirmed by the shot on the right in Figure ZI.8. This is actually the worst-case scenario for digital photographers. If you blow out the highlights, you can't do anything with imaging software to recover them. Assuming that the lighting conditions remain the same, closing the aperture or increasing the shutter speed will help the next shot.

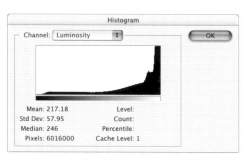

Figure ZI.8: This histogram (left) shows the values for an image that is probably too light. The histogram data is confirmed on the right.

The final shot, shown in Figure ZI.9, shows an optimal distribution of tonal values, covering a wide range of the histogram. This tells us that highlights and shadow areas are distributed equally, which is confirmed in Figure ZI.9 (right).

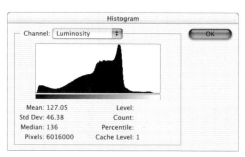

Figure ZI.9: This histogram (left) shows the values for an image that is just right. The histogram data is confirmed on the right.

The more time you spend looking at histograms and comparing the graphical representation with the actual image, the more astute you'll become.

Fine Tuning White Balance

Professional photographers Dave Harp and Richard Anderson of Baltimore, MD, have discovered an effective way of fine tuning white balance on modern digital cameras using a simple device that's been around a long time.

The Expo/Disc, shown in Figure ZI.10, was originally designed by George Wallace to turn the reflective meter inside a single lens reflex film camera into an incident meter. It did so by providing a prismatic diffusion filter, combined with color correction filters and a piece of opaque plastic, so that a perfect 18% of available light would arrive at the film plane.

Figure ZI.10: The Wallace Expo/Disc can be used to fine tune white balance settings on digital cameras.

Dave and Richard have found that the Expo/Disc also provides a perfect white balance when used with digital cameras because it presents an image to the camera's optical system in near-perfect RGB balance. They've found it to be more reliable than simply using a white card or a gray card to measure white balance. Dave and Richard both use Nikon D1X cameras, but the device will fit on most digital cameras that allow for custom white balance settings.

When Dave and Richard started experimenting with the Expo/Disc, they found that although the white balance was extremely accurate, it was too cool for their tastes. Undaunted, they "sandwich experimented" using Tiffen 82B and 82A filters with the disc, and the result produced warmer skin tones.

The beauty of the Expo/Disc, these two photographers say, is that you can fine tune the color balance—your own personal 18% gray—or even change it to suit an assignment by adding your own recipe of filtration. They suggest that it helps if you have a basic knowledge of color theory, since you'll have to add cool filtration to warm the scene, and vice versa.

The Wallace Expo/Disc comes in various filter sizes, but if you buy the largest size (72mm), you can hold it in front of just about any camera lens to preset your color balance. Cost ranges from $50 to $60, depending on size.

For more on the Expo/Disc, go to **www.expodisc.com**.

Sensors Expanded

Nothing illustrates the rapidly improving world of image sensors better than the cases of the Foveon and Fujifilm sensors.

Foveon is the brainchild of Carver Mead and Dick Merrill. The sensor is built around the CMOS technology, but with a very important difference from other sensors. As explained in Chapter 1, sensors—CCD or CMOS—are built with a red, green, or blue filter placed in some fashion over each discrete pixel. Of course, this means there are gaps. Most of the time you don't notice these gaps because the camera's onboard processing system intelligently reassembles the component colors and properly fills in the blanks with appropriate colors. However, if you look closely at the transition areas of an image, you are likely to see an effect referred to as "color fringing," where several colors are present when there should have been only one. Filtering individual pixels to respond to red, green, or blue light also reduces the overall effectiveness of a sensor because each pixel throws away the other two colors of light.

The Foveon technology ingeniously relies on the fact that different colors of light penetrate a medium to different depths. By placing a thin coating of this material over all the pixels, a pixel is activated according to the depth that a particular color reaches. (See Figure ZI.11.) Every pixel is available for red, green, or blue light, effectively making the sensor nearly three times as effective than the method described previously. At this time, the Foveon sensor is used in the Sigma SD9 SLR digital camera. While the Sigma camera is rated at 3 megapixels, in fact the effective resolution compares favorably to other digital cameras rated at 6 or 7 megapixels, thanks to the Foveon sensor.

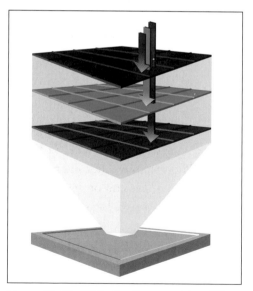

Figure ZI.11: With the Foveon chip, different colors penetrate a given medium at different depths.

Fujifilm has also developed a "SuperCCD" that they claim produces superior results. As shown in Figure ZI.12, in a SuperCCD the pixels are oriented in a diamond formation, and because of the missing pixels between odd rows, turning this into a square image requires processing that generates a higher pixel count. The Fujifilm S1 Pro has a 3.4-megapixel SuperCCD that outputs 3.07 million pixels, which is processed to generate a 6.13-megapixel image (3040 × 2016).

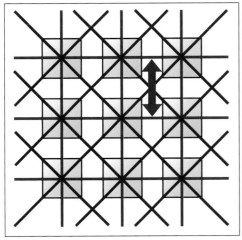 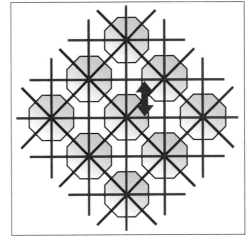

Figure ZI.12: With a Fujifilm SuperCCD, the pixels are oriented in a diamond formation instead of a traditional square.

Extending Exposure Latitude with Software

In Chapter 7 and 8 we saw how the exposure latitude of a digital camera can be extended by shooting at least two shots of the same scene at different exposures and then using imaging software to merge the shots later. Using this method, you can effectively extend the exposure latitude from a few stops to several and still maintain image detail through a wide range of tonal values.

Assuming you have followed the shooting instructions outlined in those chapters, here is one way to use Photoshop to extend the latitude of your digital camera. I'll also show you how to use Photoshop Elements to do this. (I'm assuming you already know the basics of how to use these programs.) If you are working with 16-bit files, this method won't work with the current versions of Photoshop or Photoshop Elements and you'll need to use the workaround I suggest at the end of this section, or convert your 16-bit files to 8-bit. (Future versions of Photoshop and Photoshop Elements will likely provide more 16-bit support.)

With either Photoshop or Photoshop Elements, start by opening the image files containing the various exposures. (For the sake of this example, I'll assume you are working with two image files. You can use as many as you like.)

Then:

1. Select one of the images. It doesn't matter which one. Now copy the selection.
2. Paste the copied selection into the other image file.
3. Now you have both images in the same file on two separate layers, as shown in Figure ZI.13.

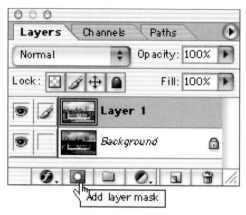

Figure ZI.13: Both images are now in the same file, as separate layers.

Next you are going to replace incorrectly exposed parts of one image with correctly exposed areas of another. At this point you can go a couple of ways, depending on your preferences and the program you are using.

If you are using Photoshop, the easiest way is to create a layer mask. To do this, all you do is select the topmost layer, then click on the Add Layer Mask icon located at the bottom of the Layers palette. (Layer Masks are not an option with Photoshop Elements at this time.)

Once you've created a layer mask, you simply select the Brush tool and paint black—as set in your foreground color palette—over incorrectly exposed areas of the image window. This blocks parts of the topmost layer and "reveals" the properly exposed areas from the image represented in the bottom layer. To reverse your work, simply set your color palette to white and paint over the image window in the areas that were previously painted black. Vary the size of the brush depending on the size of the area you are working with.

If you are using Photoshop Elements, you can simply use the Eraser tool to erase the parts of the topmost layer that aren't properly exposed and leave intact the areas that are properly exposed. Again, you can choose the appropriate eraser size and opacity for the area of detail you are working on. If you make a mistake, use the Undo commands to go back and try again.

When you are finished with either method, layer mask or eraser, flatten your layers and you are done.

Merging Images using 16-Bit Files

You can't use layers in 16-bit mode. Instead, you need to clone-stamp correctly exposed areas from one image onto incorrectly exposed areas of the second image. To do that, open two image files, and then:

1. Magnify both images to 1600 percent. This makes individual pixels visible.
2. Use the navigation tool to position your image all the way to the top and the far left of the image window.
3. Select the Clone Stamp tool. Set the brush size to 1 pixel.
4. Hold down the Option/Alt key and click a 1-pixel source at the top left of one image as shown in Figure ZI.14.

Figure ZI.14: Select a 1-pixel source at the corner of one of your images.

5. On the second image, click on the top left pixel. You've now registered the two images. You can now zoom out and choose a larger brush size. Use the Clone Stamp tool to "paint" properly exposed areas of the source image over the target image.

Index

Custom mode for white balance, 237
Cyan, Magenta, Yellow, Black (CMYK) color space
    for offset printing, 251
    selecting, 138
cylindrical objects, light for, **209**, *210*

D

Dale, Bruce
    landscape by, 174, *174*
    road trip photos by, 120–123, *121–123*
damage, camera, 115
dark current subtraction, 230
dates
    metadata for, 10
    organizing images by, **244**
daylight with camera strobe, 37–38, *37*
de-mosaicing process, 257
decisive moments in action shots, **84–85**, *84–85*
dedicated strobes, **204**, *204*
deleting images from memory cards, 243
density filters
    for landscapes, **171**, *171*
    with strobes, **217**, *217*
depth of field
    film vs. digital, 8
    for landscapes, **166–167**, *166*
    for portraits, 23, **42–43**, *42*
desktop printing, **241**, *241*, **247–249**, *248*
detail
    in interior shots, **155**, *155*
    in landscapes, 158
    in panoramas, 183
    in quality tests, 16
diffusion material, 198
Digi-frame, 253, *253*
digital frames, **252–253**, *252–253*
Digital Memory Frame, 253
Digital Photo Receiver frame, 252, *252*
digital wallets, 116
direct to print images, **240–241**, *240–241*
direction of light, 135
disc digital cameras, 116
display models, 57
distortion
    in head and shoulder shots, 29
    from lenses, 195
docking stations, 243
documentaries, minimovies for, **96**, *96*
dogs, **61–62**, *61*
Drum, Dave, minimovies shooting tips by, 93

duct tape, 80
duration of minimovies, **100–101**
dust
    camera damage from, 115
    on lenses, 195
DVD MovieFactory 2 program, 102
DVD PictureShow 2 program, 102
DVD Workshop program, 102
DVDs for minimovies, **101–102**
dynamic range
    exposure in, 139
    in landscapes, *162*, **163**

E

e-mail
    for minimovies, **105–107**, *106–107*
    for sharing, **250**
    for storing photos, 116
editing minimovies, **99–101**
electronic light capturing, **2**, *2*
electronic viewfinders, 48, 87
emotion, zooming for, **50–51**, *51–52*
environmental portraits, **37–39**, *38*
events, **64–65**
    cameras for, **12–13**
    gestures and mannerisms in, **65**, *66*
    grips and hugs in, **66**
    weddings, **67–70**, *68–70*
EXIF (Exchangeable Image File) format, 10
Expo/Disc, white balance tuning by, *265*, **265**
exposure and exposure modes
    for head and shoulder shots, 29
    for landscapes, **158**
    for panoramas, **180**
    for pet photos, 62
    for quality, **138–140**, *140*
    software solutions for, **175**, *175*
exposure latitude
    film vs. digital, **4**
    for RAW data, **267–269**, *268–269*
Extensis Portfolio asset-management software, 246, *246*
exteriors. *See* interiors and exteriors
external artificial lights, **204–205**, *204–205*
external light meters, **172–173**
external strobes
    for head and shoulder shots, 36
    for portraits, 23

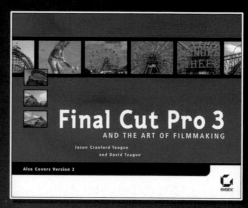

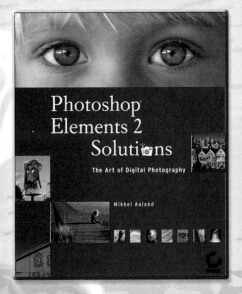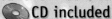

Contributors

Richard Anderson is a location photographer who has enthusiastically embraced digital technologies. Richard has been based in Baltimore since 1976. To view more of his work, visit www.rnaphoto.com.

Morton Beebe is a professional photographer and author whose work has been widely published and exhibited. To view more of his work, go to www.mortonbeebe.com.

Robert Birnbach is a commercial advertising photographer based in San Francisco who often shoots digital. To see more of his work visit www.robertbirnbachstudio.com.

Rudy Burger, formerly the Chief Executive Officer of Media Lab Europe, has over 20 years experience in high technology and digital media. Digital cameras have rekindled his love for photography.

Craig Carraher and **Tinnee Lee** together make up Lee-Carraher Photography, renowned for shooting fine jewelry and gems. They can be reached at TinneeL@aol.com.

Jorge Colombo is a professional photographer, illustrator, and designer. He was born in Lisbon, Portugal, and moved to New York City in 1989 where he now lives and works. His work can be viewed at www.jorgecolombo.com.

Doug Clark is a Seattle–based photographer who focuses on lifestyle and fine art photography. View his work at www.dougclark.com.

Bruce Dale has had more than 2,000 photographs published by *National Geographic* and twice he's earned the title "Magazine Photographer of the Year." His book, *The American Southwest*, was published by National Geographic in 1999. To view more of his work, visit www.brucedale.com.

Dave Drum is an award-winning cameraman with more than 20 years' experience shooting documentary, commercial, educational, and corporate programs for national and international markets. He can be contacted through www.palcameraswest.com.

Peter Figen is a commercial advertising photographer based in Los Angeles. Clients include Memorex, Pioneer, and PriceGrabber.com among others. You can contact him at pfigen@keyway.net.

Bitsy Fitzsimmons is a photo enthusiast who lives in Indianapolis and travels the world to take pictures of her grandchildren and flowers. She can be contacted at Bitsfitz@aol.com.

Helmi Flick lives in Texas with her husband, Ken, a freelance writer, and five cats. Her images appear regularly in a variety of cat magazines and are featured on websites all over the world. To see more of her work go to www.HelmiFlick.com.

Kate Grady is stained glass artist who used a digital camera to document her four years in Taiwan. She plans to incorporate her images into stained glass pieces. She can be contacted at gradyke@yahoo.com.

Scott Haefner is an avid kite and landscape photographer. He also works at the U.S. Geological Survey doing web design. You can see more of his work at http://thehaefners.com/kap/.

Dave Harp is an editorial and corporate photographer based in Baltimore. He is also an author, former president of the American Society of Media Photographers (ASMP), and once was nominated for a Pulitzer Prize. You can see more of his work at www.chesapeakephotos.com.

Scott Highton is a photographer and author based in the San Francisco Bay area, specializing in multimedia, corporate, and location photography. He also has an extensive background in photojournalism and documentary filmmaking. To see more of his work, go to www.highton.com.

Jack Holm is a former professor at Rochester Institute of Technology (RIT), and is currently a senior scientist at Hewlett-Packard. He can be contacted at jack.holm@hp.com.

Bruce Avera Hunter is a professional freelance photographer whose work has been published with the National Geographic Society and The Discovery Channel in print and online. To view more of his work go to www.BruceAveraHunter.com.

John Isaac worked as a photographer for the UN from 1969 to 1998 when he retired as the chief of the Photo Unit in 1998. Throughout his career, John received numerous national and international awards for his work, including Professional Photographer of the Year in 1993 by the Photo Imaging Manufacturers and Distributors Association. He now works as an independent photographer, shooting almost exclusively digital. You can see more of his work at www.johnisaac.com.

Leonard Koren is a San Francisco artist who writes books about design and aesthetics. For more on his work visit www.leonardkoren.com.

Wendi Marafino is commercial photographer based in Los Angeles who photographs both products and people. She also shoots for the Hollywood film industry. You can contact her at wmarafino@keyway.net.

Tom Mogensen is an artist in San Francisco whose clients include Oracle, Macy's, and the San Francisco Giants. His work can be viewed at www.fotom.com.

Richard Morgenstein is a location photographer based in San Francisco specializing in environmental portraiture. You can see more of his work at www.morgenstein.com.

Michael Reichman is a world renowned nature photographer and photographic educator based in Toronto, Canada. His landscape and wildlife photography is widely collected and exhibited. He is a Contributing Editor to *Photo Techniques* magazine. Michael is the publisher and primary author of The Luminous Landscape website, www.luminous-landscape.com, where you can see more of his work.

Mark Richards is an award-winning corporate and editorial photographer who specializes in people and lifestyle photography. To see more of his work visit www.markrichards.com.

Steve Rosenbaum is a graduate of the Rochester Institute of Technology, with a degree in Professional Photography. He is currently President of S.I.R. Marketing Communications, Inc. To see more of his photographic work, go to www.sironline.com.

Doug Salin is a San Francisco–based architectural photographer who specializes in textiles, lighting applications, interiors, visual merchandising, and shooting digital. You can see more of his work at www.dougsalin.com.

Terry Schmitt is an award-winning professional photographer who has worked for the San Francisco Chronicle and UPI. He currently works as a freelance photographer. He can be reached at terry@tschmitt.com.

Fred Shippey worked for Eastman Kodak for 22 years and was involved in a wide variety of conventional photography and digital imaging projects. For the last ten years he has been a consultant on electronic imaging technology and applications and has written for a variety of publications in the U.S. and abroad. www.home.eznet.net/~fshippey

Chester Simpson grew up in Roanoke, Virginia, and graduated with a degree in photography from the San Francisco Institute of Art in 1977. He has been taking award-winning photographs since. To view more of his work, go to www.chestersimpson.com.

Carol Steele is a commercial and portrait photographer living and working in the United Kingdom. In 1997, she received the coveted British award "Master Pictorial & Illustrative Photographer of the Year." To see more of her work go to www.carolsteele.co.uk.

Andrew Tarnowka is a professional architect and serious photographer who was born in Poland and now lives in Washington, D.C. He travels extensively. He can be contacted at andrew@hondracy.com.

Chris Wahlberg's passion for photography and art has taken him through studies at the University of Connecticut and the San Francisco Art Institute. He has had photo studios in Dallas as well as Chicago where he studied and produced holograms at the Fine Arts Research Holographic Center. In 1987 he opened a studio in San Francisco shooting commercial assignments for such clients as Hewlett-Packard, Rolex, NASA, Fetzer Wineries and many others. To see more of his work go to www.chriswahlberg.com.

About the Author

Mikkel Aaland is a photographer, writer, and author of several books including *Photoshop Elements 2 Solutions* (Sybex, 2002), *Photoshop for the Web* (O'Reilly, 2000), *Digital Photography* (Random House, 1992), and *Still Images in Multimedia* (Hayden, 1996). Aaland's documentary photographs have been exhibited in major institutions around the world, including the Bibliothèque Nationale de France in Paris and the former Lenin Museum in Prague. He has contributed both text and/or photography to *Wired, Outside, Digital Creativity, American Photo, The Washington Post,* and *Newsweek,* as well as several European publications. Aaland is also co-founder of Tor Productions, a multimedia and web production company founded in 1989 and based in San Francisco.

The author has led public workshops on the effective use of digital images and graphics in new media at institutions and conferences such as the University of California, Berkeley; Stanford University; Drexel University; Photo Expo in New York City; and CNET's builder.com. He has held private consultations with new media companies such as Corbis, Washington Post.com, and Newsweek Interactive. He is also a frequent guest on TechTV. He can be reached at **mikkel@cyberbohemia.com.**

About the Design and Production

TonBo designs is a full-service design studio in Sausalito, California established in 1989 by Lori Barra. TonBo provides complete art direction, design, and production services for books, magazines, marketing collateral, web design, promotional materials, packaging and corporate identity. TonBo manages and executes all aspects of communications projects, from concept through delivery of the final product. Their client list includes Apple Computer, Adobe Systems, Chronicle Books, Revo Sunglasses, Peet's Coffee & Tea, Isabel Allende, *Newsweek, Time,* Harper Collins, Peachpit Press, and IDG Books. **www.tonbo.com.**

⌘Z Command Z is a design production studio established in 1988 by Jan Martí. Based in Palo Alto, California, Command Z provides electronic graphic production services to a wide range of clients in Silicon Valley and the San Francisco Bay Area. Jan can be reached at **comz@comz.com.**